P9-AOT-381

Against the Odds

Against the Odds

Scholars Who Challenged Racism in the Twentieth Century

EDITED BY

Benjamin P. Bowser and Louis Kushnick

with Paul Grant

University of Massachusetts Press

Amherst and Boston

Printed in the United States of America

LC 2001008663
ISBN 1-55849-343-3

Designed by Jack Harrison
Set in Monotype Dante by Graphic Composition, Inc.
Printed and bound by The Maple-Vail Book Manufacturing Group

Library of Congress Cataloging-in-Publication Data

Against the odds : scholars who challenged racism in the twentieth century / edited by
Benjamin P. Bowser and Louis Kushnick with Paul Grant.
p. cm.
Includes bibliographical references.
ISBN 1-55849-343-3 (alk. paper)
1. African American intellectuals—Political activity—History—20th century.
2. Intellectuals—United States—Political activity—History—20th century.
3. African American political activists—Biography.
4. African American civil rights workers—Biography.
5. Political activists—United States—Biography.
6. Civil rights workers—United States—Biography.
7. African Americans—Civil rights—History—20th century.
8. African Americans—Intellectual life—20th century.
9. Racism—United States—History—20th century.
10. United States—Race relations.
I. Bowser, Benjamin P. II. Kushnick, Louis.
E185.96 A465 2002
305.896'073'00922—dc21
2001008663

British Library Cataloguing in Publication data are available.

To Oscar Earle, Joe Bonzell, Mack Ivory, Ben Daniels, Jerry Saunders, and Damon Johnson—men who lived through a century of lynchings, poverty, Jim Crow, "for colored only," bullets and torpedoes, racists during wars and in unions, ghettoization, and who, through it all, celebrated life and laughed to the end. May we have their strength, wisdom, and humor

—B. P. B.

To the memory of Herman Fiske, for his compassion, strength, and love.

—L. K.

Contents

Acknowledgments ix

Introduction: Moving the Race Mountain 1

1. A World Libertarian: John Glover Jackson 20

2. Portrait of a Liberation Scholar: John Henrik Clarke 27

3. A Lifetime of Inquiry: Frank Snowden Jr. 41

4. Writing about African Americans in American History: The Career of John Hope Franklin 63

5. Studies of the African Diaspora: The Work and Reflections of St. Clair Drake 86

6. Blending Scholarship with Public Service: Robert C. Weaver 111

7. Pursuing Fieldwork in African American Communities: Some Personal Reflections of Hylan Lewis 123

8. An Architect of Social Change: Kenneth B. Clark 147

9. Personal Reflections on W. E. B. Du Bois: The Person, Scholar, and Activist, *by Herbert Aptheker and Fay Aptheker* 158

10. Vindication in Speaking Truth to Power: Herbert Aptheker 193

11. Catching History on the Wing: A. Sivanandan as Activist, Teacher, and Rebel, *by Louis Kushnick and Paul Grant* 227

Conclusion: Of Jim Crow Old and New 243

Acknowledgments

The editors thank people on both sides of the Atlantic who made this work possible. In the United States, Nathalia Bowser, Blanche Pugh, and Walter Stafford were the Harlem connections to Kenneth Clark, Robert Weaver, and Hylan Lewis. Elder Cage and Herbert Parker were the Chicago connections to John Glover Jackson. Eric Cyrs, Jackson's biographer, helped complete his interview-essay. In the United Kingdom, Rebekah Delsol, Julie Devonald, Ken Sou, and other members of the staff of the Ahmed Iqbal Ullah Race Relations Archive provided invaluable assistance in the production of this book. We also acknowledge the contribution made by Jenny Bourne, A. Sivanandan, Hazel Waters, and other colleagues at the Institute of Race Relations through their principled leadership in the antiracist struggle and their support for this book.

Gary Okihiro introduced me to Herbert Aptheker, and Herbert and Faye Aptheker introduced me to John Hope Franklin and the spirit of W. E. B. Du Bois. K. Deborah Whittle, my wife, gave me the strength and continuity to see this project through from idea to completion. She not only accepted my days upon days of writing, transcribing, and traveling but also joined me in conducting interviews. Louis Kushnick, my partner in the struggle and coeditor of *Sage Race Relations Abstracts,* refused to let either time or distance stand between us in the completion of this project. His outrage at racism, his humor, and his dedication to this project were essential.—B. P. B.

I thank Huw Beynon, Dorothy Katzenellenbogen, Simon Katzenellenbogen, Patricia Kushnick, and Jacqueline Ould for their support and encouragement.—L. K.

Against the Odds

Introduction
Moving the Race Mountain

In the United States the idea of races was created by colonial legislatures to divide poor European laborers from Africans and Indians.[1] Wealthy and privileged European planters in the 1700s could not have remained wealthy without the ideology of racism, nor could their class privileges have survived without racist divisions becoming institutionalized in the law of the land and being maintained by violence and coercion. Races, as we know them, were created and sustained by government and were only dismantled as legal entities by legislation in the twentieth century. The current wisdom that government cannot bring about racial equality is interesting, if puzzling: in effect, it asserts that government cannot remedy what it created. The notions of race set forth by the state legislatures of Virginia and North Carolina in the eighteenth century are still used to characterize human beings, but the mountain of oppression and exploitation has been moved over the last one hundred years.[2]

At the beginning of the twentieth century, the two principal ways of understanding the world—scientifically and theologically—used the idea of race to explain and justify the exploitation and oppression of people of color. As a scientific concept, it explained the inferiority of African Americans through reference to natural selection.[3] The different races had varied capacities for civilization—like different animal species had different behavioral capacities—and different evolutionary trajectories. The superior European populations were destined to expand and develop, while the inferior blacks, Native Americans, and Asians suffered physical and moral degeneracy and faced extinction. Given this, the survival of a vigorous white race was dependent upon maintaining racial purity, which in turn required separation from the lesser races by any expedient method.

As a theological concept, race explained the lesser status of people of color in terms of divine selection: the God of the Old Testament had cursed the children of Ham to be hewers of wood and carriers of water. If

God had instituted racial segregation and subjugation, who were human beings to challenge his will?[4] For some, there was little reason to imagine that the races should or could be equal and it was futile even to attempt to educate or improve members of the lesser races: their inferiority was ordained and therefore unalterable.[5]

These views, which were the largely unchallenged common sense of the early twentieth century,[6] supported a culture of racial terrorism in the United States.[7] From 1882 to 1968 more than forty-seven hundred blacks were lynched. This was done to entertain, to relieve boredom, to defend white womanhood, and to remind blacks of their inferior and subservient place in society. Whites of all classes would gather to express their belief that "to kill a Negro wasn't nothing. It was like killing a chicken or a snake."[8] Here a domestic racist ideology was intrinsically linked to a culture of terrorism, and both were sustained by a racial hierarchy manifested by European colonialism and military power.

In contrast, the twentieth century ended with the theology of racism extensively challenged, as the churches tried (and are still trying) to wrest relevance from postmodern conditions and to move beyond an adherence to established structures of power and the bigotries they nurture. The late twentieth century also saw the scientific concept of race called into serious question. It is now viewed as inherently flawed, and real only because many still use it and believe that it is real.[9]

This academic questioning of racial hierarchies has been matched by a general waning of overt racial prejudice in American public life. There is less tolerance for some forms of racial terrorism and a greater acceptance of multiple identities. Furthermore, increasing numbers of Americans are less willing to identify themselves by race at all; thus the Census Bureau provided a shopping list of identities on the 2000 census form. Interracial marriages and general social relations are more frequent and more tolerated. Racial integration at work and in public accommodations is now a given. Despite those who wish to conserve the old race concept, the demise of race at the beginning of the twenty-first century is a reality. A range of factors, including legislation, public agitation, and economic shifts, drove this transformation in public thinking and behavior.[10] The mountain has literally moved.

Even so, we still have a racist national culture.[11] Poor and not-so-poor whites have consistently compromised their own class interests because of their underlying belief that they are superior to all other races.[12] People with influence and power still use race and racial differences to divide and set groups with common interests against one another. The last decade of the twentieth century also clearly showed the continuing relationship between so-called ethnic differences, racism, fascism, and genocide.[13] Notwithstanding these continuities, the questioning of the concept of race and the practices based on it is an important improvement and no minor achievement.

What This Book Is About

There is a considerable literature concerning the respective roles of social movements and governments in changing racial beliefs and practices in the twentieth century. Much less attention has been given to the scholars who provided the conceptual basis for some of those progressive changes. For example, much of the important scholarly work that supported the 1954 Supreme Court decision outlawing racial segregation and the successful civil rights activism between 1950 and 1970 has been overlooked. The theoretical work to dismantle race and racial hierarchy was in place well before the Second World War. That is not to say the world would have remained the same without the contributions of these scholars. Our purpose is simply to underline the fact of their involvement in creating the culture of resistance that made progress possible.

Many scholars and activists helped move the race mountain in the past century. This is a book of interview-essays featuring a small group of these scholar-activists who contributed to the critique of race, who recorded its distortions and omissions in history, and its negative consequences in community and international life. The fact that they are all men in no way suggests that women played no role or had no place in this endeavor. In the first half of the twentieth century, patriarchy reigned without apology or quarter given in higher education: half the population was largely debarred from university graduate programs because they were women. Where the aspirations of African American women met with the twin structures of gender- and race-based hierarchies, the result was total exclusion. Marion Thompson Wright (1904–62) was the first black woman to complete a dissertation in African American history. (She obtained a Ph.D. from Columbia University in 1941.) Black women's involvement in higher education was limited and uneven in the best of times. For example, the number of black women with advanced degrees actually dropped after 1945 with the end of the Rosenwald and General Education Board Funds.[14] Given this, women of color had few opportunities to become trained as scholars.

Ironically, the interviews in this book illustrate the contradictory impact of patriarchy on the African American community. The reader will see that while these male pioneers were denied funds and opportunities to research and write, often their greatest resource was their wives. Without the moral support, income, and understanding of their spouses, much of their work would not have happened. The nature of such affirming partnerships raises the issue of the cost and sacrifice to the community; issues much discussed by black women intellectuals over the last decades of the past century.

For most women in the first half of the twentieth century, the routes for expressing their gifts and capacities to transform society were largely directed toward community service and the arts. The fact that women of color held up over half the sky as social and political activists is now well established. However, there were few black women social scientists and historians to critique racism and patriarchy. Instead their impact was felt as activists who challenged established notions of service, community, politics, and the interdependence of structures of exploitation and oppression. Women were major contributors to the upsurge of creative writing in the first half of the twentieth century.[15] Through their writings they raised important issues and corrected a number of the distortions formulated by white male and female thinkers, as well as those offered by men of color. Projects to recover this rich legacy are already in place and will be a major feature of volume 2 of this series. Laying the foundation for a gendered comparison of critical and subversive intellectuals in the United States is one of the most exciting aspects of the current endeavor.

Many of the scholars and scholar-activists in this collection began their careers in the 1930s, a period of global upheaval. The depression years were a period of profound suffering and great hope. In the United States the collapse of the economy, the devastation of the middle class, and high unemployment encouraged the possibility of a large and influential socialist movement. These revolutionary times also produced the first generation of African American intellectuals whose work lent itself to scholarship *and* social change. This book aims to present their struggles against the odds and to provide an insight into the world that shaped them.

The scholars included in this series of interview-essays represent four approaches to the task of changing the world: community scholars, university scholars, reform-scholars, and scholars who spoke to power. These categories are not mutually exclusive nor are they exhaustive. They are primarily for convenience of presentation. The contributions of W. E. B. Du Bois are recounted by Herbert and Fay Aptheker. We interviewed all the following:

Herbert Aptheker
Kenneth Clark
John Henrik Clarke

St. Clair Drake
John Hope Franklin
John Glover Jackson
Hylan Lewis
A. Sivanandan
Frank Snowden Jr.
Robert Weaver

None of these scholars are common household names, and most have worked in relative obscurity for most of their lives. However, one of the aims of this book is to recapture the significance of their contributions and those of their contemporaries to the development of antiracist thought and practice. The African American scholars in this collection represent the first generation of black scholars with more than one or two in their respective fields. In 1914 there were only fourteen blacks with Ph.D.'s in all disciplines across the entire United States.[16] Any black person with an advanced degree was both an exceptional achiever and a contradiction to the presumption of black inferiority.

All but two of the interviewees are African Americans. Herbert Aptheker, who is white and Jewish, is included because his career and commitment show the price paid by white scholars who struggle against racism. A. Sivanandan is included because he shows the international dimension to the struggle for racial justice and that scholars of color in other parts of the world have biographies similar to their African Americans counterparts. Both Aptheker and Sivanandan show that racism has never simply been a matter of black and white: they, like many others, worked against the odds simply to survive, let alone challenge racist ideas and practices.

Another aim of this book is to reconstruct the conditions under which critical intellectuals of color produced their theoretical and political work. Despite their degrees, they experienced the same ill treatment that all other blacks experienced—Jim Crow in the South and racial discrimination in the North. The interviews allow them to tell their own stories in their own way: to detail their battles against racial and social injustice in the context of their own lives. There is plenty of fascinating autobiographical material in these essays, material that re-creates the circumstances in which people had to work and their perceptions of their causes and effects.

Despite lacking access to libraries, assistants, funding, and time to write, all our contributors produced. They were up against the race barrier, professionally and personally. Aptheker was isolated because he was a Communist and a Jew. All were inadmissible to most graduate degree programs in the United States during the 1930s. The vast majority of American universities and colleges would not consider them for academic appointments because of their race, their views, or both. Yet they produced. Their work was not widely read, and those who received recognition did so only as seniors. Nonetheless, they produced a body of work that continues to challenge established thinking, policy, and practice.

While their work is still vigorously debated and possesses a life of its own, the authors of those ideas are not with us forever. Several of this generation's central intellectuals were still alive and active when this project was initially conceived, but a sense of urgency developed over the last ten years. Key figures in antiracist and anticapitalist scholarship, such as C. L. R. James and Eric Foner, were originally included but died before we could interview them. Six of our contributors died within two years of their interviews. The task was to capture their stories before it was too late. Because of their long experience and even longer memories, these men have valuable perspectives on social change and race, insights that offer tools for changing the world in the twenty-first century. During their lifetimes, the world changed beyond all recognition. They responded to these changes and helped make them happen; their stories dramatize these national and global shifts and continuities.

The Interviews

As in any selection such as this, the choice of interviewees may be criticized. It is impossible to cater to all tastes and concerns. All choices to include are also acts of exclusion. We acknowledge three specific criticisms: we have left out key figures such as Rayford Logan, Harold Cruse, and Benjamin Quarles; we have spoken only to men; and there is no representation from other scholars of color from within the United States. Our only defense is our limited time and resources. This work was done out-of-pocket between classes and other research commitments.

The project was conceived in 1989 after an interview with Herbert Aptheker. That experience, and the connections, contradictions, and conundrums it provoked, encouraged the editors to interview other senior scholars. The selection of interviewees was based on access, capacity to contribute, and commitment to the general aims of recording stories and garnering insights. As some interviews were set up, other possible informants could not be traced or refused or for other reasons were unable to cooperate.

We soon realized that establishing a framework for the interviews would also provide us with an opportunity to compare responses. We decided we would ask the scholars the same series of general questions and then a series of unique questions based on their writings. All the interviews were tape-recorded. Most were conducted over the course of two days; the only single-day interviews were with Kenneth Clark and Frank Snowden. All interviewees spoke until they were tired on the first day. The interviewer would review the interview that evening and formulate clarifying questions for the second day. Then the interviewer would transcribe the tape for both days in order to review it and get a further sense of each person interviewed. Key moments were highlighted in the transcripts and used to formulate further questions. As part of that process, we removed ourselves from the text and edited it into a narrative form. The concern was to emphasize the dynamics of each scholar's story rather than their relationship with the interviewers.

Details had to be checked by the interviewer-editors. The interview-essay was then mailed to each scholar for his review, corrections, second thoughts, and comments. The texts were revised, based on each scholar's corrections and comments, and then returned to the scholars. This process in itself allowed us to learn more about each scholar. Although Frank Snowden was the only one who insisted on writing his own essay, they were all perfectionists, and the editing process continued until each was satisfied and approved the text. There were two exceptions to this: John G. Jackson passed away before the process was complete, so his biographer, Eric Cyrs, reviewed his text; and Hylan Lewis's declining health prevented him from completing more than one iteration of the editing process before he passed away.

The following general questions were asked of each scholar (with up to ten additional questions on his specific career and life):

1. What were the formative influences (persons, readings, and events) during your youth on developing your interest in [list major area]?
2. What were the major incentives during the early years of your career?
3. What were the major barriers during the early years of your career?
4. Please name fifteen books written by others that were most influential on your career.
5. What were the influences and events that led up to your writing the following [list major contributions]?
6. Please tell me about the scholars and community people who were supportive of your scholarship that led to [list major contributions].
7. Please tell me about the scholars and community people who opposed your work.

8. What do you consider your best work and why?
9. Briefly sketch the five most important topics that you would like to see studied in the coming decades based upon your work.

The Four Critical Intellectual Traditions

The interview-essays are divided into four groups representing critical themes. John G. Jackson and John Henrik Clarke represent the community scholars; Frank Snowden Jr., John Hope Franklin, and St. Clair Drake make up the university scholars. The reform scholars are Robert C. Weaver, Hylan Lewis, and Kenneth Clark. A. Sivanandan, W. E. B. Du Bois, and Herb Aptheker are the scholars who spoke to power.

The Community Scholars

Racial segregation in the United States during the first half of the century limited the ranks of African American scholars. The almost universal assumption that African Americans were incapable of scholarly attainment kept blacks out of most northern colleges and universities where they were not legally excluded as in the South. One of the great stories of the past century is how the racial barriers to colleges and universities did not stop blacks in the United States from discovering their people's place in world history. Denied access to formal training and to faculty appointments, black men and women with a passion for knowledge and justice still read avidly.

They understood that the history of Africa and the African peoples, either completely ignored or grossly distorted by white American scholars and commentators, were important keys to continued black subordination. Therefore, it was a common practice for scholars in the community to form reading clubs to exchange materials and information and to encourage one another in the research of Africa's past and present. For example, the American Negro Historical Society was established in Philadelphia in 1897, and the Negro Society for Historical Research began in New York in 1911. The aims of these and comparable groups were threefold: to challenge the distortions about blacks, to write Africa and African peoples back into world knowledge, and to liberate the minds of their communities. Correcting the record was considered essential and a necessary first step to the redemption and liberation of African peoples throughout the world.

Most of the people engaged in this knowledge work labored as postal clerks, small shopkeepers, janitors, hairdressers, preachers, barbers, or day laborers. They made a living however they could and spent evenings and weekends reading, writing, and teaching. Whenever they could find a forum, they would teach. In Harlem during the 1920s and 1930s, the best forums were street corners, where community scholars would encourage and inspire the many, while clashing with respectable preachers and professionals, whose accommodation with racism they despised.

The community scholars' movement had its most organized expression before World War II in Harlem—the largest African American community in the United States. The Blyden Society, led by Willis N. Huggins in the 1920s, and the Harlem YMCA History Club in the 1940s became the community university. Furthermore, the largest public collection of books and artifacts in the United States devoted to Africa and to African people was in a library just across the street from the Harlem YMCA; it is named after a founding community scholar, Arthur Schomburg. In addition, the New York Public Library's main branch and special collections downtown held the largest collection of books in the United States outside of the major universities and the Library of Congress. The entire collection was open to the public, including blacks.

Du Bois spoke in the history section in *Crisis* magazine to these community scholars. They also formed the community base of Carter G. Woodson's work and reason for establishing "Negro" History Week, which was later expanded to a month. The black studies movement that burst onto the scene in the 1960s had its origins on the street corners of Harlem. Exposure to the ideas of the community scholars equipped black students with the knowledge that the curricula of white universities and colleges were profoundly deficient. It was no coincidence then that when black studies programs were initially formed out of student protest, many of the first senior faculty were long-time community scholars.

During the 1930s these scholars had argued that the omission of Africa's past and the contributions of its people to world civilization and history were obvious even to a casual reader. By simply presenting the omissions, they questioned the official histories and social thinking, and showed their deficiencies. Even racist scholars had to respond to the early community scholars' claims that Africa was central to the ancient world and that African labor and cultures had made the modern world possible.

John Henrik Clarke often told the story of his first encounter with Arthur Schomburg. Schomburg told him: "Son, go study the history of Europe, for when you know the history of your oppressor, you will know why you were misplaced in history."[17] Schomburg then emphasized that what we call African or African American history is nothing more than the missing pages of world history. Carter G. Woodson declared, "It is not so much a Negro History Week as it is a History Week. We should emphasize not

Negro History, but the Negro in history. What we need is not a history of selected races or nations, but the history of the world void of national bias, race hate, and religious prejudice."[18]

Woodson also articulated the black community scholar movement's antiracism when he pointed out that the teaching of "scientific" truth would help eliminate prejudice among whites, as well as build self-esteem among blacks. These intellectuals were especially critical of the concept of "race" and recognized that it was racist in definition and intent. This is particularly evident in the work, however flawed, of J. A. Rogers. Rogers focused his attacks on the notion of racial purity (*Nature Knows No Color-Line: Research into the Negro Ancestry in the White Race* [1952], and *Sex and Race: Negro-Caucasian Mixing in All Ages and All Lands* [1942]). The tendency is also evident in the work of John G. Jackson.

The late *John Glover Jackson* graduated near the top of his class in New York City's elite Stuyvesant high school but received no encouragement, no college admissions offers, and no funding to attend college along with his white classmates. He spent most of his life working as a clerk in a printing factory. He was more than ninety years old when interviewed in a Chicago nursing home in 1990. His mind was very sharp and his interview-essay fascinating. He was at the center of the Harlem community scholars in the 1930s, and together with Nathaniel Willis Huggins wrote the most influential pamphlets of the period, *A Guide to the Study of African History* (1934) and *An Introduction to African Civilization* (1937). Jackson and Huggins summarized the literature around the role of the African in world civilization. Their work was the first step for those wanting to counter the notion that Africa had no history or civilizations—the missing works for a missing history.

Of particular interest is that Huggins and Jackson called attention to another community scholar, Gerald Massey and his *Ancient Egypt: The Light of the World* (1907). The current debate concerning the role of Egypt in world and African civilization was framed by Massey and addressed by Huggins and Jackson, as well as by others such as Alexander Crummel in *The Future of Africa* (1862). Through their historical work, Jackson, Huggins, J. A. Rogers, and Arthur Schomburg concluded that the notion of race was nonsense and that there were no pure and distinct races. In the first interview-essay of this collection Jackson speaks for himself on this point.

John Henrik Clarke was one of the youngest of the Harlem community scholars, and John G. Jackson mentored him. When Clarke was growing up in rural Georgia, local whites discouraged education among blacks by requiring them to pay a book tax to attend school. The only child in his family to go to school, he completed only elementary school. Yet some years later, when John G. Jackson met Clarke in Harlem, Clarke's curiosity and desire for knowledge were reflected in a personal library that is reputed to have had more than ten thousand books, documents, and pamphlets. Jackson referred to Clarke as "a natural-born scholar." Part of Clarke's importance is that he recorded the most significant persons and events in Harlem from the 1930s through the 1960s. He was one of the last of the early community scholars and helped pioneer the black studies movement. His primary works include *Harlem: A Community in Transition* (1964); *Harlem, U.S.A.* (1971); *Marcus Garvey and the Vision of Africa* (1974); and *Malcolm X: The Man and His Times* (1990). Though blindness slowed his productivity late in life, John Henrik Clarke courted controversy with his defense of Afrocentric scholars and claims of Jewish racism.

His interview is important because at the core of Clarke's critique of white America was his belief that whites still do not regard blacks as human beings equal to themselves. Furthermore, as far as he was concerned whites have no real historic reason for racial arrogance. As an expert in European and African history, he believed that if whites could see themselves with black or American Indian eyes, they would know that their world primacy is based on slavery and genocide. For Clarke, the white notion of race stands squarely in the way of recognizing black peoples' humanity and achieving their own humanity.

The University Scholars

Harvard University was one of the very few exceptions to segregated universities and colleges. When President Lowell prohibited blacks from living in the Harvard dorms in 1922 because of southern students' objections, the Harvard Board of Overseers, supported by protests from students, alumni, and faculty, overturned his decision.[19] W. E. B. Du Bois received a Ph.D. from Harvard in 1898 and was the speaker at a Harvard College graduation. Three other scholars interviewed in this collection completed undergraduate or graduate degrees at Harvard in the 1930s—Frank Snowden Jr., John Hope Franklin, and Robert Weaver. They attended Harvard and worked with its most prominent faculty. Based on their interviews, it seems that Harvard was an exception precisely because of its prominence and the stature of its faculty.

Harvard was very much a part of the early New England tradition that valued education as a vehicle for moral and intellectual improvement of the elite, regardless of the race of the students. White Harvard graduates taught at black colleges in the South and were able to send an occasional star student to Harvard. These students received professional training, opportunities for prestigious advanced degrees, and teaching and research positions at other colleges and universities. Yet despite their extraordinary training, sponsorship, and degrees, segregation in the academy seriously compromised their early promise and obstructed the production of their major works.

Frank Snowden Jr. became interested in the classics as a student at Boston Latin (High) School. Like the other black Harvard degree recipients, he had to teach in southern black colleges. By distinguished teaching he worked his way from Virginia State College to Atlanta University and then to the top black university, Howard University in Washington, D.C. In spite of crushing teaching loads in a subject far removed from the practical "lift yourself by your own bootstraps" curriculum advocated by Booker T. Washington, Snowden used his extensive knowledge to refute the historic claims that contemporary racial attitudes went back to the ancient world and beyond. His books *Blacks in Antiquity* (1970) and *Before Color Prejudice* (1983) stand as definitive statements of the ancients' attitudes toward race. Although they recognized physical differences among peoples, they offered reasoned environmental explanations for them. They did not attribute inferiority or superiority to color but to culture and what they perceived as degrees of barbarism. To the Greeks and Romans, black Africans were considered partners and equals in the ancient world. Ironically, it was the ancestors of present-day English and Germans whom the Greeks and Romans considered beyond civilization's reach.

The conclusions of Snowden's scholarship are that racial antagonism, hierarchy, and definitions are not built into human perception and behavior as some prominent modern scholars have suggested.[20] The origins of modern race and racism are found in the ascendancy of later Portuguese, Spanish, English, and German influences on modern civilization rather than the ancient world.[21] In this, his scholarship vindicated one of the central tenets of the community scholars, that racism was a recent phenomenon linked to chattel slavery and colonialism. In later years Professor Snowden attempted to correct Afrocentric scholars' oversimplification of the complex racial cultures of the European ancients.

John Hope Franklin left Fisk College and his native Oklahoma to study history at Harvard. Like Snowden, he had to go south to teach and was overworked and underresourced. Even so, he produced what remains the central text on the history of African Americans, *From Slavery to Freedom: A History of African Americans* (2000; first published in 1947 with the subtitle *A History of American Negroes*). Its distinguishing feature is that it was written in precisely the universal vein that Woodson espoused, not as a history apart from American history. Franklin is quoted as saying, "I do not teach black history at the University of Chicago. I teach the history of the South—Black and White."[22]

Franklin's career-long aim was to integrate the ignored presence and influence of African Americans into the mainstream of American history. Without their presence American history is incomplete and distorted; it requires correction to be more accurate and broader in scope. In his other major works, such as *The Free Negro in North Carolina, 1790–1860* (1943); *The Militant South, 1800–1861* (1956); *Land of the Free: A History of the United. States* (1969); and *The Color Line: Legacy for the Twenty-First Century* (1993), Franklin presented African Americans as a vital part of American history and questioned all the stereotypes of black inferiority and white supremacy. In doing so, he indirectly challenged the idea of race and the practice of racism and pointed to the necessity for white Americans to craft new historic identities not based upon racial superiority.

St. Clair Drake completed his degree at the University of Chicago and spent most of his career at the city's Roosevelt University. *Black Metropolis* (1945), cowritten with Horace Cayton, is the most comprehensive window on African American urban community life of the twentieth century. W. E. B. Du Bois's *Philadelphia Negro* (1899) is the only other that comes close. Drake and Cayton's work on the relationship between class, culture, and community was groundbreaking in itself. It also showed a so-called inferior people with a complex and extensive community life, comparable to that of any Europeans.

While serving as Stanford University's first black studies program director, Drake became very interested in the claims of community scholars and black nationalists regarding race. His response was a detailed two-volume assessment of them, *Black Folk Here and There: An Essay in History and Anthropology* (1987–90). This work, which drew on Drake's many years of study of black cultures in the diaspora, revealed the richness of black community life and provided a deeper understanding of the claims and problems posed by the community scholars' use of history.

The Reform Scholars

Robert Weaver is the third Harvard scholar. Like Snowden, he completed his bachelor's, master's, and Ph.D. at Harvard. At the height of the organization of the New Deal in the 1930s, he was attracted to Washington, D.C., with his Harvard Law School friend John Preston. An ubiquitous figure at congressional committee hearings, Weaver received a series of federal appointments focused on housing. He was able to help craft the first and most successful housing programs and to use set-asides and quotas to insure the participation of black contractors and architects in the early public housing programs. These eventually led to his appointment as Secretary of Housing in the Johnson Administration, and the programs of the late 1930s became the models for affirmative action in the 1960s.

Weaver set in motion federal programs that lasted until the Reagan administration. This experience allowed him to trace how the initial federal housing programs were compromised, discredited, and made so ineffective that many of the larger developments had to be abandoned and torn down by the 1990s. It also inspired Weaver to author two books essential to an understanding of the New Deal efforts, *Negro Labor: A National Problem* (1946) and *The Negro Ghetto* (1948). His passion for justice continued to drive his writings throughout the early 1980s when he argued against the compromise of federal programs.

Hylan Lewis completed his Ph.D. at the University of Chicago and wrote one of the last of the Chicago School holistic studies of community, *Blackways of Kent* (1955). An expert on black community life and poverty, Lewis wrestled with the theoretical and practical problems of combating poverty during the early 1960s. His work with Kenneth Clark in Harlem set the theoretical rationale and structure for the first "antipoverty" program in the United States, HARYOU (Harlem Youth Opportunities Unlimited). Lewis was frequently consulted on the development of programs to address urban poverty and, like Robert Weaver, knew what successful programs required. From the 1970s on Lewis was the most articulate critic of how these programs were actually undercut and then abandoned by a range of political actors and interests. In this, his views and critique anticipated the work of William J. Wilson's *Declining Significance of Race* (1978) and *The Truly Disadvantaged* (1987).

Kenneth Clark, a Columbia University Ph.D. in psychology, spent his entire career in New York City. Clark was able to get an appointment at the City University of New York due to postwar interest in integration and a faculty shortage.[23] He and his wife, Mamie Clark, did theoretical work and research on the negative psychological effects of racial segregation on black children. This work was featured in the 1954 Supreme Court decision *Brown vs. Board of Education*, which outlawed racial segregation in U.S. public schools. Although the Clarks' central study was later challenged on methodological grounds,[24] they clearly established that race identity and self-concept are important considerations in child rearing and educational achievement.

This was a very important development in challenging the academic and commonsense views of black people. The Clarks' work portrayed African Americans as thinking and feeling human beings, with emotions and a sense of self that can be damaged by black and white racial attitudes. Clark also suggested connections between individual and communal psychology when he extended his study of the damaging effects of racial segregation on self-concepts to examine its greater damage on black community life in *Dark Ghetto* (1965).

Scholars Who Spoke to Power

Challenging the concept of race and racism in individual psychology and in historical and contemporary scholarship is very important. However, the most critical place to challenge race and racism is in the organization of economic and political power. The very concept of race in the United States was first codified by state legislatures and was designed to control and exploit poor whites and blacks alike. This continued throughout the twentieth century, despite the federal government's initiation of major social changes during the Great Depression and the Second World War.

The scholars interviewed for this book were aware of the relationship between hierarchies of race and structures of power. All the interviewees came up through socialism's heyday of the 1920s and 1930s; they knew the literature and many socialists. Despite this, for a variety of reasons, most sought to reform the system by advocacy, education, and government action. John G. Jackson did not believe in the working class's capacity to form a better society—a point central to ideological Marxism. John Henrik Clarke rejected European and Western socialism in favor of the older nonracist African socialism. Frank Snowden had no use for socialism, period. St. Clair Drake was a radical and a socialist very early in his career. His radicalism continued, but he saw the limits of socialism in racial politics, in the attitudes of American socialists, and in Stalin's abuses, which discredited the Soviet socialist model. John Hope Franklin believed that the American social system was fundamentally sound, with big government a necessity to balance inequalities in power and resources. Robert Weaver, Hylan Lewis, and Kenneth Clark were all reformers who believed that action by the federal government could eliminate racial and other inequalities. A. Sivanandan, W. E. B. Du Bois, and Herb Aptheker are the only exceptions to this tendency.

A. Sivanandan, the best-known antiracist scholar in Great Britain today, is director of the Institute of Race Relations (IRR) in London and editor of its journal *Race and Class.* One of his first contributions to the institute was an analysis of racism in Britain and other western European countries that connected immigration policies with patterns of colonial and postcolonial exploitation. At the turn of the century, Sivanandan's concern to "catch history on the wing" entailed robust analyses of the limitations of postmodernism and the impact of globalization on the "wretched of the earth." This work extends and deepens discussions initiated in the 1980s concerning the politics of identity and the global reconfiguration of capital and has had a profound contemporary impact. These interventions sparked a reappraisal of the role of intellectuals at the beginning of the twenty-first century and fueled serious questions among activists and academics concerning these new forms of imperialism and how to combat them. Sivanandan's writings can be found primarily in *Race and Class* and in his two volumes of collected essays, *A Different Hunger: Writings on Black Resistance* (1982) and *Communities of Resistance: Writings on Black Struggles for Socialism* (1990). The passionate love of justice that inspires his "formal" political writing also drove his award-winning novel, *When Memory Dies* (1996). This book develops the themes of the struggles against imperialism and neocolonialism and the disastrous consequences of sectarianism and communalism in the context of three generations of a Sri Lankan family.

W. E. B. Du Bois's contribution to this collection is via an interview with Herbert and Fay Aptheker, who spent forty years editing Du Bois's complete works. Few people realize that Du Bois's sensitivity to the black experience in the United States, evident in *The Souls of Black Folks* (1902) came out of extensive and ongoing fieldwork in the Jim Crow South. His most engaging work on race in the South was never published. His longtime sponsor, the U.S. Labor Department, destroyed it because of his prominence as a radical. Du Bois's pre-1930 scholarship set the groundwork for research into families, communities, leadership, and public health in the United States.

Du Bois's greatest theoretical contribution is not his notion of the double-consciousness of African Americans but his connection of both domestic and international racism with capitalism and imperialism. His work far exceeded Lenin's *Imperialism* in this regard and did so long before he joined the Communist Party. An appreciation of the impact of W. E. B. Du Bois is essential for anyone who wishes to understand the struggle against racism and the major events of the twentieth century.

Finally, *Herbert Aptheker* has made major contributions to the fight against racism and suffered a fate similar to many antiracist black scholars because of it. Although only one of several critiques of U. B. Phillips's dominant school of history regarding American slavery, Aptheker's challenge was the most effective.[25] In *American Negro Slave Revolts* (1943), Aptheker documented African American resistance to slavery and successfully discredited the racist historiography and historians. Fifty years later Aptheker once more broke new ground. In *Anti-Racism in U.S. History: The First Two Hundred Years* (1992), he challenged the view of American history as simply a matter of "black versus white." There were whites opposed to racism and social injustice, as there were black accomplices to racism, slavery, and social injustice. He is now the foremost student of the history of white antiracism in the United States.

Like Du Bois, Herbert Aptheker was considered a security threat to the United States because of his opposition to the Cold War, his disdain for U.S. imperial adventures, and his membership in the Communist Party. Despite Aptheker's extraordinary contributions to history and race relations, he has never held a tenure-track university appointment. His interview highlights his political and intellectual choices, and the price he paid for them.

The St. Clair Drake, John Hope Franklin, John Henrik Clark, Kenneth Clark, and Robert Weaver interview-essays were feature articles in *Sage Race Relations Abstracts.* The Du Bois interview with the Apthekers was first published in Rutledge Dennis, ed., *W. E. B. Du Bois: The Scholar as Activist,* vol. 9 (Greenwich: JAI Press, 1996). The Frank Snowden, Hylan Lewis, John George Jackson, A. Sivanandan, and Herbert Aptheker essays were all written specifically for this collection. What follows are an extraordinary group of interview-essays.

NOTES

1. Allen; Cecil-Fronsman; Takaki.
2. Lopez.
3. Gossett; Stanton; Frederickson; Haller.
4. Jordan, 242, 416.
5. Sumner.
6. Frederickson; Eisley.
7. Tolnay and Beck 1995.
8. Allen, 12.
9. Feagin and Herman; Shanklin; Reynolds.
10. Gates.
11. Goldberg.
12. Kushnick.
13. Kuhl.
14. Meier and Ruddick, 125.
15. Roses and Randolph.

16. Meier and Ruddick, 7.
17. Boyd.
18. Meier and Ruddick, 10.
19. Kennedy, xxii.
20. Gergen.
21. Wood.
22. Meier and Ruddick, 120.
23. Ibid., 126.
24. Porter.
25. Meier and Ruddick, 108–9.

REFERENCES

Allen, Theodore. *The Invention of the White Race.* Vol. 1. *Racial Oppression and Social Control.* London: Verso, 1994.

Anthias, Floya. "Connecting 'Race' and Ethnic Phenomena." *Sociology* 26, no. 3 (1992): 421–38.

Banks, William. *Black Intellectuals: Race and Responsibility in American Life.* New York: W. W. Norton, 1996.

Boyd, Herb. "The Griot of Our Time Passes," *New York Amsterdam News,* July 23–July 29, 1998, p. 3.

Cecil-Fronsman, B. *Common Whites: Class and Culture in Antebellum North Carolina.* Lexington: University Press of Kentucky, 1992.

Cimbala, Paul, and Robert Himmelberg, eds. *Historians and Race: Autobiography and the Writing of History.* Indianapolis: Indiana University Press, 1996.

Eiseley, Loren. *Darwin's Century: Evolution and the Men Who Discovered It.* Garden City, N.Y.: Doubleday, 1958.

Feagin, Joe, and Hernán Vera. *White Racism: The Basics.* New York: Routledge, 1994.

Frederickson, George. *The Black Image in the White Mind: The Debate on Afro-American Character and Destiny, 1817–1914.* New York: Harper and Row, 1971.

Gates, Nathaniel. *The Concept of Race in Natural and Social Science.* New York: Garland, 1997.

Gergen, Kenneth. "The Significance of Skin Color in Human Relations." *Daedalus,* 96, no. 2 (1967): 390–406.

Goldberg, David. *Racist Culture: Philosophy and the Politics of Meaning.* Oxford: Blackwell, 1993.

Gossett, Thomas. *Race: The History of an Idea.* Dallas: Southern Methodist University Press, 1963; New York: Oxford University Press, 1997.

Haller, John. *Outcasts from Evolution: Scientific Attitudes of Racial Inferiority, 1859–1900.* Urbana: University of Illinois Press, 1971.

Ignatiev, Noel, and John Garvey, eds. *Race Traitor.* New York: Routledge, 1996.

Jones, James, and Robert Carter. "Racism and White Racism Identity: Emerging Realities." In *Impacts of Racism on White Americans,* ed. Benjamin Bowser and R. G. Hunt, 1–23. Thousand Oaks: Sage, 1996.

Jordan, Winthrop. *White over Black: American Attitudes toward the Negro, 1550–1812.* Chapel Hill: University of North Carolina Press, 1968.

Kennedy, Randell. "Introduction: Blacks and the Race Question at Harvard." In *Blacks at Harvard: A Documentary History of the African American Experience at Harvard and Radcliffe,* ed. Werner Sollors, C. Titcomb, and T. A. Underwood. New York: New York University Press, 1993.

King, William. "The Triumphs of Tribalism: The Modern American University as a Reflection of Eurocentric Culture." In *Toward the Multicultural University,* ed. Benjamin Bowser, T. Jones, and G. A. Young. Westport: Praeger, 1995.

Kuhl, Stefan. *The Nazi Connection: Eugenics, American Racism, and German National Socialism.* New York: Oxford University Press, 1994.

Kushnick, Louis. "The Political Economy of White Racism in the United States." In *Impacts of Racism on White Americans,* ed. Benjamin Bowser and R. G. Hunt, 48–67. Thousand Oaks: Sage, 1996.

Lopez, Ian. *The Legal Construction of Race.* New York: New York University Press, 1996.

Malcolm X. *February 1965: The Final Speeches.* Ed. Steve Clark. New York: Pathfinder Press, 1992.

McBride, David. *From TB to AIDS: Epidemics among Urban Blacks since 1900.* Albany: State University of New York Press, 1991.

Meier, August, and Elliott Ruddick. *Black History and the Historical Profession, 1915–1980.* Urbana: University of Illinois Press, 1986.

Moses, Wilson. *Afrotopia: The Roots of African American Popular History.* Cambridge: Cambridge University Press, 1998.

Porter, Judith. *Black Child, White Child: The Development of Racial Attitudes.* Cambridge: Harvard University Press, 1971.

Reynolds, Larry. "Retrospective on 'Race': The Career of a Concept." *Sociological Focus* 25, no. 1 (1992): 1–14.

Romanucci-Ross, L., and G. De Vos, eds. *Ethnic Identity: Creation, Conflict, and Accommodation.* Walnut Creek: AltaMira Press, 1996.

Roses, L. E., and R. E. Randolph, eds. *Harlem's Glory: Black Women Writing, 1900–1950.* Cambridge: Harvard University Press, 1996.

Rushton, J. Philippe. *Race, Evolution, and Behavior: A Life History Perspective.* New Brunswick, N.J.: Transaction Publishers, 1995.

Shanklin, Eugenia. *Anthropology and Race.* Belmont, Calif.: Wadsworth, 1994.

Shockley, William. *Shockley on Eugenics and Race: The Application of Science to the Solution of Human Problems.* Washington: Scott-Townsend, 1992.

Sollors, Werner, C. Titcomb, and T. A. Underwood, eds. *Blacks at Harvard: A Documentary History of the African American Experience at Harvard and Radcliffe.* New York: New York University Press, 1993.

Stanton, William. *The Leopard's Spots: Scientific Attitudes toward Race in America, 1815–1859.* Chicago: University of Chicago Press, 1972.

Sumner, William G. *On Liberty, Society, and Politics: The Essential Essays of William Graham Sumner.* Indianapolis: Liberty Fund, 1992.

Takaki, Ronald. *Iron Cages: Race and Culture in Nineteenth-Century America.* New York: Oxford University Press, 1990.

Tolnay, Stewart, and E. M. Beck. *A Festival of Violence: An Analysis of Southern Lynchings, 1882–1930.* Champaign: University of Illinois Press, 1995.

Vaughn, Alden. *Roots of American Racism: Essays on the Colonial Experience.* Oxford: Oxford University Press, 1995.

Ware, Gilbert. *William Hastie: Grace under Pressure.* New York: Oxford University Press, 1984.

Wellman, David. *Portraits of White Racism.* New York: Cambridge University Press, 1977.

Wood, Peter. "'If Toads Could Speak': How the Myth of Race Took Hold and Flourished in the Minds of Europe's Renaissance Colonizers." In *Racism and Anti-Racism in World Perspective,* ed. Benjamin Bowser, 27–45. Thousand Oaks: Sage, 1995.

Yinger, J. Milton. *Ethnicity: Source of Strength? Source of Conflict?* Albany: New York State University Press, 1994.

1

A World Libertarian

John Glover Jackson

One of the most important writings in the series of books and pamphlets that kept Africa alive as an essential part of world history was Willis Nathaniel Huggins and John Glover Jackson's *Introduction to African Civilization* (1937). By the turn of this century, slavery, colonialism, and long internal conflict had reduced Africa to a shadow of its past glory. Two centuries of European exploitation of African labor and the belief that Africans were inferior led prominent European and American scholars to literally write Africa out of history. The centrality of Africa to the ancient world and the abundant written evidence of Africa's influence were systematically omitted from classic texts and authoritative world histories. Where developments and events in Africa could not be ignored, they were attributed to Europeans or Asians. By the turn of the century, the prestige of the American university community was solidly vested in the omission of Africa from world history.

Educated and non–university affiliated scholars such as Gerald Massey (*Ancient Egypt: The Light of the World* [1907]), Willis N. Huggins and John G. Jackson (*An Introduction to African Civilization*), and others kept the truth alive. The many university scholars who are now researching and writing to properly put Africa back into world history and the study of civilization owe a great deal to these men, who devoted their lives with little support or recognition for keeping the evidence alive and for showing its potential.

The Interview

I grew up in New York City. My family was from Aiken, South Carolina, and had been directly involved in South Carolina's Black Reconstruction in the 1870s. During holiday visits, they told stories about those days that seemed at odds with what I later read about that period. The difference between what I had learned from my family and what was written led me to write an unpublished history of Black Reconstruction in South Carolina.

History was not my initial love. If I had had the opportunity, I would have become a scientist rather than a historian. I would have gone into astronomy in which I have had a lifelong interest. As a youngster I read many books on it. I was quite good in science at New York's Stuyvesant high school. I also did well in English and was encouraged by my teachers to write. But the differences in opportunities because of race became very apparent after graduation. The white students got good jobs and went on to college, and I got nothing. What I did in school meant nothing. I had to take manual labor jobs, the only ones open to Negroes regardless of education.

It was my mother who encouraged me to read, despite the fact that she did very little reading herself. I read newspapers, magazines, and books. After high school I read C.-F. Volney's *Ruins; or, Meditation on the Revolutions of Empires (1926)* and *The Martyrdom of Man* (1943) by Winwood Reade. Then I read W. E. B. Du Bois's *The Negro* (1915). From that point on, two major interests have dominated my life and work. The first is my interest in civilization, which began with reading Du Bois. I immediately realized that Africa and Africans had been barely mentioned in my prior readings and that works such as those by Du Bois and Gerald Massey were very important despite their omission from the official university histories. My second interest was in studying religion. I wanted to study religion because I did not have any and could clearly see how it controlled and limited people's lives. I had rejected religion from very early on in childhood. My family knew about my disbelief.

In the 1920s I became a member of Harlem's Blyden Society, led by Willis Nathaniel Huggins. We were a group of writers and historians who were interested in learning about our suppressed history and culture. The Blyden Society and the Schomburg Library were our universities, since we were cut off from the white-dominated and segregated university libraries and research sources. The Blyden Society was our forum for discussion, debate, exchanging ideas, to read and encourage each other's writings. We also used to have African scholars come and talk to us about Africa. But even in the streets, there was debate and discussion. One could get an education in Harlem by just listening to the many street-corner speakers. Hubert Henry Harrison was the most informative and the most entertaining of the street corner speakers. The others such as A. Philip Randolph and Carlos Cooks were not as good.

It was Hubert Harrison who introduced me to Albert Churchward's *Signs and Symbols of Primordial Man* (1913), and Churchward's writing introduced me to a work even more significant than Du Bois's, Gerald Massey's *Ancient Egypt: The Light of the World*. Churchward had died in

1929, and Massey died the year I was born. Dr. Harrison also introduced me to Joel Augustus Rogers (*From Superman to Man* [1957], *World's Great Men of Color* [1947], *Nature Knows No Color Line* [1952], *Sex and Race: Negro-Caucasian Mixing in All Ages and All Lands,* vols. 1–3 [1940], and *One Hundred Amazing Facts about the Negro* [1957]). It was J. A. Rogers who introduced me to Dr. Willis N. Huggins. Huggins and I worked together on two pamphlets, which were well read in the 1930s: *A Guide to the Study of African History* (1934) and *An Introduction to African Civilization* (1937). We had planned to do more work together, but Huggins committed suicide. He was in substantial financial debt. We were all in poverty and read, researched, and wrote when we could. I had manual labor jobs during the day. Eventually I got into a union shop at the Thompson Time Stamp Company (in New York City) after working for a while as a Red Cap at the train station.

I attended college for four years at New York City College night school. There were no teachers at City College that I can remember who inspired my scholarship. My intellectual excitement came from the Harlem community. The people I learned most from were J. A. Rogers, Hubert Henry Harrison, and Arthur Schomburg. I never met Carter G. Woodson or W. E. B. Du Bois. I never got an advanced degree. I taught secondary school briefly, but not until I retired from the union in 1971 did I get an academic appointment at New York City College in black studies.

I entertained myself by going to polo games and band concerts. I also used to go to the Apollo Theater in Harlem. I especially liked the comedian Eddie Green. Sometimes I would take a girlfriend. Once I was engaged to be married, but she lost her mind and had to be taken to an asylum in 1940. She accepted my lifestyle and devotion to scholarship, so this was a great loss to me. My closest friends over the years were Hubert Harrison, J. A. Rogers, and John Henrik Clarke whom I mentored. Clarke is a natural-born scholar. He never went beyond the seventh grade, yet he had a library of almost ten thousand books before I met him. I was also a friend of Zora Neale Hurston. All except Clarke have passed away, and it has been lonely all these years without them.

There were many others who were politically active. Bayard Rustin was a member of the Blyden Society but left because of his interest in the Communist Party. I was not attracted to Communism because I frankly think the Communists overestimate the ability of the masses to see their best interest. In this country, "the masses" vote Democratic or Republican and do not see that they are letting the capitalists pick and control their candidates for office. I have never been politically active because I could never see where it made any difference to blacks and the masses which party was in office.

The closest I ever came to being involved in a political movement was writing for Marcus Garvey's *Negro World* in 1925. But I was never a member of the Garvey movement or the United Negro Improvement Association. My writing consisted of summaries of what was called Negro history in those days. I never lectured and have intentionally been a very private person for most of my life. The reason is poverty. I did not have the money to travel. I have acquired my information from libraries located primarily in New York City. Of particular importance were the Schomburg Center in Harlem and the Oriental Division of the New York City Public Library's main branch.

Despite poverty and debt, I took great pleasure in my research and writing. This is why I did it, and what else was I to do with my time? I would have written even if few people read it. A greater and more long-term problem for me was getting my work published. Fortunately, John Henrik Clarke solved this problem for me. He found a publisher in the early 1970s. Otherwise, why would I have spent my life working full-time during the day at a stamp company and then devote nights and weekends to research, reading, and writing?

Some Personal Views

My intellectual approach to history goes back to the British diffusionists of the 1930s. It was their belief that civilization and cultures diffused throughout the world over thousands of years of contact between different peoples. No one culture is solely the product of its own isolated history. I first became interested in diffusionism after reading G. Elliot Smith (*The Ancient Egyptians and Their Influence upon the Civilization of Europe* [1911]; *The Ancient Egyptians and the Origin of Civilization* [1923]; G. E. Smith, et al., *Early Man, His Origin, Development and Culture* [1931]; *In the Beginning: The Origin of Civilization* [1928]; and *The Diffusion of Culture* [1933]). I never met Smith, nor did I ever correspond with any of the diffusionists.

My longest membership has been with the anarchist Rationalist Press Association in London. In fact, I would define myself as a philosophical anarchist. This is someone who believes that everyone should be free to do what he wants as long as he does not infringe on the freedom of others. This is a peaceful anarchist, unlike violent bomb-throwing anarchists like the early Communists. I believe J. A. Rogers would have agreed with this view.

Furthermore, I do not think that there is spirit after life. And I make no distinction between religion and spirituality. They are the same. The philosophical views I am closest to are that of the Scots philosopher David Hume (*On Human Nature and the Understanding* (1965 [1758]), Robert G. Engersoll, and Benedictus de Spinoza. My disbelief in spirituality and religion has been very disconcerting to many over the years. In some ways I have enjoyed challenging others on this point. The spirit is a religious myth used to keep people under control just like the notion of a white race is a myth.

There are only two races of man, both of whom originated in Africa. There are the peoples of Africa and there are the peoples of China. The significance of the African origins of all humans is that everyone has African origins. The so-called white race is, in fact, a mixture of African and Asian peoples. In one way, this is self-evident. Europe is not a continent. Its peoples have never been separated from contact with the larger and more influential centers of civilization throughout the ancient world in Africa and China. So clearly, I disagree with the north-south, black race versus white race, peoples of the sun versus peoples of the ice dichotomy (Michael Bradley, *The Iceman Inheritance: Prehistoric Sources of Western Man's Racism, Sexism, and Aggression* [1978]). I favor racial integration because the races have always been integrated and always will be. It is just a matter of whether people will accept this fact and reality. J. A. Rogers wrote a book on it—*Nature Knows No Color-Line* (1952).

I consider *Ages of Gold and Silver* (1990) to be my best work because it covers the history of the world more thoroughly than *Man, God, and Civilization* (1972). I would especially point out the final chapter, "The Future of Civilization." In this chapter, I suggest that there is not much of a future for civilization. This is a radical departure from my prior works where civilization continued regardless of human folly. Why do I take this position? In this century, there have been two World Wars, and it is absurd to think that there will not be others. There is no place in history where you will find that men and nations have not fought each other merely because of the potential horrors of war and its destruction. The next world war will probably wipe out the human race as we know it because of nuclear weapons. I do not agree that the end of the Cold War is also the end of the nuclear threat. Nations that hold nuclear weapons may destroy the ones they no longer need, but all these nations are going to keep some of these weapons. It is inevitable that someone is going to use them. I would not want to be a young person today, because there is little reason to think that there is going to be a future.

Topics for Future Research

I have spent my life working toward two goals. The first goal has been to bring Africa back into world history and the second goal has been to let people know about the religious myths that have been so destructive and controlling in people's lives. If people knew of the myths of religion, they would have to face reality. Religion is helping to bring the world to an end, because religions promote wars. My book *Christianity before Christ* (1938) is self-explanatory. A lot more work like this needs to be done.

The debate between Booker T. Washington and W. E. B. Du Bois was no debate at all. It was strategic. They were friends and pretended to disagree. They were both advocates of education and knew that black people needed both kinds—the practical and liberal arts. They got together before the debate and planned how they would use it to get concessions from whites. You can find evidence of this in the Schomburg Center in New York.

I would encourage younger scholars to do their own independent research. Through most of my career, the university has stood opposed to researching the truth about Africa and African peoples. I believe that universities are still barriers to the serious pursuit of knowledge. In particular, we need people trained in anthropology and other areas that can help recover African life and civilization.

Finally, there were other scholars like me who had no place in the university and, because of that, have been free to pursue research unrestricted by the European academy. They have manuscripts that publishers will not print just as I had. One such nonuniversity scholar was Richard B. Moore. These people need to be found and their work published.

If I had an opportunity to rewrite any of my works, I would leave them just as they are. Also I cannot write another book. I have written myself out. If someone else wants advice from me, I say read my books. It may seem something of a contradiction to ask that someone read my books and at the same time see no hope for civilization. But I do have one hope. Maybe those who read my books may prevent World War III. If there is no war, there is a basis for hope and a future.

I would not describe myself as among the giants of Africana scholarship. I would let others make that assessment. I have been called a man of great principles. I will accept that. I have been called a purist. I just did the best I could to make it accurate. I felt strongly about this because I wanted to put Africa back in history, and I do not consider this to be a bias in my writing.

You cannot write a serious history of the world and leave Africa out. I wanted to write about the world, but you cannot do that without including Africa.

I am satisfied that I have done all that I could do. Now I spend time reliving my life. All the information I wanted to get out is in my books.

This essay is based on the research of Eric Cyrs and on interviews with John Glover Jackson. Mr. Cyrs is John Glover Jackson's biographer. Benjamin P. Bowser, associate editor of *Sage Race Relations Abstracts,* Herbert Parker, and Elder James Cage also contributed to this essay based on an interview with John Glover Jackson on August 17, 1992, in Chicago.

Elder Jackson passed away October 14, 1993.

2

Portrait of a Liberation Scholar

John Henrik Clarke

Almost from the beginning as a child I started to raise essential questions inside myself about the things I observed and about the things people declared "true" and literally dared me to question. These who would impose the "truth" on me had no control over me when I was alone. I would question their truth and keep my conclusions to myself. I did not argue with them about what I thought or felt because I never told them. I lived inside myself seemingly forever and hoped for the day when I could speak my mind.

The earliest and most persistent question that came to my mind while growing up in a strict Baptist household and a very religious family was why do we use God to excuse so many man-made things, so much man-made misery? People in my family, community, and race attribute to God a lot of things, which are ungodly, and then claim that God will straighten them out in the by-and-by. We seem not to want to understand that God did not mess things up in the first place. We have made folklore out of this limited view of God and out of God-dependency as a spiritual necessity when we gave up on others or ourselves. We say that we have done all we can for them and then leave them alone. God will fix it by-and-by. Why must God fix something that God did not initiate and did not cause? What kind of God is this, or more precisely, what kind of faith is this?

I believed that if God was merciful enough to give you a brain, two functioning hands, and two legs where you put one in front of the other, then God has given you the facility to take care of yourself, to be responsible for your actions and for what happens to you. This is as self-evident to me as the ability to taste and to distinguish between a flower and an ear of corn. We use God as an excuse for not taking responsibility for our lives. This is not an anti-God argument. We have drawn the wrong conclusions from religion. Instead of being a source of liberation, our religions have become psychological traps. It is ironic that people have to leave religion as it was (and still is) practiced in order to understand and appreciate its meaning and to enjoy its benefits.

While in Baptist Sunday school, I began to look at the images they presented of God—that God was all-loving and that God was universal. If these claims are true, why do some people work very little and have so much, and why do others work so hard and have so little? If he is merciful, show me the mercy in this case? If he is a God of love, show me the love in such cases? As a child, I could not ask these questions aloud because I would have been slapped. I would have been called "a child of the devil."

Something grew in me early that I would have to grow to adulthood to understand. I am as religious as any person on earth, but I have something that is above religion—spirituality! Spirituality is the big umbrella under which religions function and out of which religions came. To be truly spiritual makes you a part of all religions without having to adhere to the mythology in any of them. But while growing up I had to brood and keep these impressions to myself because I had not worked them out inside myself. I had not worked out the images of all those white angels, a white God, and white saints. I could not understand how of all the people who died through the years, why not a single black or brown person got into heaven. Heaven was snow-white and even the devil was red.

What I grew up brooding over and was confused by were the millions of impressions, ideas, and beliefs where I saw my people and myself outside the context of history. It appeared that we had no place in history, no place in religion, had contributed nothing to civilization, and therefore, could not exist or be acknowledged as of value as human beings in the present. This is what drove me to study history seriously and at an early age. After I read the Bible, my curiosity led me to encyclopedias, almanacs, and out-of-town newspapers. I used to even read movie magazines. Since I had a good memory, I could remember the names of all the movie stars, as well as the names of the stars' wives. This was pure nonsense and rubbish of no meaning to black people or to anyone else. Devoting my mind to nonsense occurred in school as well. Because I was a good student, I had to memorize all the state capitals. I had to ask essential questions inside myself amid a clutter of irrelevant information that those around seemed to think important.

Family and Racial Segregation

When it became apparent to me that I wanted to do more serious reading, I left Jim Crow Columbus, Georgia. I was eighteen. There was very little to hold me since my mother had died in 1922 when I was about seven. She was from the Mays family out of which came the famous baseball player Willie Mays. My father's income was not enough for us to survive on. So she earned extra money as a washerwoman taking in white people's laundry. She did whole bundles from one white family for one dollar—wash and iron. Sometimes they would throw in the soap. Now, these same white people would call us "lazy people" on welfare. Yet for three hundred years during our slavery and during Jim Crow, white people were on welfare, and we paid for it.

After my mother nearly worked herself to death, I will never forget seeing her in that racially segregated hospital. The hospital was totally inadequate and it stank, literally stank. No one deserved to be put in such a place. But there she was, a beautiful woman, dying needlessly because whites denied us access to adequate hospital facilities. She died from pellagra, a disease caused by an inadequate diet. It was bad enough being poor, but it was far worse being regarded as so utterly worthless as not even to deserve to be alive.

My mother was a beautiful, quiet woman who loved all her children and tried to keep it a secret that I was her personal favorite. She told me so on her last day in the hospital. I knew that she would never come home. I hate hospitals to this day. Despite our short time together, she and two other women helped me to form a positive concept of myself. Besides my mother, there was my great-grandmother who witnessed the last slaves brought over from Africa, and there was my fifth-grade teacher who taught me to believe in myself. I feel the presence of those three women even today.

My mother's death was not the only event that prompted me to leave the South. There was my own circumstance. After my mother died, my father went back to Union Springs, Alabama, chose another wife, and returned to Columbus, Georgia. I finished grammar school, and then I had to work because my family needed my financial support. Our poverty did not care that I was a good student. My jobs were to haul wood and take breakfast to my father and his coworkers. He worked in a brickyard where the men had to go to work very early. I would go to their houses, take their breakfasts to them, and then go to school. There were six men. At the end of the week, I would get five cents from each. So I made thirty cents a week.

I was fortunate to be able to go to school at all. Only one child in each family living outside the city limits could go to the city school because you had to pay $3.75 for a book fee. My father only made $12 to $15 per week, and we needed every penny of it. So I was the one chosen from my family. All my brothers and sisters believe to this day that they should have been chosen to go to school. For example, the last time I saw my brother Alvin in Detroit, we were eating together, and I answered a question for his wife. He said smugly, "my brother went to the city school"—meaning that I had an advantage over him.

I read as much as I could by picking up books from the white people I worked for and by borrowing books. Most of these white people had books for decoration and had not read them. I would go to the public library as if I was on an errand for a white person. Blacks could not use the library at the time. I would forge their name to take books out. My experience just calls to mind that the story has yet to be told of what black people in the South did in order to survive. We lived in an atmosphere tantamount to Nazism right here in the United States. I swore that I would get out of the South when I could. Eighteen years was long enough.

Being "Taken In"

Miss Roselee took me in. She was a maid and cook in one of the white homes that I did chores in. I went to Miss Roselee's and stayed there for four years. She had an old boarding house that was an undeclared house of prostitution. That did not faze me because the ladies were nice to me and gave me school, lunch, and church money. "Taking in" was a custom, a substitute for adoption among blacks in the South. Taking in a young person was part of our humanity that we then took for granted and that has now passed from us unnoticed. This was part of our extended family practices. But now extended families can no longer afford to do this for economic reasons.

We have not discussed taking in and other indigenous customs as part of how we survived. How is it that people would just take in a child with no paperwork and raise that child as their own straight up into manhood or womanhood, ask no questions, and not be compensated in any way? The people who explain blacks to white people have ignored our customs and the things we did to survive and, in doing so, have done black people a great disservice. Clearly, I was better off being taken in at a house of prostitution than I was at home because of our poverty. While taken in, I was able to go to school where I completed the eighth grade.

I traveled by boxcar to Chicago in an unsuccessful attempt to get into the World's Fair in 1932. If you did not know anyone in Chicago to stay with and had no money, the police would not let you enter the city. I found myself back on a freight train and on my way to Jersey City—a nickel ferry ride from New York City. I have lived in New York for more than fifty years. What attracted me initially was the opportunity to go to WPA school at night. It did not matter then whether or not I graduated from high school.

What was important to me was that I could read anything I wanted and as much as I could and could question anyone. My readings and associations led me to further questioning.

I was immediately drawn to radical elements. They were the only ones who acknowledged our plight and attempted to do anything about it. I became active in the Young Communist League. I was never a member of the Communist Party, contrary to what many believed. As a matter of principle, if I had been a member of the Communist Party, I would have said so unashamedly. I was active with radicals who were committed to doing something. This is where those who claimed that I was a Communist got mixed up. There were Communist-sponsored activities where non-Communists like me were effective and active. For example, I was active in the Scottsboro and Angelo Herndon cases as a young street speaker and fund-raiser. I went to the rallies held for such causes.

My first act with the Young Communist League was to prevent Henry Winston and family from being evicted from their Lower East Side apartment. The law was written in such a way that if you were evicted and someone put your things back in the house, the marshal had to wait another thirty days to give you another eviction notice. In thirty days you could find another place to stay. So I was head of a group of young Turks who put the Winstons' furniture back in the house. Henry and I remained friends, though we had some strong disagreements about Marxism. When Henry wrote his book *Strategy for a Black Agenda,* I was the only one to raise the question of whose black agenda.

I had arrived at an important position in the 1930s—a position that has been verified by events in the Communist world today. Communism and socialism were not monoliths to be applied in the same way in all nations. Each country has to approach socialism based on its own needs and character. Poland is a good example. No matter how Communist Poland becomes, it is going to remain Catholic. You can say religion is the opiate of the people and I might agree with you, but that will not change anything. Poles are going to remain Catholic. You can declare that Russia is an atheist nation all you want, but there are going to continue to be millions of religious people in Russia, including 30 million Moslems. I told Henry and other Communists that they had to work from reality not their ideological declarations. So if black people become socialist, we become Baptist socialist, Methodist socialist, holy-roller socialist, father divine socialist, and Moslem socialist. That is reality.

But a more telling critique of the Left is in the study of African tribal societies —a study that Karl Marx missed. It is very clear that African tribal societies have successfully functioned for their people far longer than any nation devised by European thinkers. These tribal societies in their structure and administration were fundamentally socialist. They were socialist not only before Karl Marx was born but also before Europe was born. They did not wait for someone to ordain them "socialist" and say that they were "socialist." They never said once that they were socialist; they did not have to. Examine African tribal societies before foreigners interfered with them. There is nothing in socialism that they did not have. Africans had the purest form of socialism that has ever existed on this earth.

So I have no problem with socialism if you take it from its African universal base. But if you take it solely from its European base, then I have an extreme problem with it. Then it is still based on the assumption of European dominance of the world. What European ideologies of the Left and Right do not understand is that they assume continued European dominance. They believe that, if the world is to be socialist, it will be socialist under European dominance. If it is to be capitalist, it is to be capitalist under European dominance. I have problems with either assumption. In contrast, if Africa had built its own enduring socialist societies all over the continent, it would be evident by no network of jails, no psychiatrists, no orphanages, and no old people's homes.

All the social services we in the West have built outside the family would exist inside the family if the West had any kind of humanity. African tribal societies were far beyond where we in the West are right now and beyond where we say we hope to go. So it is time to examine what Africans had as a basis that we still need. Clearly we need to stop calling African societies "primitive." If they were primitive, why is it that their social order came before and has outlived every form of government and social order that this alleged Western civilization has ever devised? The key to our salvation as a people here, in Africa, and in Europe may be in the social wisdom of African tribal peoples.

Harlem

When I came to New York I first learned of the Harlem "street speakers." I do not know of any other place in the country where there was this tradition. The street speakers were men who stood on street corners expounding on the topics of the day. They had to be knowledgeable, relevant, good speakers, and able to hold their own, because their audiences were not passive. People would speak up from the crowd and boo them away if they were outdone. The speakers on Lenox Avenue were considered to be the junior or "undergraduate" speakers. The speakers on Seventh Avenue were the senior graduate speakers—the elite. You had to speak first on Lenox Ave. and could do so for years before you could get to Seventh Ave.

On Lenox Ave. there was Ras DeKiller, who I believe became the role model for the street speaker in Ralph Ellison's book *Invisible Man*. On Seventh Ave., Arthur Reed was king and trained a young man named Ira Kemp, who went door-to-door selling dresses made by his family. Ira Kemp became the king of street speakers. Also on Seventh Avenue there was a young Dominican named Carlos Cooks—arrogant as hell and a good speaker. Unknown to the audience, Cooks's people owned brownstone houses in Harlem and were slum landlords. I coined the phrase "Carlos Cooks is a crook." When he saw me in his audience, he would start blasting away, "We got to get rid of the traitors in our midst." When I would say something, he would turn toward me and say, "This man is a disgrace to the skin he wears." I was the only one to say that Carlos Cooks was a hustler. Nonetheless, he was a very effective speaker and had a segment of the Garvey movement in his following. Unfortunately, Cooks and his Garveyite following misinterpreted Garvey. Carlos Cooks passed on in 1966.

My formal introduction to history began in Harlem in the 1930s. I was active in the Harlem history club at the Harlem YMCA under Willis N. Huggins. I was fortunate enough to have met Arthur Schomburg and remembered reading his famous essay "The Negro Digs Up His Past" while I was still in Georgia. I can say that it was Arthur Schomburg who taught me the interrelation of African history to world history. Willis N. Huggins taught me the political meaning of history. I would go to the lectures of William Leo Hansberry on the philosophical meaning of black history. The Harlem history club was literally a graduate-level history department with some of the most important figures in black history right there in the middle of Harlem. I learned all that I could.

Some of the club's publications would include John G. Jackson's and Willis Huggins's *Guide to the Study of African History*. In this work, the references on Africa alone made it an important contribution. Besides his essay "The Negro Digs Up His Past," Schomburg wrote a book entitled *The New Negro*. Huggins and Jackson later wrote *Introduction to African Civilization*. I was being introduced to material and books I had never seen or heard of before. This would lead me to read more deeply. It might surprise you that H. G. Wells's *Outline of History*, despite its white supremacist views, is a good outline of history. It led me to read other works in history like Spengler's *Decline of the West* and the early works of Will Durant such as his *Story of Philosophy*.

John G. Jackson's works still have a great influence on me, and this is evident in my enquiry into the role of religion as a force in history and the African origins of the legend of the garden of Eden. He was one of the earliest scholars who attempted to separate myth from truth in biblical history. (See his book *Pagan Origins of the Christ Myth,* as well as his pamphlet "Christianity before Christ"—later made into a book.) His writing indicates that in some cases biblical stories were not true and were not meant to be true. The Bible was meant to provide fables and myths to illustrate the truth. If you understand the truth from the illustrations, the Bible has done what it was meant to do. For example, the story of the exodus is told to illustrate that, at a given hour, God will come to the rescue of his people. It is a story on the ultimate goodness of God, who will rescue his people in their most desperate time. If you have real faith in yourself and in God, the story is nothing more than that and has served its purpose.

Of particular value to me were William Hansberry's "Sources for the Study of Ethiopian History" and the writings of Charles Seiford, especially his unpublished "Who Are the Ethiopians?" In addition to the historic readings, I enjoyed a lot of good general writings such as the early fiction of Richard Wright. My writing style has been influenced by white writers such as Sherwood Anderson, Ernest Hemingway, James Joyce, and other great writers who tried to take their writing into other dimensions.

I appreciate people with insight, white or black, who have looked for the fifth side of a square. Insight is always the fifth side of a square. This is what I have learned from writers who write well and thinkers who think well. Many young people, and older ones as well, have not developed the sense of challenge to seek out and find people who do things well. We can all benefit from being exposed to the masters and respect the fact that what they do is something well done. Unfortunately, many scholars and writers today do not see the standard that they have to move up to. I am clearly partial to the works, writings, and thinking of our people's freedom movement, but I have no hesitation in going outside the movement to get any truth, idea, or theory that I think will add to what I have learned from my own people.

The writers and scholars in the Harlem history club were good writers and scholars who were dedicated to their people and to history. They had little comfort or financial advantage. Being scholars meant they had to pursue their work and live with economic uncertainty. There was uncertainty in their personal relations as well. They were expected to be ordinary men with ordinary interests when they were in fact extraordinary in who they were and what they did. They were not masochistic, yet many of them suffered at the hands of their wives, children, and friends. Despite lack of support and misunderstanding from those closest to them, they stuck to what they set out to do as men of dedication.

An Englishman named Edmund O'Brian expressed the necessity for dedication some years ago. He said "thinking is at its best when you make a priesthood out of duty." A writer cannot do his best work before he understands the priesthood of his endeavor. You cannot express ideas well externally until you have made sense of them internally. All the external material measures of success do not motivate or really reward the dedicated scholar. I know O'Brian's point well. My deepest disappointment has not been financial or for the years that I could not get a teaching position. My disappointment was in the lack of support from the two women I married.

For years I could not get a regular teaching job. I taught in high schools, in the community, and in oddball places in the depression years and after I came out of the army in 1945. I did odd jobs for almost twenty years to support myself, my family, and my historical studies and research. Finally, in 1949, the administrator at the New School for Social Research had to fund an African Studies Center and I was allowed to give courses in the community. Later, I became head of the heritage teaching program for HARYOU (Harlem Youth Opportunities Unlimited), the first antipoverty program in Harlem. Then I was training Head Start teachers at New York University.

All these positions were on soft money lines. When the grant ran out, the job ran out. I could get that kind of job. I became known for my radical approach to teaching and as a teacher who documented things and proved my points. Sometimes I would work in the bank at night to supplement my income. Then James Turner expressed an interest in my coming to Cornell University, and the black and Puerto Rican students at Hunter College wanted me to develop their curriculum as well. I was making a little money then (1970) as a consultant for CBS and was not ready to teach yet. So I told the dean at Hunter College that I would do two courses for fifteen thousand dollars thinking they would tell me to go to hell. They accepted. To my surprise I was hired at Hunter College and, for the first time in my life, I was paid fifteen thousand dollars per year to teach two courses. The students told them to hire me, and this was a time when administrations did not ignore their students' wishes.

Research Topics

If I were able to direct a new generation of students in historical studies, I would have them do a number of studies that are not being done. We need to see general studies as well as detailed specializations on the peoples and cultures of the world. The work on Africa, Asia, and Europe, which European scholars initiated in the nineteenth century, needs to be carefully reviewed. We will undoubtedly find much to redo without the assumptions and bias of European supremacy. We need to see students trained in the different periods of African history, doing studies of European peoples in the same periods. What they would look to study are the connections and interactions between Africans and Europeans.

In particular, there is a need for Africanists to study the emergence of Europe from A.D. 1400 to 1600. This period was a critical turning point in the history of the world. We need studies of the 700 years before A.D. 1400 when Islamic Africans, Arabs, and Berbers had isolated Europe, controlling commerce in the Mediterranean. Europe was hemmed in and struggling with its own internal conflicts. The Crusades gave Europe an external reason for certain ideas and certain people to dominate. In the process, a lot of pressure was taken off the Catholic church to reform, and Europe was forced to look at the world beyond itself.

Europeans looked at the world beyond Europe and realized they could not conquer it, not until they learned maritime skills. Arab, African, and Berber scholars translated this maritime knowledge, primarily from China, at the University of Salamanca in Spain. The acquisition of this knowledge by Europeans in the 1400s is an essential turning point in world history. Europe would now punish the world for what it had suffered at its own hands and because of its own failures during the period between the decline of the Roman Empire and the second rise of Europe in the fifteenth and sixteenth centuries. Within this two-hundred-year rise, they would turn to Christianity to justify their criminal assault on the rest of the world. With religious justification or at best the church's indifference, they created and expanded the slave trade and the expansion of European people in settler nations beyond Europe. This period needs to be studied specifically with attention to the impact it had on African and Asian peoples.

Consider two small points. First, Europe is not really a continent. It is a part of Asia. Europe does not qualify as a continent in comparison with others. Second, Europeans are multiracial. These two points have major implications for how we view European cultures and the European identity. We need more work that looks at the ways that European scholars used to argue that Egypt was not a part of Africa. We need to study the relationship of Egypt to the rest of Africa, especially before the European distortion of their own and Egyptian histories.

For students to understand the twenty-first century, they must understand the centuries of disruption that led us to where we are today. We really have to study the last five hundred years of world history and the last five hundred years of disruption in favor of Europe and the downgrading of other peoples. Once things are placed in their proper historical perspective, we might have a better idea of where the world can go tomorrow.

We need to study South America, where the majority of the population is neither black nor white and could go either way in whom they identify with, depending on the future flow of world power. South Americans, in particular Brazilians, claim white or European preferences because they assume that blacks and African peoples will not come to power in the world community. We need to study the formation of nations in South America and the slow destruction of Indian cultures in Mexico and in Canada. There need to be in-depth studies of the destruction of indigenous cultures in both South and North America. There have been no in-depth studies of how these people came to America since they are supposed to be of Asian descent. The Asian ancestors of North and South American Indians could have come due to curiosity or overcrowding. They could have been cattle-raising people who needed more space. By studying the Asian migration patterns I have not been able to identify a disruptive period in Asian history that would have made that many people want to leave Asia.

What happened to the indigenous people of the Caribbean? They have disappeared. We need to study the Caribbean mentality after 1850 because the Caribbeans had a rebellious mentality up until the middle of that century. They identified themselves specifically with Africa, but they lost this after 1850 and became imitation-English, imitation-Dutch, imitation-Spanish, and now they have a color complex indicative of a confused racial identity. At what point did they lose their revolutionary attitude and start to refer to their heritage from the viewpoint of their colonial masters?

Africa as a place of history, migrations, cultures, and influences on the world is older than Europe and is rich and diverse in all human experiences. Yet we still know so little about Africa as a place with people central to world history and to the future. We need studies of the migration patterns of the peoples of Africa and the impact those migrations have had on present cultures. This would mean looking at the infusion of one African culture into another, creating still another culture that had vitality. The Ashanti and the Fante social order and world systems are examples. These people of the Upper Niger migrated and blended cultures.

We need to study cultural retentions where Africans have held on to their culture through centuries of wars and all sorts of other difficulties. They have held on to their concept of nation and concept of self. A good example is the Zulu. The Zulu nation is not South African in origin. They have East African origins and were called "Inguna." They migrated to central Africa and then down to South Africa. We need to study the marital and courtship habits of Africans, such as the Herro who pledge to bring virginity to their wedding bed, in contrast with the Mandi who have trial marriages. Among the Mandi a couple lives together and has two or three children before being married later with a big ceremony. In cases where they do not marry, the children belong to the family of the wife because their lineage is matrilineal. Whoever later marries her becomes the guardian of the children she had by the previous man. This is a very civilized custom.

We need to study Africa since 1957 with the beginning of the independence explosion when African states started to receive their so-called independence. What happened? Africa may have gone down the wrong road to freedom because we did not first have stable African states. There was no African state methodology, and we did not observe African political traditionalisms. What we adopted were European parliamentary forms. Africa should have adopted some form of African traditionalism in government. As a result, I see where so-called independence has done more harm than good. The methods and directions toward independence we took should be an issue within critical studies of neocolonialism. It would have made a great difference if there had been one African state in existence with stability and vitality. It would have been a role model for other African states. But the former colonial powers do not intend any one state to be such a role model.

We need to study the period between 1619 and 1776 in American history. Very little is said about what happened between the arrival of settlers in Jamestown, Virginia, and the American Revolution. Very little has been said about the contradictions of the American Revolution. In fact, the American Revolution and its proclamation of liberty and democracy was a contradiction because it was clearly not meant for African Americans. We had not been accepted as citizens. Northerners and southerners had no difficulty in classifying us as three-fifths of a person.

Southerners voted according to our presence in their political constituency. A white man could cast votes for us without our consent as though we were cattle. Liberty and justice for all did not include people of African descent. We need to study the small number of freedmen in the South who were stripped to the point of not being free—who were they; why did they stay; what did they think; and how did they maintain their free status? Many of them were craftsmen, barbers, builders, and blacksmiths. They were restricted in where they could go and what they could do.

When they went into a new town, they had to give notice. They were watched and had to carry papers on them at all times. This was humiliating. I challenge the idea that they were free. They just had a little more ability to move about, a little more than bondsmen. We know even less about the status and experiences of New England freedmen.

We need to investigate the large historic African presence in Asia, especially in India where there are 100 million people of partly African descent. We need to investigate the African presence in the Pacific Islands. There are entire nations made up of people of African extraction. We need to investigate Australia before the British destroyed its black inhabitants. Tasmania was black before the British destroyed every man, woman, and child on the island.

The Future

African Americans will play a key role in the new and second political awakening of African peoples. Despite our subordinate domestic status, African Americans are already the most politically active Africans outside Africa. The first political awakening was with Nkrumah in the independence of Ghana. The second will have to be based on the various nationalisms, pan-Africanism and other forms of African unity, that go across all religious and political lines. We can no longer discuss who is Baptist, who is Protestant, and so on. If you are African, even if you are a Moslem, being African will have to take precedence over what else you are.

Asserting that there will be a new African awakening does not mean that I am ignoring the declining African American domestic plight. The destruction of black communities in the United States is very deliberate, and the power and responsibility for this destruction rests squarely on the shoulders of government and economic leaders. They know that if we succeed in building sound communities after all that we have been put through, we can build and run a nation. Successful communities are small role models for a successful nation. It is from the community that you get the ideas and impetus to build a nation. Those who do not want us to come to power are intent on keeping our community so disrupted that we will never build a sound community. The people behind the destruction are not black, do not live in our community, and cannot succeed forever. No black men or women have that kind of power.

We have a lot of scholars, writers, and politicians doing more talking than writing and more talking than acting. We have enough actors. We have enough people to talk about us and to beg. We now need people who understand what real liberation is all about and who will act to make positive change for black people happen.

Our people and scholars are focusing on their "blackness" as a historic and cultural value. They struggle and are confused about whiteness that is everywhere and touted as everything good and of value in this culture. But this does not always mean that self-appreciation is lacking. What is lacking is a proper value on blackness. I think a lot of black scholars are misleading us with statistics and charts and examples that do not make sense. They are explaining us to whites, and their explanations make no sense to black people. Their unwillingness to come before black people and explain their explanations suggests that they do not believe their own explanations. Once we solve the internal problem of who we are, we can solve the external problem of what we will be.

It is understandable why I would grow up to fight Jim Crow and racial prejudice and the separation of races. I have literally risked my life fighting these things because I knew racial hatred and ignorance was so damned unnecessary. I also knew one other thing: if there is a superior race in the world, it damned well is not white people. I have always been clear on this point from early in my life. No superior people could do to other people what they have done to the world. European culture has produced people who are terribly insecure and frightened. No one on this earth should tremble at the sight of them. I would fear because a coward has the upper hand and not because he is brave. He is not brave. That is something I will never get out of my mind.

If I ever have any influence over a state, the first thing I would build is a decent hospital—some place to take care of children and old people. A civilization has to be measured by how it takes care of its old and its very young.

3

A Lifetime of Inquiry

Frank Snowden Jr.

Both my parents were born and raised in Virginia. Although I was born in Virginia, I spent nearly all my early life in Boston. By the time I was ready to enter the first grade, my father, who was a civilian employee and personnel officer of the War Department in Hampton, Virginia, moved our family to Boston. My father made this move to the North to provide a more cosmopolitan environment, to get better educational opportunities for his children, and to escape the racial segregation of the South. The move had a good effect. He continued to work in personnel, but he also got into the military and eventually rose to the rank of colonel in the army reserves. In Boston I attended elementary and junior high classes in which I was the only Negro. I experienced no racial discrimination because of my color. In fact, my teachers often pointed to me as an example of proper classroom behavior. We lived in Roxbury, which was then a racially mixed neighborhood, as were all the other neighborhoods in which we lived. White playmates were always a part of my childhood experience.

Early Life in New England and the Boston Latin School

My father had learned that the Boston Latin School offered the best background for a college education in Boston. At his suggestion, I took the entrance examination and was admitted. My years at the Boston Latin School were unquestionably one of the greatest influences in my life. The school, which was the first public school in the United States, was founded in 1635—a year before Harvard College. In my day, Boston Latin admitted only those students who excelled in elementary school and who passed a rigorous entrance test. Youngsters were urged to take the full six years by entering into class six, which corresponded to the seventh grade in the regular system. Such students were considered to be better prepared for college and for life. The standards were high. According to Philip Marson, a master at Boston Latin School for thirty-one years, only one-third of the boys who entered completed the course and graduated. But those who did graduate were highly successful in college, and astonishingly large numbers of them went on to high distinction in national life.

My six years at Boston Latin School from 1922 to 1928 left a lasting impression on me. There I learned the importance of regular study habits. Two of my teachers encouraged preparation by basing their grades largely on the results of daily quizzes, which they gave in all their classes and returned the following day. Exhortation to the attainment of excellence was a popular theme in assembly hall programs at which attendance was required. On the walls of the assembly hall were engraved the names of eminent Latin School men such as Benjamin Franklin, Cotton Mather, Samuel Adams, John Hancock, Ralph Waldo Emerson, George Santayana, and others. My interest in the classics began at Boston Latin School, where I studied Latin for six years and Greek for three. I received the Dixwell Prize given to the pupil in each teaching section whose grades were highest in Latin, Greek, and ancient history. At graduation in 1928, I received one of the seven highly coveted Franklin Medals from a legacy left by Benjamin Franklin, distributed annually to top-ranking students based on the marks of their last two years. At Boston Latin School I also began to look forward to teaching as a career, because excellent teachers inspired me. Several of these teachers were later honored by the establishment of scholarships, medals, or prizes in their honor. Two of them—Robert B. Drummey and Leon Otis Glover—were my teachers who gave the daily quizzes.

A common witticism at Boston Latin was that Harvard College was founded so the boys at Boston Latin would have a place to go after graduation. Along with a number of other classmates, I took a great risk and applied to no other college than Harvard. I was accepted and granted a scholarship based on my record at Boston Latin School and my College Board scores. You ask who were my mentors. My mentors in both high school and college were my teachers, who were an ever-present source of inspiration and encouragement. My experience in the 1920s stands in contrast to the current emphasis on black students' having black role models. Of course, black role models are important, but there are no substitutes for gifted teachers of whatever color or for highly motivated, serious students.

In this regard, the important contributions of white teachers in New England schools have often been overlooked. In my day, most blacks did not have black role models at any time. If having such role models had been a sine qua non for their success, few blacks would have graduated from New England colleges. W. E. B. Du Bois, for instance, was from New England, where he did not have any black role models. In my case, there were few such figures. One black role model, however, was a graduate of MIT who had an engineering job of importance in the Boston city government and lived in our neighborhood. Whenever he passed my friends and me as we were playing, he said, "Boys, you have to study hard or you'll never make it." Neither of my two children had black role models in school. Yet both excelled in their university studies and have been very successful in their careers.

My interest in classics at Boston Latin continued at Harvard and determined my major field of study. I won scholarships for each year at Harvard, and in my senior year I won the Bowdoin Prize in classics for an essay I wrote in Attic Greek. After graduating in 1932, I continued my studies at Harvard and in 1933 received a master of arts degree in classical philology. Some of my best friends at Harvard had been classmates at Boston Latin. They lived at home as I did. There was a house at Harvard called Phillips Brooks House, which had a room for commuters. We commuters could go there and get hot chocolate and go upstairs to relax and read. I also knew some students who lived on campus. Another black student in my class at Boston Latin, William Edward Harrison, also went to Harvard. After college he worked at the *Boston Chronicle* newspaper for most of his life. Several other black students who were at Harvard at the same time were Edward Hutchins, Howard Fitzhugh from Washington, and Thomas Patrick, who was denied admission to Harvard Medical School because of its racial policy at that time. He went to medical school in Germany instead. I knew Ralph Bunche, who was in graduate school. There was another black graduate student named William H. Dean from Baltimore who had gone to Bowdoin College, where he was the only student at that time who got all A's. His father-in-law was Channing Tobias. When it was time for William to get a job, his father-in-law told him that he would see if he could be considered for a position at New York's City College. William Dean went to one of his professors at Harvard and asked for a letter of recommendation. The professor told him that his letter would specify that Dean was a Negro. Dean told the professor, "Then don't write the letter." Instead he went to Atlanta University.

Teaching in the South

I left Boston for teaching positions in Virginia and Georgia, where I faced day-to-day discrimination. In Boston I had never experienced any racial discrimination in housing, public accommodation, transportation, or any other aspect of my daily life. I had enjoyed genuine friendships with classmates at Boston Latin School and at Harvard. These friendships have continued to this day. After graduating with a master's degree in 1933, I took the examinations for a position in the Boston Public Schools and achieved the highest scores in Latin and French. An important part of the examination was an oral test conducted by three administrators who questioned me extensively about the classics. These examiners gave me the highest rating in Latin, which meant that I was in the number one position for an appointment. There had never been a black person at the top of such a list. I did not get a position, however, because in the depression there were few openings. If I wanted to teach, I would have to go to the South. At that time, virtually no blacks held positions on college faculties in the United States, except at the black colleges in the South. William Hinton was one exception. He held a nonteaching position at Harvard Medical School from 1905 to 1949, when he was appointed to a professorship on the eve of his retirement.

Going south was no casual matter. With strong apprehension, I went to teach at Virginia State College for Negroes. I had heard of another young man who received a teaching position in the South. As he got farther and farther into the South, his depression finally became so overwhelming that he jumped off the train, committing suicide. I discussed the offer of my appointment at Ettrick, Virginia, with my father, with Ralph Bunche, and with others familiar with the college. They all encouraged me to go. My father reminded me that he was from Virginia, and that Virginia was not as bad as the Deep South.

The telegram from the college offered me a salary of $1,055 per year. This salary, it was explained, was lower than the normal salary because of retrenchment due to the depression. The position involved the assignment of three college classes in Latin and the supervision of two other classes in Latin and in English in the laboratory high school. After I arrived, I found that there were no laboratory teachers in Latin and English. Hence, in addition to my three regular Latin classes, I was assigned four classes in the laboratory high school. I found student interest in Latin to be great, and my frequent references to Greek created such interest that several students asked if I would be willing to teach them Greek for two hours on Saturday evenings before their weekly dance. In all my classes, I required students to bring in fifteen English words that were new to them as well as the sentences in which they were used and the derivations of the words. The students were struck by the large number of words derived from Greek and Latin roots.

During the three years that I taught in Virginia, enrollment increased in Latin, and several students decided to major in it. One student I taught in the laboratory high school later majored in Latin in college and became a high school teacher. I taught the way I did because of my Latin School role models. I gave daily quizzes. Students could see exactly where they stood. Like all faculty members, I lived on campus in Ettrick. The nearest city was Petersburg, where blacks were completely segregated. We blacks could not eat in a restaurant anywhere there, and if we went to the theater, we had to sit up in the balcony.

By my third year at Virginia State, John Hope, then the president of Atlanta University, became aware of my credentials. He requested that Florence Read, the president of Spelman College, interview me for a position in the Atlanta University system. Shortly after my interview I was offered a position in Latin at Spelman and Atlanta University. I explained that I would be reluctant to accept their offer unless my wife, Elaine, whom I had met and married at Virginia State, also received a teaching position. She received an offer also. In 1936 we moved to Atlanta, where we remained until 1940, when I was offered a position at Howard University in Washington, D.C. In the mid-twentieth century, Atlanta and Howard Universities were the meccas for outstanding black academics who at the time were not appointed to faculties outside the South. A number of them later received appointments at northern universities and in government. The professors at Atlanta when I was there included Du Bois, Ira Reid (who later went to Haverford College), William Stanley Brathwaite (the eminent literary critic from Boston), Ruppert Lloyd (who later went into the U.S. Foreign Service), and William H. Dean. At Howard there were such distinguished faculty members as Ralph Bunche, E. Franklin Frazier, Abram Harris (who later went to Chicago), David Blackwell, the mathematician (who later went to the University of California), Charles Drew, Hildrus Poindexter, and Mercer Cook (who later became an ambassador). Today, the southern tour for black academics is no longer necessary. My son, for example, after receiving a B.A. from Harvard and a D.Phil. from Oxford, taught at the University of London and at Yale, where he is now a full professor.

In Georgia and Virginia I experienced antiblack bias at its worst. The evils of Jim Crow included segregated water fountains, restaurants, train coaches, rest rooms, and theater galleries. Once I was flying from New Orleans to Atlanta. When I reached the airport, it was early morning and I had not had breakfast. I knew that blacks were not permitted in the airport restaurant. Therefore, I told an official that I was hungry and asked where I could eat. He said, "Sure, follow me." He then took me into the kitchen and said to the cook, "Here, Susie, feed him good." I refused, of course, to eat there. I will never forget that.

There are many other examples. On one occasion, a white cab driver refused to pick me up, yelling, "I'll call you a nigger cab." Similarly, a photographer in an Atlanta department store refused to take my daughter's picture with the explanation that he did not take "little nigger pictures." And then there were the constant references to all of us blacks, regardless of age, as "boys." A clerk in a clothing store took my measurements for two suits and commented that he knew another "boy" at Atlanta University. He was referring to the elderly and distinguished professor William Stanley Brathwaite. I told him to cancel my order, and I encouraged others to boycott that store.

Yet at the same time there were occasional pleasant surprises. For example, I requested that the *Atlanta Constitution* end the disrespectful practice of failing to capitalize the word "Negro." I took a petition to the Woolworth store in the Negro neighborhood and sought the signatures of the white clerks. They all refused. The manager approached me and asked the reasons for my speaking to the clerks. After I explained, he read the petition. Then he yelled to the clerks, "Sign it. 'Niggra' is a proper name, ain't it?" Thus armed, I sent the petition to the newspaper. A few days later I received a letter from the *Atlanta Constitution* stating that, "The matter you called to our attention is important and will be taken care of immediately." The change was made the very next day.

More frequently, however, the surprises were unpleasant. While driving north on one occasion with two students, we stopped at a gas station late one night in North Carolina. When I was charged twenty-eight cents more than the meter indicated, I brought the discrepancy to the attention of the attendant. He told me to go inside and speak to the owner. When I explained the reason for my appearance, he asked an employee to bring him a blackjack and instructed me to get the hell out of his store before he killed me. He then followed me to the car and poured twenty-eight cents' worth of gas all over the back of the car. He repeated his threat to kill me and added that, if he heard another word from me, he would set a match to the car. The two students had preceded me in returning to the car. As I sped away, one student said, "Prof, now I know that there's a God. I prayed that you wouldn't open your mouth one more time, and you didn't."

While I suffered such discrimination with anguish, I was heartened by my success in the classes of the Atlanta University system. The number of majors in classics increased. I introduced courses in Greek and Roman literature in translation that attracted large numbers of students. I also devised a course entitled "Vocabulary Building: English Words of Greek and

Latin Origin." To my surprise, seventy students enrolled. I later wrote articles in classical journals on the importance of this course.

Howard University, Continued Segregation, and Italy

I was invited to come to Howard University in 1940. My wife and I were very anxious to get out of the Deep South. But even in the nation's capital, blacks encountered segregation. The public schools were separate and far from equal. My daughter attended Slowe School in Washington. While she was there, I was chair of the Parents Education Committee. In that capacity I told the parents that the only thing we could do to protest the overcrowded conditions in the classrooms was to go on strike. A newspaper article reporting the event carried the headline "Slowe School Too Slow for Snowden." I also said at a meeting that we were not going back to the school unless the superintendent of schools met with us. When the superintendent finally invited us to his office, I noticed a map of separate black and white educational districts on the wall. "There is the problem," I said. "You have deliberately planned a segregated system." "One more word from you," he responded, "and I'll call this meeting to a close." I told him to go ahead and do so because the press was waiting outside to report on the outcome of the meeting.

Even the playgrounds were segregated. There was one playground close to our house where blacks could not go. Once a group of students came to me and said they wanted to play basketball there, but the white boys would not let them. They asked if I would go with them. I did. When we arrived, I told them to go ahead and play. They left their belongings with me. When I looked down, I saw that they had brought knives. To defend our rights but prevent violence, I went across the street and called the police, who responded right away. Just as the police arrived, a group of whites arrived to attack the black kids on the playground. The police stopped them. Later I went to the police station to thank the officers for interceding. One officer said, "What did you expect me to do? My name is Sullivan and I'm from Boston."

A striking example of racial segregation was in the area of culture. Negroes were refused admission to the National Theater. In 1946 my students at Howard and I were interested in attending a performance of Katharine Cornell in Jean Anouilh's version of Sophocles' *Antigone*. I called the theater to say that I wanted to bring my students to see the play. The person who answered the phone said, "Certainly, bring them." But when I revealed that I was from Howard University, he hung up. The irony, of course, was that both Sophocles' original play and Anouilh's French version were important landmarks in the history of freedom. In Sophocles' play Creon was denounced as the type of tyrant whom the Athenians loathed. During the Nazi occupation of France, audiences crowded into a tiny theater in Paris to see Anouilh's play, which gave secret courage and hope to the French because of its attack on dictatorship.

The content of the play also led to Cornell's decision to bring a production to the United States. After my students' disappointment, I wrote a letter to the *Washington Post* pointing out that the transmission of this democratic tradition was vitiated because of racial segregation in the theater where the play was being performed. After a Second World War waged in the name of freedom, Negro citizens were not allowed to attend the National Theater in Washington. When the *Washington Post* did not publish the letter, I wrote to Joseph Alsop, a Harvard classmate. Alsop, the most influential journalist in Washington at that time, was astonished and told me that he would bring the matter to the attention of the editor of the newspaper. Shortly afterward, therefore, I wrote a more detailed letter that was published in its entirety. A few days after the publication of the letter and a related editorial, Katharine Cornell wrote to me that she had not been aware of the theater's policy and that she was shocked by it. She informed the management that, unless the policy was changed immediately, she would not continue to appear. The theater called her attention to a line in the small print of her contract that referred to the theater's "Negro policy." Cornell informed me, however, that neither she nor anyone else in Actors Equity would ever appear again in the theater unless the policy was changed. That was the end of racial segregation in the National Theater and an American chapter in the transmission of *Antigone.*

I was at Howard from 1940 to 1990 except for leaves of absence to accept scholarly appointments. My wife taught in the D.C. public schools until her retirement. I received a Fulbright faculty research grant to go to Italy in 1949–50. I went to Italy again in 1954–56 as cultural attaché to the U.S. Embassy in Rome. While I was there, my two children visited Italy for the first time. My daughter completed high school there, and my son attended third and fourth grades. I later wrote to Senator Fulbright to tell him how my going to Italy had influenced my children. Neither of them ever forgot Italian civilization. In college, our daughter majored in Romance languages. She then taught Italian, and has been deputy chief of a government language school. Both of them also received Fulbrights to return to Europe—my daughter to Portugal and my son to Italy. Senator Fulbright responded, telling me that my letter was an eloquent statement of the aims of the program and inviting me to the Senate, where I met with him for an hour. At a later date the senator spoke on the Fulbright program. When he was asked a question, he said, "Ask Snowden. He knows more about the program than I do." My other absences from Howard University were as a fellow at the Woodrow Wilson International Center for Scholars in Washington in 1979 and scholar-in-residence at the Rockefeller Center in Bellagio, Italy, in the fall of 1977.

When I arrived at Howard in 1940, I was the only classicist. In order to convince the president of Howard that I needed assistance, I once taught a course in Greek literature in translation in which I accepted 70 students. I often taught classes of 100 to 150 students. In addition to teaching Latin, I introduced courses in classics in translation and in vocabulary building—English words of Greek and Latin origin. The growing enrollment in classics led to a gradual increase in the number of faculty. By the time I retired, the department had grown from one in 1940 to nine full-time faculty members in 1990—three blacks and six whites. Some of my Howard University majors became teachers, and others followed legal, government, and medical careers. One student who enrolled in vocabulary building and minored in Greek scored in the 99th percentile on a legal aptitude test. He graduated from Harvard Law School and later became attorney general of St. Croix in the Virgin Islands. Another student, who received a perfect score on a civil service examination, was called down by the examiner, who wanted to know if he had seen a copy of the examination before he took it. "No," he replied, explaining that he had come across many of the words in his course in vocabulary building and was able to decipher the meaning of other words from his knowledge of Greek and Latin roots. The well-known actress, Debbie Allen, took Greek with me. When she later visited the campus, I invited her to my class on Greek literature. The students were delighted by her explanation that acting is not mere mechanics and that she had learned much that was useful to her professionally from her knowledge of Greek tragedy. Andrew Young was a student in the introduction to the humanities class in which I lectured on Greek and Roman literature.

Others recognized my teaching as well. I was featured in a Howard University magazine article "The Unquiet Life of a Master Teacher." A *Washington Post* article (October 10, 1982) featured me as one of Washington's "wizards of wonder" and surprised me by declaring me to be one of the city's authentic geniuses. The article pointed out that my books on blacks in the ancient world had launched a new academic discipline. It explained that I found that in the ancient world Romans and Greeks did not consider color important. Blacks were soldiers, actors, diplomats, and slaves. They were assimilated culturally and physically. Their public image was favorable. Homer spoke of them as "blameless." When asked how long it would take our society to reach the ancients' concern with character rather than color, I recalled two examples from the recent news: five Boston youths slaying a black man for walking into a white neighborhood and the boycott by blacks of an outstanding white professor at Harvard Law School lecturing on civil rights. These events suggested that we had a long way to go before we approach the ancients' view of race.

I not only taught but also took on administrative appointments. I was chairman of the Department of Classics, director of the Evening and Summer School, and dean of the College of Liberal Arts from 1956 to 1968. While dean, I was responsible for improving academic programs and for introducing the college's first honors program.

I should also point out that long before the black-consciousness movement of the 1960s, I was investigating and writing about blacks in the ancient world. My first articles on the subject were published in 1947 and 1948, "The Negro in Classical Italy" (*American Journal of Philology* 68 [1947]: 266–92), and "The Negro in Ancient Greece" (*American Anthropologist* 50 [1948]: 31–44). While I was doing this work, racial discrimination against blacks was still an ugly reality in the nation's capital and beyond. My father's experience gives you some idea of what blacks faced in the way of subtle and not so subtle discrimination. My father served in World War II as a major in the army. Since the army was segregated, he had to go to Petersburg, Virginia, to serve with black troops. He told me of an incident when he and several other black soldiers were transporting German prisoners of war on a train. When whites saw them together, they demanded that the black soldiers go to the segregated car. Of course, the white Germans could not go there, leaving the problem of who would guard the German prisoners. The Germans, even as prisoners of war, had more rights in the United States than their black U.S. Army guards. This is an illustration of how ridiculous Jim Crow was. On another occasion some years earlier, my father and mother were driving me through New Jersey. They stopped to get something to eat in the afternoon at a Howard Johnson restaurant but were told that they could not eat there. There was a white witness who gave them his name. Learning that there was a law against racial discrimination in New Jersey, I sued on my father's behalf. Our lawyer argued a good case during the jury trial, pointing out that an army officer and his wife could not be served at a restaurant in the state. My father won the case, but did not receive any funds from the fine imposed on Howard Johnson. Money awarded in racial discrimination cases in New Jersey went to charity, not to the plaintiffs.

In 1990 although seventy students had signed up for my classes beginning in September the president of Howard informed me in July that I would have to retire because the university could not keep me on full salary at age seventy. In August the Department of Classics at Georgetown University invited me to become a member of the faculty. I taught there as an adjunct professor from 1990 to 1992. And in 1992 I served as Visiting Blegen Distinguished Research Professor at Vassar College.

When I was still at Howard in 1953 I received an invitation from the U.S. Department of State to make a six-month lecture tour of Africa and western Europe under the sponsorship of its Educational Exchange Program. I received the invitation because my research articles on the Negro in the Greek and Roman world had been called to their attention. My tour included French West Africa, the Gold Coast, Nigeria, Libya, Turkey, Greece, Italy, and Austria. I gave lectures in English, French, and Italian. My lecture topics included general education in American colleges and universities, blacks in the ancient Greek and Roman world, and the Negro in America. The success of my tour was indicated in a letter addressed to the president of Howard University from the State Department's International Educational Exchange Program: "His lectures drew maximum attention with listeners occupying not only all seats and standing room, but also verandas and windows." By the way, in Lagos, after I had gone to bed and was under a mosquito net as a protection against contracting malaria, there was a knock at the door at about 2: 00 A.M. The visitor said, "You said you would answer questions at any time." To answer the questioner, I stepped out from under the net and saw all the mosquitoes flying around. I asked my visitor, "Don't they bother you?" He answered, "No, we have no faith in the white man's drug." As soon as he left, I got back under the net and took the white man's drug. An evaluation letter I received on that tour said that I was one of the most effective lecturers the program had sponsored.

While in Italy under the auspices of the program, I lectured in thirteen cities. In Milan, there was unreserved enthusiasm, and the consulate received twenty to thirty telephone calls from people wanting to meet me or to invite me to lecture once again. My lectures, especially those devoted to the issue of race, it was pointed out, could have gone on indefinitely if the chairman had permitted. On one occasion, someone asked me about intermarriage in the United States. Tracing briefly the history of the "separate but equal" doctrine proclaimed by the Supreme Court, I said that intermarriage was illegal in sixteen states. But I also pointed out that, in spite of the law, intermarriage occurred. Then I said in Italian, "As your poet Virgil said many years ago, 'Love conquers all' [L'amore vince tutto.]" The audience went wild. I taught myself Italian when I was doing my dissertation because much of the material I used was in Italian. Then when we went to Italy, my wife and I had an apartment in Rome. We had a maid to whom we spoke Italian. When I prepared lectures for Italian audiences, I asked her son, who was a senior in high school, to listen to them. I made him promise not to treat me as a professor. If I made any mistakes, I wanted him to let me know. So he went over all my lectures. The newspapers commented on how well I spoke Italian.

As I was about to complete my lecture tour, I received a letter from the newly appointed ambassador to Italy, Clare Boothe Luce, who invited me to meet with her. In our conference, she informed me that she had received enthusiastic reviews of the Italian portion of my tour. She said that I knew much about Italy that would be helpful to her, and she hoped that I would return. The next year I received an offer to serve as the cultural attaché to the U.S. Embassy in Rome. I accepted the offer and took leave from Howard University for two years, 1954 to 1956. While I was on this assignment, I lectured at virtually every university in Italy. No U.S. cultural attaché had ever done that.

One of my other assignments was to host distinguished American visitors to Italy. One of them was William Faulkner in September 1955. When he arrived, the press interviewed him because they knew that he was from the South and wanted to know his reaction to the Emmet Till lynching, which had just occurred. He told his interviewers that he had been on an airplane and was therefore not informed but that if they returned the next day, he would have a statement for them. The next morning he came to my office with a prepared statement. On September 6, 1955, Faulkner wrote:

> When will we learn that if one county in Mississippi is to survive, it will be because all of Mississippi survives? If the state of Mississippi survives, it will be because all of America survives. And if America is to survive, the whole white race must survive first because the whole white race is only one-fourth of the earth's population of white and brown and yellow and black. So when will we learn that the white man can no longer afford, he simply does not dare to commit acts that the other three-fourths of the human race can challenge him for, not because the acts are themselves criminal, but simply because the challengers and accusers of the acts are not white in pigment. Not to speak of the other peoples who are already the western world's enemies because of political ideologies.

> Have we, the white Americans who can commit or condone such acts, forgotten already how only fifteen years ago what only the Japanese, a mere eight million inhabitants of an island already insolvent and bankrupt, did to us? How can we hope to survive the next Pearl Harbor, if there should be one, with not only all peoples who are not white but peoples whose political ideologies are different from ours arrayed against us after we have taught them, as we are now doing, that when we talk of freedom and liberty, we not only mean neither, we don't even mean security and justice and even the preservation of life for peoples whose pigmentation is not the same as ours. And not just the black people in Boer South Africa; but the black people in America too. Because if America is to survive, it will have to be because we choose and elect . . . to present to the world one homogeneous and unbroken front whether of white Americans or black ones or purple or blue or green.
>
> Perhaps we will find out now whether we are to survive or not. Perhaps the purpose of this sorrow and tragic error, committed in my native Mississippi by two white adults on an afflicted Negro child is to prove to us whether or not we deserve to survive. Because if we in America have reached that point in our disparate culture when we must murder children, no matter for what or what color, then we do not deserve to survive and probably won't.

Faulkner's statement surprised everyone, and although it was covered in the Italian press, it has not received the publicity it deserves.

At the time of my departure to the United States, Ambassador Luce wrote a letter to the State Department in which she expressed her regret that I was leaving and emphasized that Rome had never had a more successful U.S. cultural attaché. She added that I had officially visited other countries in Europe, where my reputation in Rome had created a spontaneous demand for my appearance. The State Department called me afterward and had me do lecture tours in Brazil and India during later leaves of absence from Howard. I never considered a career in the Foreign Service, however, because I was committed to teaching, writing, and doing research.

Research on Blacks in Antiquity

The study of blacks in the Greek and Roman period had not crossed my mind as an undergraduate at Harvard in 1932. My initial interest in this topic came about from my Ph.D. dissertation, "Slaves and Freedmen in Pompeii," written in Latin and completed in 1944. One of my findings in the examination of the written and archaeological evidence was that there was a presence of blacks in Pompeii and surrounding areas. This prompted me to investigate further whether there was a black presence in the rest of Italy. And if so, whether they were free from the type of color prejudice that has created major problems in the modern world. This inquiry led to an extensive investigation for more than half a century through Greek, Roman, and early Christian literature, as well as visits to archaeological sites in Greece, Italy, North Africa, Egypt, and museums in Africa, Europe, and the United States. Other scholars emphasized the importance of my early findings in their work. For example, in July 1948 I received a letter from Sir Alfred Zimmern, the Oxford scholar and author of *The Greek Commonwealth* (1931). He wrote as follows in response to my article "The Negro in Ancient Greece," published in the *American Anthropologist:* "I am much obliged to you for your courtesy in sending me a copy of your article on the Negro in ancient Greece. You will, I hope, excuse me for not writing until I had leisure to read it during the holiday season. It is gratifying to find that my generalization ('the Greeks showed no trace of colour prejudice') made so many years ago has stood the test of time and has been verified by so careful a scholar as yourself. I have found the whole paper most interesting and instructive."

William Westernman, professor of ancient history at Columbia, to whom I sent one of my earliest articles, invited me to New York to talk with him. He told me that I had discovered something important and that I should publish more of it. "Get offprints and distribute them widely," he advised. There were classics professors in other places who also encouraged me. There was also Herbert Bloch, a well-known professor at Harvard who was well acquainted with racism in Nazi Germany. I was his first doctoral student in the 1940s. I sent my first two major articles to him. He wrote back: "Thank you so much for sending me your two critical essays which I have been only able to read now. May I say that reading them was a great pleasure. First of all, you have reached a mastery in the subject of blacks in the ancient world in which no one can compete with you. At the same time I admire the objectivity with which you have treated questions that others have not tackled without being influenced by modern prejudices. I agree with every sentence in the two articles and with all of your criticisms."

And there was a letter (September 26, 1948) from Martin R. P. McGuire, former chair of the Department of Greek and Latin at Catholic University in which he predicted that the development of my research on blacks in the Mediterranean world would make a very important contribution to classical scholarship. The letter added, "It seems to me that you ought to write a comprehensive monograph on the Negro in Greek and Roman civilization. You have already published preliminary studies which can be developed further in a monograph. Such a monograph, making full use of the epigraphical and archaeological as well as literary data, and also all the evidence provided by physical and cultural anthropology would be a very important contribution to classical scholarship."

Professor McGuire's letter was a correct assessment of the importance of my later studies as attested by the evaluations of well-known scholars in a variety of fields—Egyptologists, archaeologists, anthropologists, and historians of art, religion, Christianity, and sociology. My findings on the attitudes of early Christians toward blacks led to a request for me to write the article "Blacks and Early Christianity" in *The Interpreter's Dictionary of the Bible: Supplementary Volume* (1976). My early findings also led to a request to write the article on Aithiopes [Ethiopians] published in *Lexicon Iconographicum Mythologiae Classicae* (1981).

Donald L. Noel, writing in the *American Journal of Sociology* (1984, vol. 90), observed of *Before Color Prejudice* (1983) that "Snowden's reasoning is sound and complements Steven J. Gould's assessment in his *Mismeasure of Man* of latter-day scientists who perceive and interpret racial differences through lenses severely distorted by prevailing racism. . . . He has given us the clearest and most thorough assessment of the ancient view of blacks that we are likely to have until new evidence is found." It also should be noted that I received the Charles A. Goodwin Award of Merit from the American Philological Association in 1971 for my *Blacks in Antiquity.* This is the only honor for scholarly achievement given by the association and is named in honor of a longtime member and generous benefactor. The award is presented at the annual meeting for outstanding contributions to classical scholarship published by a member of the association within the prior three years.

P. W. Hollenbach, in *Religious Studies Review* (vol. 9, 1983), wrote that *Before Color Prejudice* should be of great interest to historians of religion and race relations. The classicist John E. Rexine in *Platon* (vol. 36, 1984) wrote that *Before Color Prejudice* should be required reading in all university courses in classics and ancient history and added, "It deserves to be in every classicist's library and its findings included in all university courses in classics and ancient history."

The most detailed treatment of the Negro somatic type and presence in Western art for a long time was G. H. Beardsley's *The Negro in Greek and Roman Civilization: A Study of the Ethiopian Type* (1929). Beardsley recognized the importance of considering literary evidence. This pioneer work, however, gave only scant treatment to the Ethiopian in Greek and Roman literature. Very little was done since then until *Studies Presented to David Moore Robinson on His Seventieth Birthday* (ed. G. E. Mylonas, 1951). David M. Robinson asked the editor of this collection to get me to write an article. I did, and it is entitled "Rome and the Ethiopian Warrior." From Beardsley's work and my own in the Robinson collection, I knew that the most compelling case could be made by combining visual evidence with information from Greek and Roman literature.

Early in my investigations I knew that visual materials were important to showing the place blacks held in the ancient world in comparison to today. Hence, I set out from the beginning to get photographs made of the most important artifacts. In my travels to museums, whenever I saw works that illustrated my findings, I would make arrangements to have photographs taken. For example, when I was in the Soviet Union, I knew what I wanted to see. I had the photographs made and they got back to the United States before I did. The photographic side of the research led to my involvement in *The Image of the Black in Western Art* (1976). Volume 1, *From the Pharaohs to the Fall of the Roman Empire,* made special use of my research. The editor of the collection, Dominique de Menil, wrote to me about the project in its planning stage. My wife and I invited her to have lunch with us in Washington. At lunch she invited us to come to Paris for a planning meeting. The second planning meeting, the following year, was also in France. In the introduction to volume 1, she wrote: "The collaboration of Frank Snowden was invaluable. His research on Greek and Roman antiquity antedated our own. For twenty years he had investigated the museums of Europe and America, gathering references to blacks in the classical period. *Blacks in Antiquity,* published in 1970, represents the sum of his work."

In 1989 I received a letter from the Department of Classics at the University of Cape Town in which the chairman of the department wrote:

> Thank you very much for your letter of January 11th. I am delighted and honored to know that you have accepted our invitation to be keynote speaker at our January 19, 1991, Conference of the Classical Association of South Africa. We would be very grateful if you could present two papers. The first would be for a scholarly audience related in some way to the conference theme, Religion in the Greco-Roman World. The second would be for a general audience, including members of the public, on blacks in antiquity and / or the relevance of the lack of racial prejudice in the ancient world would be very appropriate for this second lecture. But, of course, it is open to you to speak on any topic you choose.

Originally I accepted the invitation because of the significance of my lecturing in South Africa at that time. In the end, however, I did not go because the symposium wanted me to stay for two weeks, and I did not want to leave my wife for such a long time. These responses to my work clearly indicate that this line of investigation is very important and should be continued. Further administrative or diplomatic appointments would have prevented or delayed my completing this work.

Reaction to Afrocentrism

Even before I began to collect the long overlooked and copious ethnographical, literary, and iconographic evidence relating to blacks in the ancient Mediterranean world, there were well-known scholars who, on the basis of their general knowledge, had commented on the absence of color prejudice in the ancient world. A. Zimmern pointed out that the Greeks showed no trace of color prejudice. T. J. Haarhoff said there was never any racialism in ancient Italy. In R. F. Hawtrey's opinion, the view that there was no hint of color prejudice in antiquity was not new. He pointed out, however, that it was not until the publication of *Blacks in Antiquity* that the evidence had been assembled with such completeness. W. R. Connor, in *Good Reading: A Review of Books Recommended by the Princeton Faculty* (vol. 25, 1975) noted that *Blacks in Antiquity* "made it possible to correct errors and omissions that have passed for the truth and has given us glimpses of a society which, for all its faults and failure, never made color the basis for judging a man." B. Warmington in his review of *Before Color Prejudice* in the *International Journal of African Studies* (vol. 17, 1984) wrote that the demonstration of the lack of color prejudice expressed in both my books is certainly correct. Though some scholars have doubted my findings, Warmington went on to point out that the doubters are of two types. There are a few classical scholars who have misread the ancient evidence. Then there are Afrocentrists who have adopted a practice of identifying the Egyptians as blacks, or Negroes, and who have maintained that the history of blacks has been distorted by a "white conspiracy" that has whitened historical figures such as Eratosthenes, Septimius Severus, Cleopatra, and Hannibal. Then there is Martin Bernal, who in *Black Athena: The Afroasiatic Roots of Classical Civilization* (1987) joins the Afrocentrists in his misreading of the ancient record. He has written that his emphasis on the African nature of Egypt and "the presence of people *whom one might usefully call black* among its rulers" are important to counter the cultural debilitation of people of African descent [emphasis added].

Several important points relevant to the blackness of Africans in the ancient world emerge from an examination of the iconographic and written evidence. Both Bernal and the Afrocentrists, overlooking this evidence, have mistakenly assumed that the term "Afri" (Africans) and various color adjectives for dark skin pigmentation used by Greeks and Romans were always the classical equivalent for "Negroes" or "blacks" in the modern world. Not all people described by classical color words such as "melas" or "niger" were blacks or Negroes as understood today. Only the inhabitants of the Nile Valley south of Egypt, known to Egyptians as Kushites, Ethiopians, and Nubians were the rough equivalents of modern blacks. These Africans were characterized by various combinations of dark or black skin, woolly or tightly curled hair, flat or broad noses, and thick lips. The color of these Africans, one of their most characteristic features, was highlighted in the name Greeks and Romans invented for them, "Aithiopes" (Ethiopians) meaning literally burnt-faced peoples. The color of these Africans, the blackest known to the Greeks and Romans, was different from that of other dark-skinned peoples such as the Egyptians, Moors, and Indians. They were dark, but not as dark as the Ethiopians, whose hair was the woolliest and most tightly curled of all mankind. Although the ancient Egyptians were darker than their Greek and Roman neighbors, they were not black in the sense of negroid or Afro-Caribbean. The Egyptologist David O'Connor has written on this matter in "Ancient Egypt and Black Africa and Early Contact" published in *Exploration: The Magazine of Archaeology and Anthropology.* He pointed out that "thousands of sculptures, paintings and representations from Egypt as well as hundreds of well-preserved bodies from their cemeteries show that the typical physical type was neither Negroid nor Negro" (14 [1971]: 2).

Some Afrocentrists have gone beyond Bernal in invoking a white conspiracy by highlighting how Eurocentric racists have "whitened" historical figures such as Cleopatra, Septimius Severus, and Hannibal. In a chapter in Ivan Van Sertima's *Black Women in Antiquity* (1989) entitled the "African Warrior Queens," John Henrik Clarke argues that "until the emergence of white supremacy, Cleopatra was generally depicted as a distinctly African woman, dark in complexion." In this chapter, Clarke ignores all the ancient sources to the contrary. In support of his claims, he offers inter alia a nonexistent Cleopatra in the Book of Acts. As further proof of Cleopatra's blackness, Clarke cites a reference to the queen as "fat and black" in Ripley's *Believe It or Not*. His final "evidence" is a *modern* painting of a negroid Cleopatra. There is no reference at all to the Macedonian lineage of the entire Ptolemaic dynasty that includes non-negroid features. There are also images of the queen on her own coinage that contradict Clarke's racial characterization of her. G. M. Jones in *Stolen Legacy* (1954) charges that the Greeks were not the authors of Greek philosophy and misused African and blacks as equivalents. He tells us that the geographer Eratosthenes, the head of the great library in Alexandria and a native of the Greek colony of Cyrene, was black because Cyrene was in northwest Africa. E. L. Jones wrote a passage of emotionally charged rhetoric in *Profiles in African Heritage: Black Studies Series in Classical History* (1972): "Any time a person achieved fame or became outstanding in ancient or medieval history, it was taken for granted that they *[sic]* were white." As proof, James cites the Emperor Septimius Severus, although none of the numerous portraits of the emperor provide any evidence at all of negroid features. The Carthaginian Hannibal has been frequently considered by some Afrocentrists as black. J. A. Rogers maintained that the Carthaginian people were negroid and that Hannibal was a full-blooded Negro with woolly hair. I. Van Sertima (1958) also referred to Carthaginians as "Africoid peoples." Timothy Kendall has pointed out significantly that one of the great ironies of the Afrocentrist position is that their emphasis on ancient Egypt has led to a very distorted and myopic view of history. Ironically, the modern bias of the Afrocentrists has led them to neglect the great significance of ancient Ethiopia or Nubia, which really was a black African culture of enormous influence and power. I have dealt with the Afrocentric misreading of history elsewhere in detail. Furthermore, Mary Lefkowitz, in *Black Athena Revisited* (1996) and in other publications has accurately pointed out the distortions of the Afrocentrists.

The differences between black and white relations in the ancient and modern worlds are striking. First, in the ancient world there were prolonged black-white contacts from the earliest times. Second, initial white contacts with blacks frequently involved soldiers and not so-called savages. Ethiopia or Nubia was perceived by Egyptians, Greeks, and Romans as an independent country rich in resources and inhabited by the blackest people known in their experience. Despite Egypt's centuries-old conflicts with its black southern neighbors, the *Great Hymn to the Aten* looked impartially at diversity of speech, skin color, and character, and acknowledged all peoples, whether Egyptian, Syrian, or Nubian as creations of the Aten, the sun disk. Greeks and Romans selected the fair Scythians of the distant north and Ethiopians of the deep south as examples of an environment theory of human physical differences and as dramatic examples of "the other." Both groups exemplified the broad scale of human potentiality. As Menander wrote in the fourth century B.C., it makes no difference whether one is as physically different from a Greek as a Scythian or an Ethiopian: it is merit, and not color, that counts. The same northern and southern peoples also appear in a highly spiritual context in early Christian pronouncements that all whom God created, he created equal and alike.

The color of blacks presented no obstacles that excluded them from opportunities available to other newcomers living in Egypt, Greece, or Italy. Ancient slavery was color-blind. Both blacks and whites were slaves, and the ancient world never developed a concept of the equivalence of slaves and Negroes. Nor did they create theories to prove that blacks were more fit than whites for slavery. The majority of slaves in the ancient world were white, not black. Prisoners of war accounted for the majority of black slaves. At the same time, however, the advantages of cosmopolitan centers such as Alexandria and Rome were as attractive to blacks as they were to Jews or Syrians. Like other slaves and freedmen, blacks often engaged in occupations at the lower end of the economic scale, but blacks with special talents and qualifications found places for their talent and skill. In Egypt, blacks had long found careers in the military a means of attaining positions of security and prestige. Roman imperial armies included Ethiopians like those in the *numerus Maurorum*—a unit of Moors of the Emperor Septimius Severus in Britain. There is an image of a black soldier depicted in a scene engraved on a third-century A.D. sarcophagus, apparently a member of the emperor's elite bodyguard. In the Roman world, blacks were popular in the theater. A famous black animal fighter was praised by the poet Luxorius in the fifth century A.D. in these words: "The fame of your renown will live long after you, and Carthage will always remember your name."

Included among the distinguished followers of the philosopher Epicurus was a black from Alexandria named Ptolemaeus. A black known only as Memnon was the most celebrated disciple of Herodes Atticus, the celebrated sophist and patron of the arts in the second century A.D. Racial mixing between blacks and whites gave rise to nothing resembling modern strictures about miscegenation. Intermarriage between Nubians and Egyptians was not uncommon and dated back at least to the fourth dynasty, about 2600 B.C., attested by the limestone head of a prince from the court of Memphis and his black wife. Greeks and Romans, like many blacks and whites then and now, used their own physical traits as a yardstick in their aesthetic preferences. Some scholars have read nonexistent antiblack sentiment into the Greco-Roman somatic norm image, but they have overlooked the fact that there were Greeks and Romans who praised the beauty of blacks, and there were still others who preferred blackness and had no hesitation in saying so.

Herodotus, the first European to describe the physical appearance of Ethiopians, describes them as the most handsome of men. In the first century B.C. one of the love poems of Philodemus to a certain Philaenion described her as "short, black, and with hair more curled than parsley, and skin more tender than down" and concluded, "May I love such a Philaenion, golden Cypris, until I find another more perfect." Greek and Roman writers such as Aristotle and Plutarch, who had occasion to refer to interracial marriages or any other aspect of black-white racial mixture, developed no theory of white purity. It should be noted also that realistic portraits of mulattoes and other black-white mixed types in ancient art illustrate dramatically the result of black-white mixture and at the same time point to the physical assimilation of blacks into the predominantly white populations of Greece and Italy.

Religion also knew no color bar. Blacks and whites worshiped Isis, a national deity of Egypt, at the same shrines and played an influential role in the spread of Isiac worship not only in Egypt but also in Greece and Italy. Christianity reinforced the strong bond that united blacks and whites in the common worship of Isis. Scythians and especially Ethiopians figured prominently in the imagery of the early Christian church. When Origen, the Alexandrian theologian (A.D. 185–255), the influential pioneer of exegesis and systematic theology, declared that God created all men equal, whether they were born among Hebrews, Greeks, Ethiopians, Scythians, or Taurians, he was using a formula well known in classical thought that left no doubt as to its meaning and comprehensiveness. Saint Augustine stated that under the name "Ethiopians" all nations were signified, a part representing the whole, and that that nation at the end of the earth was chosen to be mentioned by name. Augustine referred elsewhere to man's common descent and his common human nature in these words: "Whoever is born anywhere as a human being, that is, as a rational and moral creature, however strange he may appear to our senses in bodily form or color or emotion or utterance, let no true believer have any doubt that such an individual is descended from the one man who was first created."

The baptism of the minister of the Ethiopian queen by Philip the Evangelist, described in the Book of Acts was a landmark in proclaiming that consideration of color was to be of no significance in determining membership in the Christian church. Blacks not only were humble converts but also were influential figures such as Saint Menas, sometimes portrayed as a Negro, a national saint in Egypt. The black Ethiopian monk Moses, a patriarch of the Egyptian desert, was frequently cited as a model of humility and of the monastic life, as an excellent teacher, and as a father's father. He left some seventy disciples when he died at the end of the fourth or early fifth century A.D.

In the entire body of evidence relating to blacks in the ancient Egyptian, Greek, Roman, and Christian worlds only a few concepts such as the classic somatic norm image have been cited as evidence of so-called antiblack sentiment. This misinterpretation and similar misreadings of the ancient evidence, however, are examples of modern and not ancient prejudices. In treating a subject that is so alive today, nothing is easier than to read back twentieth-century ideas into documents that in reality have quite another meaning. This is precisely what many modern scholars have done. Misled by modern sentiments, they have seen racism where none existed. Further, it has sometimes been argued that color prejudice is inherent in human nature. Scholars may disagree as to the precise stage in the history of black-white relations at which color acquired the importance it has assumed in the modern world. One point, however, is certain. The onus of intense color prejudice cannot be placed on the shoulders of the ancient Egyptians, Greeks, or Romans.

Even if I had received no encouragement, I would have pursued my research. Once started, I realized that the investigation had to continue and that it would be necessary for me to conduct the type of fifty-year inquiry required to collect the relevant materials. Look where it led! You have seen the encouraging comments on even the early investigations: "Get offprints and send them out widely." Even in recent Harvard University Press publications on the classics, sections on popular Harvard paperbacks still include my *Blacks in Antiquity* and *Before Color Prejudice.* I have also been frequently invited to lecture at public schools, museums, and universities. If I had found Washington, D.C., and Howard unsupportive of my work, I could have left after the 1960s like other faculty members when the doors opened at many institutions from which blacks had been previously excluded. In fact, I had a variety of offers, but I enjoyed seeing the wide student interest in the classics grow at Howard. And the continuation of my research was facilitated by my access to the invaluable asset of the Library of Congress.

A chapter entitled "Attitudes toward Blacks in the Greek and Roman World: Misinterpretations of the Evidence" appears in *Africa and Africans in Antiquity,* edited by Edwin Yamauchi (2001). I have also completed two articles on attitudes toward blacks in the ancient world in *Encarta Africana,* edited by Kwame Antony Appiah and Henry Louis Gates Jr. of Harvard University. So much for my investigations on blacks in the ancient world pursued for more than half a century.

4

Writing about African Americans in American History

The Career of John Hope Franklin

I was born in the small town of Rentiesville, Oklahoma, which is seventeen miles south of Muskogee and sixty-five miles southeast of Tulsa. It was an all-black village. My father moved to Rentiesville in 1912 and found it lacking in opportunities, not to mention amenities. He was postmaster, justice of the peace, notary public, and president of the Rentiesville Trading Company. Out of all that he did, he still could not make a living. So he knew very early on that we would have to leave. My mother taught school, and this helped feed and clothe us, and send my older sister and brother to private school.

Living in an all-black town had its advantages. The only time we were exposed to racial prejudice was in traveling on the railroad to Checotah, five miles south of Rentiesville. We had no other means of transportation to and from Rentiesville. The first racial incident that I can remember was when my mother, sister, and I went to Checotah. As the train approached Rentiesville, we flagged it to stop. It barely did. So we got on wherever we could. It so happened that the coach where we boarded was for whites only. We did not know it at the time and the train was already moving. When my mother sat down, the conductor told her that she was in the wrong car. It made no difference that this was the only place that we could get on. She told him that we could not go back to the coach for blacks since the train was already moving. The conductor stopped the train. We thought that he did it so we could move to the segregated coach. But he put us off the train. By this point, we were well into the woods and had to walk back to Rentiesville. I must have been about seven years old. I wrote about my early years in Rentiesville for my 1994 Cosmos Club (Washington, D.C.) lecture entitled "Vintage Years: The First Decade."

In 1921 my father moved to Tulsa. We would have joined him when school was over in early June. But the Tulsa riot occurred on the first day of June. (See Scott Ellsworth, *Death in a Promised Land: The Tulsa Race Riot of 1921* [1982].) Whites looted and burned much of the black section of the city and killed a number of blacks. We did not know whether my father was living or dead. The only news we got was from the Muskogee newspaper. Everything he acquired in Tulsa had been burned to the ground. It was four more years before the family could move to Tulsa. So instead of moving in June 1921, we left Rentiesville in December 1925 when I was ten years old.

After the riot, black and white people were very careful in their etiquette and everything else in dealing with each other. There were no new racial flare-ups. I experienced no serious racial incidents in Tulsa because it was absolutely, completely, unequivocally, and inescapably racially segregated. You could not go to any white movie theater in Tulsa. You had to go to one of the two black theaters. The parks and all the recreational facilities were racially separated. Of course, the schools were segregated. The one place in Tulsa that we could go and be with white people, but segregated, was Convention Hall. This is where the musicals, recitals, concerts, and traveling entertainment came. The Chicago Civic Opera appeared there after the close of their season in Chicago. My mother and father would not go to Convention Hall or any place where they had to segregate themselves voluntarily. It was unavoidable on trains and buses. I went to Convention Hall because I was very fond of music. They were very liberal parents in that they would let me go despite their opposition to segregation. Their feeling was that if I wanted to humiliate myself by going and sitting in the Jim Crow area, that was my problem. So I enjoyed Gershwin playing *Rhapsody in Blue,* Paul Whitman's orchestra, and John Philip Sousa's band, as well as the Chicago Civic Opera.

I was expected to go to college. My father and mother had gone to college. My brother and sister had gone to college. My brother had gone to Fisk University, and my father had gone to Morehouse College. It was not a surprise that I graduated from high school as valedictorian at age sixteen. The question was not whether I would go to college but *where* would I go. My brother was more influential than my father. My younger sister and I followed him to Fisk University, rather than to Morehouse College where our father had gone.

At Fisk University in Nashville, Tennessee, one of the first things you learned was to avoid the downtown. I had a very unpleasant racial experience my first time in downtown Nashville. To this day, every time I go to Nashville I remember it. There was a transfer point in downtown Nashville where all the streetcars converged. We were in transit to Fisk. I only had a

$20 bill, which I gave to the attendant for the 25-cent trolley ride. I apologized to the attendant and explained to him that I only had a twenty and that he could give me dollar bills if he could not spare fives or a ten. He pointed his finger at me and said, "No nigger is going to tell me how to make change." He gave me $19.75 in dimes and nickels to teach me a lesson. But staying out of the downtown was not enough. Racism in Nashville was not limited to downtown. Fisk University owned some properties near the university that it rented out. A young tenant named Cordie Cheek was alleged to have struck a white child. Cordie was taken from the house by a white mob not a block from Fisk University and lynched. This was in 1934. We were all traumatized and protested afterward.

In the fall of 1934, after the lynching, I was a senior and president of the student council. Franklin D. Roosevelt came to visit Fisk University on his way to Warm Springs, Georgia, for his annual vacation. People in Nashville could not believe that he would come to Nashville and not stop in the city for a public presidential visit. There was no stop at all-white Vanderbilt University and no stop at the governor's mansion. The morning of his visit the radio announcer said the president would make only one stop and that was at the Hermitage outside the city. Everyone knew, but whites could not believe that he was also going to stop at Fisk, which had made extensive preparations. The president wanted to hear Fisk's choir. I was in the choir. Black and white people began to come to campus to see the president. A white man about sixty years old came up to me and asked where white people sat. I told him that there was no special place. He could sit wherever he liked. He became angry, but not at me. He said, "I have voted the Democratic ticket all my life. But if the president can come here and countenance Negroes and whites sitting together, I will not vote the Democratic ticket any longer. This is too much for me."

When I first arrived at Fisk, I wanted to be an English major. While I was in a course on contemporary civilization, I heard a series of lectures given by Theodore Currier, who was chair of the Department of History. It was fascinating to hear a historian handle problems as he did. I decided to take a course with him, and that was my undoing as an English major. I knew that history was what I wanted to do with the rest of my life. The way he projected history was so exciting; the questions he raised were so concise and penetrating; and the answers were so dramatic. The whole flow of human experience was laid out in such a way that I found it was the most exciting and attractive intellectual activity I had ever engaged in. I knew then that I wanted to be a historian. This was in 1932, and I declared myself a history major in 1933 with a minor in political science. Fisk prepared me for graduate school with great care. Especially important were Professor Currier's history seminars and tutoring. He was my mentor in every sense of the word. I graduated in 1935.

Harvard

Professor Currier encouraged me to apply to Harvard University where he had done his graduate work. He felt that this was the place I should go. I had no feelings one way or the other as to where I should have gone to graduate school. I was admitted to Harvard, but with no financial aid whatsoever. I was told that I was the first African American admitted without conditions and from a black college. Just that spring, the Association of American Universities put Fisk on its list of approved undergraduate colleges. Based on that, Harvard admitted me without conditions. Du Bois was admitted to Harvard from Fisk with conditions because at that time Fisk was not an approved undergraduate institution. My father wanted to help financially, but this was at the depth of the Great Depression. By this time, he was an attorney in Tulsa, but most of his clients were unemployed. We had already lost our home in foreclosure. Professor Currier went to downtown Nashville, borrowed five hundred dollars, and gave it to me as a loan. He said that money alone would not keep me out of Harvard. Once at Harvard I got a job washing dishes for my evening meal, and I took other jobs typing term papers and dissertations. I managed to exist. Then, it was not expensive to go to Harvard. Occasionally, my father was able to send me some money. I got a scholarship after my first year and was able to complete my degree.

I did not find Harvard openly and blatantly prejudiced toward me. I was socially inexperienced and had been somewhat sheltered in Tulsa and at Fisk. I had no unpleasant racial experiences at Harvard. Part of the reason for this was probably because I lived off campus in a house with other African American students. I did not want any more dormitory living after the dormitories at Fisk, and I preferred the rooming house that many of the black Harvard students had lived in. I washed dishes at the Pi Eta Club, and got to know a number of people. One was Joseph Kennedy, the oldest of the Kennedy brothers.

The only social encounters I had with white students were in the History Club and the Henry Adams Club for American history students. That is where I had the most jolting experience of my years at Harvard. At the end of my first year, I was placed on the nominating committee of the Henry Adams Club. We were to nominate and vote on the officers for the following year. As I look back on it, I am certain I was placed on the committee so that I would not be a candidate for office. When the committee met, the question was asked who should be the next president of the club. I suggested that there was only one person who should be considered because he was the leading student and a wonderful person. They asked me who that was. I said confidently, "Oscar Handlin." There was dead silence. One student for whom I had a lot of regard up to this point responded, "Well, one thing is for sure, he does not have all the objectionable characteristics of Jews. But he is a Jew."

I was shocked and speechless. I did not know anything about anti-Semitism. I did not know Oscar Handlin was a Jew. To me, he was white, just like the others. I began to realize that these white people were talking about another white person and were capable of doing anything to destroy him if necessary because he had some alleged strange qualities that I had not discovered. Later, they said that he was this or that—all racial stereotypes. This was mind-boggling. I had been so busy all my brief life worrying so much about the race thing that I had never realized there was ethnic, cultural, and religious prejudice as well. This was very disturbing to me and the only major experience I had at Harvard with prejudice.

On another occasion, a professor told a racial joke in class. He was a distinguished professor of economic history. He said something to the effect that if a white man was unhappy about something, he would protest. If a black man was unhappy, he would mope and go to sleep. I did not think it was funny, and there was no reaction from the other students in class.

Race relations in Boston were not ideal. I remember that in the fall of my first year at Harvard, during the Harvard-Yale game, I took a young lady to Child's Restaurant in Boston. We sat there for about an hour. They were not about to serve us. I realized then that things were not all right in Boston. Juanita Jackson, who at that time was the youth secretary of the NAACP, came to Boston to have a meeting with people interested in the NAACP. They did not have a chapter there. The meeting was at a home of the Women's League for Community Service. I attended the meeting and was asked to say something. I said that Boston should start a strong chapter of the NAACP. Boston needed it and I told of the experience I had had. A local woman who was one of the grande dames of the black community stood up and took serious objections to a little black southerner coming up to Boston trying to tell them what to do. She turned to all the young people in the audience and told them to ostracize me. They were not even to speak to me because I did not know what I was talking about. That was my initial contact with organizations in Boston.

Despite the grande dame's opposition, I had a number of black friends in the Roxbury community who were good to me. I spent a good deal of time with them. I did not have the money to leave town or to call home, so I was with them for dinners on Thanksgiving, Christmas, Easter, and all the other holidays as well. A young black man at Harvard was unusual and very attractive. So their doors were open to me and the other ten to twelve black Harvard students. We all knew each other and were spread across the different schools. The exceptions were the business and medical schools. They had no black students when I was at Harvard.

My mentor in history at Harvard was Arthur Schlesinger Sr. who edited, with Dixon Fox, *A History of American Life* (1927–48). When I arrived at Harvard, he became my counselor. When it got to the point of selecting a dissertation topic, it was clear that I wanted to work in southern history. I approached Professor Schlesinger, the most popular American history professor in the department. He already had many graduate students. He said to me that while he would be very pleased to supervise my dissertation, there was a young associate professor in the department whose field was southern history. It would be good for him to have a graduate student and, frankly, he could give me more time. This was Professor Paul Buck, who had just won the Pulitzer Prize in History for *The Road to Reunion, 1865–1900* (1937). Professor Schlesinger made it clear that if I did not like Professor Buck, he would work with me on my dissertation.

I went to meet Professor Buck. He was thrilled that I would consider having him as my adviser. He said that he would work with me under one condition—that I did not audit his class. He said that I knew more southern history than he did. I was his first Ph.D. student. Most of the professors in the department had twenty dissertations going at one time. Paul Buck had one. So he gave me all the time I needed. When I came to North Carolina to do research, he and his wife, Sally, came to visit. When I was writing my dissertation, I could send a chapter to him on Monday and I would have it back by Friday. There was no airmail then. He must have received the chapter on Tuesday and read it on Wednesday for it to go into the mail by Thursday. This was important, because his responsiveness enabled me to finish my dissertation while I taught five courses at St. Augustine's College in 1941.

Doing Research in the South

I took my general oral examination in February 1939. I came down to North Carolina that spring. By then I just wanted to leave Harvard. I came to feel that the Harvard faculty was arrogant, that Harvard students were very pretentious, and that it was not a very healthy environment. So when Professor Buck asked me if I wanted a fellowship after my examination, I said no. Instead, I came to Raleigh, N.C., to work on my dissertation. I had several friends from Fisk University who were teaching at St. Augustine's College. They told me that the woman who had taught history for many years, Professor Jessie Gumsey, was retiring and I should apply for the job. This was a good position because I would be able to continue my research that was based in Raleigh. Starting in the fall of 1939, I taught. In the spring, summer, and on weekends, I did research.

In 1939 I began work on *The Free Negro in North Carolina, 1790–1860* (1943). This was a formidable task, because the libraries were racially segregated. I had to figure out how I would get access to primary documents. I will never forget my first entry into the archives of the State of North Carolina in the spring of 1939. The director, Christopher Crittenden, was taken aback by my presenting myself. He was very frank and told me that when they planned the building, they did not take into account that blacks might want to use it. So there were no accommodations for blacks. He meant that there was no segregated place in the facility where they could keep black researchers. He said that I was entitled to work there like anyone else, but that he would have to have some time to accommodate me. "Come back in a week," he said. I just sat and looked at him. I was paying room rent and did not want to pay for those extra days. He then suggested I come back in three days. When I did, he had cleared out a small conference room across the hall from the main research room. He put a desk, chair, and wastebasket in there. He presented me a key to the stacks and archives. He was concerned that the pages who brought materials to white patrons would not bring materials to me. It was considered a privilege to have materials brought to you. So I had to leave my room, go into the research room, walk across it, and use my key to go into the stacks. Not wanting to go through the room often, I loaded my dolly with materials to take back to my room. I did that for about two weeks.

One day Mr. Crittenden called me into his office and said that he would have to relieve me of my key. I was dismayed. Were they going to make me come in by the back door? I could not imagine what was the problem or what they were going to do. He said the library patrons were coming to him complaining that they were being discriminated against. I was the only one with the freedom to come and go at will through the stacks and archives. The "privileged patrons" did not have this privilege. They had to wait for the pages to bring them one box at a time. He said he could not give out keys to everyone. He had to take my key to satisfy them. So from now on, the pages would bring my materials to my separate room. Some of the white researchers took great satisfaction in seeing me come in, turn in one slip for one box, go back to my little room, and wait there until the page brought my box.

There were three racial patterns in the libraries of North Carolina. The first pattern was as I described it above. I was segregated, but had my own room. The second pattern could be found in the State Library of North Carolina where they were much more accustomed to black students using the library. They had their system all set. They had a table back in the stacks for black people. We could not go into the search room or reading room other than to deliver our requests. But since we were in the stacks, we could read newspapers and go down the aisles and read what we wanted. The third pattern was evident in the library of the Supreme Court of the State of North Carolina. They had no segregation. You could sit wherever you liked and use whatever you wanted. Thus there were three different patterns, and all within three blocks of each other. It was just as C. Vann Woodward described it in *The Strange Career of Jim Crow* (1966). They simply did what they felt they could do or wanted to do with regard to blacks.

You never knew what you were going to run into going into libraries and archives in the South. When I went to Alabama to do research in the State Department of Archives, I was very apprehensive. After all, this was Alabama, not North Carolina. I expected the very worst and was even hesitant about going into the building—not knowing whether I would be thrown out. But I went in. An older white woman on staff asked me what I wanted and to fill out an identification form. To my surprise, she went and got the papers. After she gave them to me, she just stood there and watched me. There I was holding this box and I did not know what to do. Was I supposed to go downstairs into the basement, was there a room for me, or what?

So I looked around and saw some white people sitting at a table on one side of the room. I went to the other side of the room to sit. She called to me and told me that I could not sit there. "Well," I said to myself, "why didn't you tell me in the first place where I was supposed to sit?" She then said, "That's the hottest part of the room. There is no fan over there. Sit over here [where the whites were sitting], on this side of the room where these other people are sitting. There is a fan over here and a place at this table. Come over here. They need to meet you anyway." I thought, this is Alabama! She stopped all the whites at the table and introduced me. She had read my identification form and knew I was from Harvard. She said to them, "This man is from Harvard University. You ought to meet him." She was an odd woman for 1945 in the South. I talked with her later. She said that she got a kick out of upsetting these people down here and pointed to the dark splotches on her arm. "I tell them that this is the Negro blood in me."

I worked for two to three weeks at the archives in Alabama. I wanted to read the papers of Alabama governor John Winston, who served just before the Civil War. When I asked the clerk for the governor's papers, I was told that those papers were not open. I would have to get the permission of Mrs. Owen, the head of the archives. Her full name was Marie Bankhead Owen. One of her brothers had been a senator. Her other brother had been Speaker of the House of Representatives. Her husband was the founder of the Alabama State Archives. He was dead, and she was carrying on as his successor. The clerk said that I could get her permission when she came in. Since she came in when she felt like it and at no particular time, I asked the clerk how I would know when she was in. The response simply was that I would know. Everybody knew when she was in. Try again the following afternoon.

I came back the next afternoon and was told to go up to see her. She had a huge office. She was this little old woman with a big hat on. She sat in a large chair behind an enormous desk. She looked like she was getting ready to go out to tea. I asked the secretary if I could see Mrs. Owen. As I went into her office, I immediately learned two things about racial etiquette. First, her secretary did not close the door so that there could be a witness to everything I was doing. Second, Mrs. Owen did not ask me to sit down. There were a number of elegant chairs in her office. She told me that I could see Governor Winston's papers and any other materials in the archives. Then she asked me how they were treating me in the building. I said very well indeed. She said if I had any problems, just come to her. As I was about to take my leave, she said to me, "They tell me that there is a Harvard nigger here. Have you seen him?" Her secretary, who was overhearing the entire conversation, rushed in and said to Mrs. Owen, "That's him, Mrs. Owen, that's him!" She then said, "I would have never known. You don't act like a Harvard nigger. You got right nice manners. Sit down." So I sat down for the first time. She asked me where I was born and raised. I said Oklahoma. She asked where I went to college. I said Fisk University. She said, "That's it. That's where you got those good manners." In her mind, my parents could not have properly raised me in that "foreign" state Oklahoma. I had to be raised in a good old southern state.

Mrs. Owen then began to go on about her upbringing, her background, and her views. She talked about her closeness to the people at Tuskegee (the black college founded by Booker T. Washington), and her fondness for Dr. and Mrs. Moton (see *Robert Russa Moton of Hampton and Tuskegee*, ed. William Hughes and Frederick Patterson, 1956). She was a newspaper reporter in Montgomery, Alabama, when Booker T. Washington died. She decided to write a piece favorable to Dr. Moton. In the following years she became very friendly with the Motons. Years later, when she learned that Dr. Moton was perhaps terminally ill, she went to Tuskegee to visit him. When she called at the Moton home, Mrs. Moton came to the door. She very pointedly asked me if I heard her say "Mrs. Moton." White women in the South did not call black women "Mrs."— this was considered a title acknowledging respectability and status. She made an exception with Mrs. Moton, because she was a "great woman." Mrs. Owen went on, "But I do not want you to get any ideas. I am not going to call you mister. I will call you reverend, professor, anything. But I will not call you mister." She talked for two hours. I was trying to get out of her office to do my research. Since I had good manners, we were the "best of friends." During a later visit with her, I found her very upset with President Truman. She thought that breaking down segregation in the armed forces was the worst thing. This would divide the nation and soon we would be back in the Civil War. Talking with her was the best course I ever had in southern history, because she was the embodiment of the old South and a historic figure herself.

From there, I went to Baton Rouge to the Louisiana State Archives on the campus of Louisiana State University. They had a policy of not admitting blacks at all into their archives. When I got there, the archives were closed. The Second World War had just ended and there was a week of celebration. The archivist Edwin Davis, who did not share this view of total segregation (see Edwin Davis, *Plantation Life in the Florida Parishes of Louisiana, 1836–1846, as Reflected in the Diary of Bennet H. Barrow*, 1967), told me that he would be working during this time in the archives and that I was welcome to go in with him. I worked there peacefully and profitably for a week, only because Louisiana was celebrating the end of the war. In the proceedings of the Citadel Conference I have an article on these experiences called "Pursuing Southern History—A Strange Career."

I decided to do my first book, *The Free Negro in North Carolina, 1790–1860*, after reviewing a number of options. I went to graduate school with the intention of doing work in England with a focus on British social history. But if I could barely get to Cambridge, Massachusetts, it stood to reason that I would not ever get to England. I was washing dishes in 1935 just to get my next meal. It did not make sense to think I would get to England. I learned at Harvard that doing serious research required working with primary materials at the source. London was as far away for me in 1935 as Mars is today.

I wrote a paper for Professor Schlesinger's class on Lyman Abbott and the Social Gospel. I became very interested in Abbott and that whole movement. When I was selecting an area for my general examination, I thought I would do something on the Social Gospel. But then I found out that James Dembrowski at Columbia University had just finished a dissertation on the Social Gospel and was about to publish on the same subject. I decided that I would not pursue that subject anymore.

During my undergraduate work at Fisk University, Professor Theodore Currier had me write on the free Negro in the antebellum South. There were thirty thousand free Negroes in North Carolina before the Civil War. I had to go to the archives in Nashville and was fascinated by the subject. So when I was trying to figure out what to write on at Harvard, I remembered this paper. My initial research was to make sure there was nothing already written on this subject. I talked to Professor Buck about the topic and he was also fascinated by it. By the time I did my oral defense for the Ph.D., I knew this would be a good subject to work on and announced that this was what I would do.

My next book interest came in a similar way. By the time I had done the reading for the free Negroes in North Carolina, I had become fascinated with southern belligerence and romanticism. William J. Cash's *Mind of the South* came out in 1941, and he talked a lot about the southern mood and spirit. The more I read about and looked at the plantation, the more it became clear to me that the mood and spirit was one of an armed camp. The armed patrols looking for runaway slaves were omnipresent. I was curious about them. This is the research I was doing in Alabama and Louisiana. I learned a great deal.

I went regularly to the American Historical Association meetings. I did not go to the Southern Historical Association meetings until I was invited. It was said that any Negro who was smart enough or who had sense enough to want to go would also be smart enough and have sense enough *not* to go to the southern meetings. Why would you want to humiliate yourself at racially segregated meetings? In 1949 C. Vann Woodward was chair of the program committee of the Southern Historical Association. He invited me to read a paper, to the great dismay and distress of the other members of the committee. They were upset over having an African American on the program. They asked where I was going to sit, where I was going to stand, where I would read my paper, and so on. They asked why Vann Woodward was doing this to them. He responded that Professor Franklin was very resourceful and would take care of himself. I gave the paper and no one got excited; no one dropped dead or got hurt. The room was packed. Henry Steele Commager volunteered to preside, and Bell Wiley and several others agreed to be on the panel with me.

Meanwhile, the word got around that I was working on a nonblack subject. New correspondence relevant to my interest in militancy in the South had recently been discovered, primarily at the Huntington Library. There were white historians who were dismayed and outraged that I would undertake such a study. When the manuscript went to Harvard University Press, it was sent to a major historian of the South. This historian wrote back to the director of the Press that he could not understand why they were interested in a Negro's view of the South. But if they were, John Hope Franklin's view was about as good as they could get. When the director of the Press called me, I told him that I did not have a "Negro view" of the South. I called it as I saw it, and I do not think any fair-minded historian would do any differently. The editor said they were going to publish the book. That book is *The Militant South, 1800–1861* (1956). Those who were surprised at this book were familiar with *From Slavery to Freedom: A History of American Negroes* (1947). They thought of me as a Negro historian doing the Negro's history.

Historians were also familiar with me because of a review I did of E. Merton Coulter's book, *The South during Reconstruction, 1865–1877* (1948). I had been asked by Charles Thompson, the editor of the *Journal of Negro Education,* to review Coulter's book and several others for the journal. The journal was not widely read among my colleagues in American history. When I met with Charles Thompson, I told him that, based on my reading of Coulter's book, I could not review it and the other works in one article. He told me that I could take as much space as I wished. So I wrote an article in which I took Coulter's book apart piece by piece in a withering review. I have not done anything like that since. This was an awful book, even for the late 1940s. In his book, Coulter had every stereotype ever imagined about black people. I ordered 250 copies of the review issue and sent them to every major historian I could think of. I did not deal with what was debatable in Coulter's book. I addressed only the things that were indisputably bad and so clearly erroneous that they could not be debated. The responses were amazing; I have a huge file of responses from other historians. I would say that this review more than anything else is responsible for my achieving a certain level of recognition among historians.

Ideologies and Scholarship

I have a very specific view of political radicalism. In the first place, I am more of a puritan than a pilgrim. I am for taking this house and cleaning it up. I was opposed to the Communists. They were very active in trying to recruit students when I was an undergraduate at Fisk University in the early 1930s. Neither then nor now can I make the distinction between totalitarians and Communists. So I was never tempted. I cannot tell you how vigorously they were pushing students to join the Party. I could name some who fell for it. In fact, some of these former Communists are now more to the right than I am. I guess I have always been something of a centrist. You cannot be a good scholar and an ideologue at the same time. I did not have as much of a problem with working through existing institutions to improve society as others did.

My criticism with regard to inequality in American life has been with specific economic practices such as monopolies, price fixing, and racial discrimination. At the same time, I think there is a lot to be said for an economic system with the potential to give real opportunities without discriminating. I have always had problems with a system that controls or restrains freedoms. I felt that the Communists were all about limiting freedoms, just like the fascists. We would all be restrained come the revolution. So I have never been impressed with Communists to the point of thinking about joining the Communist Party. At heart, I do not think institutions are the fundamental problem. It is the people who run institutions. The same applies to the Republican Party today. I have no patience with either totalitarian government or the view that the best government is the least government. I have no fear of big government, which has gotten a bad name like liberalism. In a system as large and as complicated as ours, you have to have some institution that can stand over other powerful institutions with real authority. If you want to have a free market economy, then you have to have someone strong enough and powerful enough to keep those who would restrain the market from abusing the public. That means a government with power.

The big theme in *The Free Negro in North Carolina* was the anomalous position of blacks who were free in the midst of a slave system. They experienced the tensions of living as free persons in a society that did not want them to be free. They were indicative of the capacity of blacks to desire and live in freedom, and they were living contradictions to everything that was said about blacks. They were a reminder to whites that there was an alternative to slavery, and to slaves. They reminded them that freedom was possible. What fascinated me about free Negroes was that they refused to leave the South. They saw it as their country and their future.

From Slavery to Freedom was a huge educational project. I was asked to write the book by a publishing house's college department and not the general marketing division. My editor, Roger Shugg, wanted the book for the college-educated reader. I wanted to teach the American people about the history of black people in this country. They did not know this history and that it is an intrinsic part of American history. They cannot know their own history without knowing about the role blacks played in it. This is true for the black and white general public alike. I wrote *From Slavery to Freedom* to be part of the general history of this country so that Americans could see the connections and relationships. This is very different from what Carter G. Woodson had in mind with *The Negro in Our History* (1922). *From Slavery to Freedom* was not written as a textbook, and at the time I had no notion of it becoming one. While I was aware of the need for more courses on blacks, *From Slavery to Freedom* was not in response to that need.

The reason why the book became so well known is that in the years after World War II there was recognition of the need for a general body of knowledge to be available to the public about "Negroes." So when the need arose for such a work, *From Slavery to Freedom* was there. This postwar need for such a work increased dramatically in the 1960s and 1970s with the interest in incorporating African American history into the general university curriculum. There was already an awareness of Afro-American history at the primary research universities such as Columbia and Harvard. The greatest need was at the large state universities and the historically black colleges. No one was more shocked than my publisher at the demand for *From Slavery to Freedom*. They could hardly keep the book in print. They would print five thousand more copies thinking that this would meet the demand, and then that lot would sell out. This kept happening until they realized that they had to keep the press rolling.

I became interested in the culture of the slave South from my research on *The Free Negro*. I wrote *The Militant South* because I was impressed with the South's attempt to reconstruct medieval feudalism and its belligerence well before the Civil War. They fought each other, dueled over honor, and had military schools, militias, medieval ring tournaments, and celebrations with knights in armor. I have to confess that I wrote the book partly to make fun of white southerners—their militancy was somewhat silly. This is a book I wanted to write. No one asked me to.

My essay "Lincoln and Public Morality" is a published address I gave in

1959 at the Chicago Historical Society. This was a time when there was great concern regarding the appropriate behavior, role, and conduct of public servants. President Eisenhower's chief of staff Sherman Adams was given a fur coat. There was such a storm of protest over this gift that he had to leave office. I went back to see what was the sense of public morality in the middle of the last century. This essay begins with President Lincoln receiving a coat from one of his constituents. He was not hounded from office. Then I went on to note what pressures there were on public officials and what their responses had been.

I wrote *Reconstruction: After the Civil War* (1961) as part of the History of Civilization Series of the University of Chicago Press. Dan Boorstin asked me to write that book. I had already written it in my head after reviewing Coulter's *The South during Reconstruction*. After reading Coulter, I knew what a book on Reconstruction should have been. So it was easy for me to write that book. I was very familiar with the literature and especially admired W. E. B. Du Bois's *Black Reconstruction* (1935). But Du Bois's was an angry book. It was not tempered by the judgment that one needs to convince someone of one's argument. Dr. Du Bois and I were good friends and I admired him. He was certainly one of the greatest thinkers and writers ever. But I could have never divided a bibliography as he did by those who were fair, somewhat fair, and hostile to my point of view. My Reconstruction book was written to show what I thought a Reconstruction book should contain. It is revisionist because it took on one by one the stereotypes first established by Thomas Dixon's *The Clansman: An Historical Romance of the Ku Klux Klan* (1905; which was the basis for the 1915 movie *Birth of a Nation* by D. W. Griffith), *The Tragic Era: The Revolution after Lincoln* (1929) by Claude G. Bowers, and others. My point was that they did not have it right.

Color and Race (1968) is a book I edited as a result of a conference on color held in Copenhagen, Denmark. The objective of the conference was to assess the meaning given to color in various parts of the world. In areas where we least expected it, there was a very strong sense of color consciousness. There was a paper by a Japanese scholar on the great sensitivity of the Japanese to various shades of yellow, not white or black. There was another paper on color in India, as well as a very striking paper by a Brazilian. According to this writer, the Brazilians had a very detailed sense of color awareness and consciousness. This scholar lost his professorship because of his writing. He was later vindicated through the legislature.

Land of the Free: A History of the United States (1965) was an eighth-grade textbook written with Ernest May and John Caughey. The California state legislature said they wanted a textbook that reflected the diversity of the population and the spirit of equality and democracy. We decided to write a book that would do all these things and submitted it for adoption. The trend toward diversity was just starting. We noticed that some of the new "diversity" textbooks were ludicrous examples. Some included diversity materials after the index as an afterthought. Since Caughey, May, and I did not have a book to revise, we wrote a book that was historically accurate and had diversity as an intrinsic part of the text and submitted it. The Textbook Commission of the State of California adopted it. But adoption was followed by a period when the book was available in public libraries throughout the state so people could comment on the content of the book. The reaction to our book was open hostility, primarily from whites. There were specific objections to the pictures, to the cartoons, and to the content. The campaign against the book took form in Land of the Free clubs. At club meetings, those who wanted to misrepresent the book would show slides of the authors and then slides of the book's content. At this point, when my picture was shown, they would begin reading from the Communist Manifesto. At one point, there was even a motor caravan that went from Los Angeles to Sacramento to protest against adoption of the book. The book was finally adopted and used for five years in most classrooms in California, but the opposition continued. In fact, one man was sued because he did not want his child in the same room with *Land of the Free.* Finally, it was superseded by another book.

One of my other books is *A Southern Odyssey: Travelers in the Antebellum North* (1976). I wrote that book because when I was working on *The Militant South* I was struck by the large numbers of southern whites who spent a great deal of time in the North. They traveled in the North; they sent their children to school there; they went to resorts in the North and went shopping and sightseeing. Yale, Harvard, and especially Princeton were very popular places to send their children. Meanwhile, for the public record, they spoke bitterly of the North, while clearly enjoying everything about it. In fact, when the Civil War broke out, many Southerners were in the North and had to scramble home. Then when the war was over, they went right back North in the spring and summer of 1865. My book is about their claim for the superiority of the South while their actions showed otherwise.

The Nineteen Eighties: Prologue and Prospect (1981) was written with Kenneth Clark. The Joint Center for Political Studies asked us to set up a committee of the best black scholars in the country to talk about the problem of race. We called it the Committee on a Policy for Racial Justice. We issued a series of statements about the problems of race. Kenneth Clark and

I extracted from these statements and projected what we thought were the problems faced by the nation in the coming decade and how we should go about solving them. It was a great exercise for us, but it is questionable what impact it had.

I edited *Black Leaders of the Twentieth Century* (1982) with August Meier. We were trying to get a handle on the kinds of leaders that have emerged in black communities in this century. It too was a very successful project.

Reflections on a Career

My focus has expanded from the 1960s on. The more I revised *From Slavery to Freedom,* the more I became convinced that it was the general public we needed to educate and work with rather than simply the college and university audiences. Then, as my reputation went beyond the academy, I was called upon by various groups to contribute. I started by giving expert testimony. I worked very hard on the famous *Brown vs. Board of Education* case. I began to feel that this was an arena that I had to deal with and where some of the big battles would have to be fought. The more I got out there in the community, the more I found out that education is a problem, as is housing, employment, and everything else. So over the last twenty years I have had an increasing interest in the larger problem and the larger arena. This is reflected not only in the committees I have worked on but also in my writings. A good example is the book *Racial Equality in America* (1976), which is based upon my Jefferson Lectures. This is probably my first major attempt to use history to project into the larger sphere my views about the burden of race on American history.

So it is no coincidence that my most recent book is *The Color Line: Legacy for the Twenty-First Century* (1993). The point I make in this book is that we have not solved the problem of the color line and that it will be inherited by the next century. We have not honestly and fully confronted the problem of race; it is alive and well, and more vigorous and robust than any African American can solve. I opposed the war in Vietnam and the Gulf War. I was at the night vigils in Durham addressing the concerns of those who gathered in opposition to the war. In my later years, I have become more of an activist. I was in the March 6, 1965, Selma, Alabama, march when the nation witnessed the unmerciful beating of white and black civil rights demonstrators. My evolution is rather odd, because it is the opposite of Churchill's dictum that there is something wrong with a young man who is not radical, while there is something wrong with an old man who *is* radical. But here I am, more radical at eighty-one than I was at fifty-one.

One cannot sit and see what is happening to this country and be passive. I have to get up and shout and do something.

There are a number of keys to why I was able to be productive. When I started teaching at St. Augustine's College in Raleigh, North Carolina, I had to finish my dissertation. This set the circumstance for the first key to my productivity: the necessity to teach, do research, and write simultaneously. I was also chair of a one-person history department for years. This is where and when I developed the work habits that propelled my career. The second key is that I did not resent my heavy workload at all. I was glad to be there. Remember, this was the 1940s and the U.S. Army was after me because a war was going on. I had a low draft number and was the right age. I was determined not to be drafted and was glad to be at St. Augustine's College. The third key to my productivity is that I enjoyed teaching. I taught for two decades before my first leave in the early 1950s when I got a Guggenheim Fellowship for part of the year. I maintained my dissertation-writing pace and habits during all this time and afterward. My next leave from teaching was almost twenty years later in 1973, when I went to the Center for Advanced Study in the Behavioral Sciences at Stanford University.

At St. Augustine's College I had a teaching load of four or five courses, at Howard University three courses, and at Brooklyn College in 1956 I had two courses and was chair of a department with fifty-two people. Not until I got to the University of Chicago did I have a load appropriate with my standing as a professor. But even there I taught because I had such a habit of teaching. I always taught a course and a seminar. Sometimes I taught two courses and a seminar. I taught the history of the south and at least once a year an undergraduate course on American civilization. Many of my colleagues did not teach in the college. It turns out that when you were appointed to the Department of History, you had no obligation to the college. By the time I reached Chicago, I was able to take the spring quarter off from teaching each year.

In doing research and writing, I do not believe that I neglected my teaching. My students remember me. The fiftieth class reunion at North Carolina Central had me as their guest of honor. They testified about what I taught them. The fiftieth class reunion at St. Augustine's College had me as their guest of honor as well. They talked about me, and discussed what and how I taught them. This reassures me that when I talk about my students I am not misrepresenting what I did.

The fourth key to my success is that I have enormous energy and do not tire easily. I go on and on and on, and enjoy what I do. Part of the habit is working wherever and whenever I can. At North Carolina Central I did not have an office. There were no offices even to share. I worked between classes in my classroom, an hour here and an hour there. I had this feeling that I ought to use every moment, and I did. In fact, I wrote *The Free Negro in North Carolina* and *The Militant South* by snatching moments here and there. I am not a morning person, afternoon person, or night person. I am a person who will use any hour I can get. When I open my eyes, I am as awake as I am going to be that day. I do not have to work with the radio and TV on. I can do without it. In fact, they painted my bedroom some years ago, disconnected the TV, and I have yet to reconnect it. People ask me, "Did you see such and such?" I say, "No, I did not." I cannot watch TV and do what I do.

The fifth and most important key to my success was my wife. We were classmates at Fisk and married after nine years of courtship. She had her own career as a librarian in Goldsboro, Raleigh, Durham, and Washington. She was solidly behind me. I know that I could not have had this kind of career and achieved all that I did without her support. I feel sorry for people who do not have a happy marriage and instead have a wife or husband weighing them down at home. I had a friend once at Howard University. He and I went to a conference and arrived home late one night. He had to call me after midnight for his wife to get verification that we were at the meeting together. If I had a spouse like that, I would have gotten nothing done. Despite the demands of her own career, my wife was as cooperative and supportive as she could be. For example, when I contracted to write *From Slavery to Freedom* we were living here in Durham in a small apartment. There was no place for me to work in that apartment. We had a small living room, bedroom, and kitchen. There was no study space. My wife suggested that I go to Washington to work in the Library of Congress, where I could get a study room and write *From Slavery to Freedom*. But I did not have the money to support myself in Washington. My publisher gave me all of five hundred dollars as an advance. My wife sent me money every month. I started work on the book in Washington at the end of the summer of 1946, and I wrote that book in thirteen months.

There are other examples of my wife's support. I went to all the historical meetings, yet St. Augustine's College had no travel money. I used my own money to go to these meetings and again my wife helped me to do that. I could not have done that without her support. If it meant making social and material sacrifices to advance my work, she would do it. On another occasion, I had noticed on my way home that new homes were being built not far from us. I told her that we could build a brand new house. She asked me, "Why would you want to do a thing like that? Don't you know that you are only going to be here a couple of more years?" I asked, "Where am I going?" She said, "I don't know, but you are going." Two years later I was a full professor at Howard University. You have to do something with your career if you get support like that. Hers was a remarkable display of loyalty and support. When I was finally able, I took her everywhere—to Europe, Australia, Japan, Russia, and India. She had earned it.

A sixth key is to do what needs to be done despite the obstacles, whether they are graduate courses or segregated libraries. I learned early to compensate for whatever deficiencies or disadvantages I have. I am most conscious of first doing this at Harvard. I used to look at the other students who were from the finest prep schools and colleges in the East. I was up against them. I realized that where I have deficiencies I just had to compensate for them. I will never forget a course I took on medieval English constitutional history. The professor came into the room and announced that the course text was Stubbs's *Select Charters*. The book was in Latin. The professor told us there were no good translations and we would have to read it in Latin. Many students got up and walked out of the class. I asked the ones who left how much Latin they had. Some said they had two years in prep school and two years in college. Several others who were leaving had four years in college. I had only two years in high school. I stayed in the class. My approach was that I would have to learn Latin. I worked as hard as I could. I wrote a term paper entirely from Latin sources and got a B in the class. I suspect that no matter how good my work had been, the best I would have gotten was a B. I could have written *Select Charters* and it would have been the same.

Finally, it is important to stay ahead of those who might resent you. I have tried all the time to ignore them or be two steps ahead of them. By no means do I think that I am above criticism. I have not done all that I could do. As I have already indicated, where I have deficiencies I have attempted to make up for them with my strengths and hard work. For example, I am deficient in languages, philosophy, and economics. I could have written very different kinds of histories if I was better trained in the social sciences. But I am not and have done the best I could with the training I have.

I involved my students in my work whenever I could. They were not as involved in the publishing side as is the case in the sciences. In my research seminar at the University of Chicago, students had access to limited research materials on southern history. So I brought my seminar down to Raleigh, and we spent several weeks at the archives. Ironically, the same man who arranged my little room at the archives in 1939 was still there. I had the unique pleasure of seeing my students, all of whom were white, working in the search room I could not use in 1939. I now had an office in the archives where my students could come to me to ask questions. This was in 1967. Since then, other scholars have validated much of the work I did. A number of former students have been involved. Also, several of my former research assistants have published and have served with me as coeditors and coauthors. Just last year, I published an edited collection of conference papers with a former student who is now a full professor at the University of North Carolina, Chapel Hill. The book is *African Americans and the Living Constitution* (1995) with Genna Rae McNeil.

Some years ago, I decided that *From Slavery to Freedom* was still so vigorous and had such a life of its own that I needed a coauthor. So I invited another one of my Ph.D.'s, Alfred A. Moss, at the University of Maryland, College Park, to help me with the sixth edition. That was the fortieth anniversary edition. Since then, we have produced a seventh edition. In more recent years, I have been working on a project looking at runaway slaves. Here again, I have invited to work with me a former student who had done significant work in this field. That is Loren Schweninger at the University of North Carolina at Greensboro. We are fairly near the end of writing that book. It is a source of great personal satisfaction for me to have former students work with me. By the way, Loren is white, as have been several of my other cowriters, and this is a message to the scholarly community that scholarship can be color-blind. If black and white scholars share the same views and interpretations of the antebellum period why should we not work together? Again, my students have taken note of their involvement in my work, and reacted to my writing, and written about it themselves. Their book about me is *The Facts of Reconstruction: Essays in Honor of John Hope Franklin* (1991). They talk about me in there. They presented it to me at a dinner in my honor. I had no idea they had worked on such a project. They all spoke and then gave me some time to defend myself.

I taught at Howard University from 1947 to 1956. Then I taught eight years at Brooklyn College before going on to the University of Chicago. When I returned to Durham, N.C., I had retired from the University of Chicago and had not planned to teach another day in my life. I came here to write the biography of George Washington Williams as a Senior Mellon Fellow at the National Humanities Center for two years. In my second year at the Center, Duke University offered me the James B. Duke Professorship in History. That is the topmost university chair at Duke. I had been the John Matthews Manly Distinguished Service Professor of History at the University of Chicago. So the offer was not at all flattering to me. But Duke University had never had an African American hold a named chair. At first,

I thought that I need not do it, but then I realized that they needed it. They needed the experience of having me at Duke with that chair.

As far as my scholarship is concerned, I do not believe I have done enough on Native Americans. I have been criticized for this recently. There is not enough about Native Americans in *From Slavery to Freedom*. This is an interesting point, because I am a descendant of Indians, slaves, and free blacks who were removed to the western territories by Andrew Jackson in the 1830s. My people have been in that area since then. Yet I have not addressed the question of slaves among Native Americans. I feel bad about this. I was once going to do a book entitled *Red, Black, and White,* but I never got around to it. Yet I have done work on race and ethnicity in *Ethnicity in American Life* (1971) and "Land of Room Enough" in *Race and History: Selected Essays, 1938–1988* (1989). Both address immigration policy. I take the view that there is plenty of room in the United States for all of us. "Land of Room Enough" is a favorite piece of mine. I also wish that I had done more work in cross-cultural processes. In a sense, I backed away from it, partly because there is more and more work being done in this area in Canada, the Caribbean, and South America. I welcome the work being done on the African diaspora. I felt I needed to remain focused on the United States. Because of this, I have pulled out of *From Slavery to Freedom* chapters on Latin America. Earlier, I even had a chapter on blacks in Canada.

George Washington Williams: A Biography (1985) is nearly my favorite work. It is clearly my best effort. I spent forty years on it. It is a level of biographical writing that is not common. This book represents the kind of digging and spadework and character construction that not many people are required to do. I had to assemble Williams's papers myself. I have been to Europe, Canada, Africa, and England more than once to find documents regarding this man's life. I think I got him. It has been a great adventure. If you live with someone for forty years, you learn to like him or you grow to hate him. Williams was a remarkable man. The *New York Times* got from my book that he was a trickster. Indeed, he was slick. There was no question about that, but I did not mean it in a demeaning way. He was as close to a genius as I have ever seen, and he was flawed. I worked on that book so long that I got to a point where I did not think I could live without it. I did not want to finish it. What would I do if I was not working on Williams? I finally finished it. It was a runner-up for the Pulitzer Prize and it won the Clarence Holte Literary Award. I have always wanted this book to be done as a movie. I talked to Sidney Poitier sometime ago about it but have not heard from him.

My favorite writing is to be found in *Race and History: Selected Essays.* It is my favorite because it reflects the full range of work that I have done and the issues that have concerned me during my career. In a way, this book says it all. One will find some monographic interpretations there as well as a chapter on Williams. This book is an object lesson on how to do research. I can read it now and get excited. My favorite work is not the most important book I have written. Certainly the most important is *From Slavery to Freedom.*

We need institutional analyses at two levels—the nation and the community. We need histories of the black churches. We do not have the big picture of the national black churches, nor do we have histories of churches at the community level. The same applies for our national organizations. Charles Kellogg did the first volume of *History of the National Association for the Advancement of Colored People* (1973), followed by Jacqueline Harris's *History and Achievement of the NAACP* (1992). But that is all there is. There should be a lot more on this important organization. There is a history of the National Urban League, but it concentrates on Whitney Young's administration. These histories could help us get a better focus on what kinds of black leadership we need—what works and does not work and for whom. Nor do we have any well-done and thorough histories of the historically black colleges. There is recent work on Fisk and Atlanta Universities, but there are more than one hundred other black colleges. The black schools constitute a movement that has not been properly studied.

We need to know a lot more than we now know of the relationships between whites and blacks in the post-Reconstruction period between 1880 and World War I (1917). This was a very important period. We need a history of the early national period from the time of the American Revolution (1776) to the Jefferson administration (1801–9). This is the John Adams era. This is the period when policies were put in place that defined and redefined the role of blacks in American society. Another is the period of *Plessy vs. Ferguson* and of the Civil Rights Act in the late nineteenth century that was aimed at addressing the policies of this period. This was the time of the most degrading writing about blacks, such as "The Negro: A Beast" and "The Negro: A Menace to American Civilization." We have not dealt with this period, and it haunts us to this day.

5

Studies of the African Diaspora

The Work and Reflections of St. Clair Drake

My seventy-eight years can be divided into three periods that have shaped my scholarly interests. The first period was the prewar years spent in a racially segregated South (though my very earliest years were spent in Pittsburgh). My experiences as a student at Hampton University in Virginia and contact there with Professor Allison Davis moved me to want to study, understand, and change the odd world of Jim Crow. This desire led me during my post-Hampton years to the Quaker Graduate Center, Pendle Hill, for a year, and then later to fieldwork with Davis in Mississippi helping to gather data for the book *Deep South: A Social Anthropological Study of Caste and Class* (1941). After that I went on to the University of Chicago for graduate work in sociology and anthropology. It was there that Horace Cayton and I gathered the data that resulted in *Black Metropolis: A Study of Negro Life in a Northern City* (1945).

The second period began with the end of the Second World War. There was the excitement and promise of a new world free from fascism and racism. The war had shown that deep and rapid change in America's race relations was possible. But this promise and possibility were frustrated by Cold War politics at home and neocolonialism abroad. This is the period when my interest in race relations as an international and diasporic experience developed. In 1951 I published "The International Implications of Race and Race Relations." In 1954 I went to Africa for a year of teaching and research in Liberia and Ghana. In 1958 I returned to Ghana for two years at the national university and then helped to train four teams of Peace Corps teachers for the country. I went back again to the University of Ghana in 1965. After the coup of 1966, I shifted the focus of my field research to the Commonwealth Caribbean. One of the results of these experiences was a book (not yet published) "Africa and the Black Diaspora: Impact of Africa on the New World."

The third and current period began in 1969 when I was fifty-eight years old. Black students' reactions to the traditional humanities and social science curricula in American colleges resulted in some very provocative questions asked about the respective roles that Europe and Africa have played in the history of Western civilization. For the most part, black scholars of the older generation, with a few exceptions (a significant one was Carter G. Woodson), wrote with white readers in mind. Now there were a significant number of black readers who had a deep personal interest in race, culture, and the African diaspora. It also became apparent that there were serious flaws in the portrayals and assessments of the roles that Africans have played in the New and Old World. A number of black scholars have been quick to address these issues and this is where my current work focuses with the series *Black Folk Here and There: An Essay in History and Anthropology* (1987–90).

This essay goes into the background of these three periods of my life. My intent is to outline the underlying contexts that have influenced my work and that of other black scholars since 1935. An understanding of context is important in determining how current and future scholars will interpret mid-twentieth-century scholarship on race relations and ethnic cultures. The importance of seeing black scholarship in context is that it has set the stage for the development of a comparative scholarship on the African diaspora that is new and exciting.

The Prewar Years

My early years were spent first in Pittsburgh, Pennsylvania, and then in Staunton, Virginia, where Jim Crow was moderate relative to the Deep South. My earliest attitudes toward racist practices were formed in communities in the North and upper South, but my knowledge about Africa and the variety of cultures within the black world was developed earlier by my father. He was from Barbados in the British West Indies, a Baptist preacher who left the ministry temporarily to become international organizer for Marcus Garvey's Universal Negro Improvement Association. I spent one year in the West Indies with my father's family. A then-famous black minister, William H. Shepperd, would periodically visit our church and home. He had been a missionary among the Bakuba in West Africa, where he had attacked the colonial policies of the Belgians and was jailed for being outspoken. He and my father's other missionary friends talked often of events and experiences in Africa. Thus I had to deal with the cultural similarities and differences between Africa, the West Indies, and the United States as a youth.

Africa was not an uncommon topic in black homes before the Second World War and the coming of television. All the black religious denominations had missionaries working in the "ancestral continent." Black newspapers and opinion magazines like Du Bois's *Crisis* were the major sources of information in black communities about African affairs and prominent personalities. They kept Africa very much before us. This point is documented in my chapter "Negro American and the Africa Interest" in John P. Davis, ed., *The American Negro Reference Book* (1966).

During the 1920s and 1930s young black students could walk right by a big white high school to reach their underfinanced segregated school, as I did, and not give much thought, if any, to segregation. Our classes were lively. Basketball was exciting and the annual Negro History Week inspirational. However, I could not use the city library. I was told that I could have access to books if one of the white students at the college where my grandmother was a maid checked them out for me. My first publication was a letter to the editor of the Staunton daily newspaper protesting their practice of calling black women in their newspaper articles by their first name rather than by "Miss" or "Mrs." To my and everyone else's surprise they actually changed. This taste of victory spurred me on to become a habitual protestor. We were segregated, but it was not with the same harshness of the Deep South—Mississippi, Alabama, Louisiana. Later, I read C. Vann Woodward's discussion about the gradual growth of segregation in *The Strange Career of Jim Crow* (1966).

In 1927 I graduated from the Booker T. Washington High School and went to Hampton Institute (now University), the school that produced Booker T. Washington. I did not know what I was in for. The students at Hampton were in revolt during my first month in college. The 1960s was not the first time black students rebelled, marched, and protested. Hampton had a largely white faculty and administration. The presence and influence of the old post–Civil War, New England schoolmistresses were still very strong. They believed they were on a "civilizing mission" and saw as a part of their role curbing their black students' "natural passions" and maintaining proper decorum. Dancing was taboo and semi-military discipline was imposed on the men.

Initial conflict began over whether the lights were to be left on in the back of Ogden Hall where movies were shown. Only seniors could "escort" girls to these films. When lights were kept on in their section of the hall, these young men felt that this newly adopted policy was insulting to "Negro womanhood." They began chanting, "Lights Out, Lights Out." The protest spread to the dormitories. A decision to strike was taken, kicked off by a refusal to sing spirituals at Sunday night services. There is an excellent history of this period at Hampton in Enoc Water's *American Diary: A Personal History of the Black Press* (1987). But Hampton was not the only black school with protests at the time. There was a general mood of protest, impatience with segregation, and willingness to change outdated practices all across the South. An analysis of the strikes in black schools can be found in Raymond Wolter's *New Negro on Campus: Black College Rebellions of the 1920s* (1975).

There was a close relation between Hampton Institute and Tuskegee Institute. Thus I came to know of the historic conflict between Dr. Du Bois and Booker T. Washington over a desirable policy for educating former slaves. But not until I visited Tuskegee as a representative of Hampton Institute's student council in 1931 did I experience the Deep South's segregation, which impacted Booker T. Washington. White and black guests stayed at different guesthouses on campus! Our visit came when racial tension was high in Alabama and Mississippi. Sharecroppers were restless. The Scottsboro case had gripped the attention of the entire world. International pressure generated by the involvement of the Communist Party saved them from being lynched or executed. The mobs that smashed the windows of the U.S. Embassy in Hamburg, Germany, in protest at the treatment of the Scottsboro Boys seemed a long way from the rural Alabama I saw that spring. But consciousness of Africa was not.

Booker T. Washington had been competing for more than thirty years with W. E. B. Du Bois for influence in Africa. Instead of the conferences of intellectuals that Du Bois sponsored, Washington was proud to have sent teams of agricultural experts to Togo as early as 1900. Another team was sent to the Anglo-Egyptian Sudan in 1906. King Leopold had invited Washington to set up little Tuskegees in Africa from the Atlantic to the Pacific Ocean. The king wanted to whitewash his brutal rule of the Congo and his reputation as an oppressor. Fortunately, Robert Ezra Park, who was Secretary of the Congo Reform Association, saved Washington from being used. Later, he was Washington's assistant at Tuskegee for seven years. Then he went on to the University of Chicago and became one of the country's leading sociologists. In my introduction to *The Man Farthest Down: A Record of Observation and Study in Europe* (1984), which Washington wrote in collaboration with Park, I discussed the interaction between the black educator and sociologist. I did not know of this close relation until the 1960s.

While I was at Hampton, I read W. E. B. Du Bois's column in *Crisis*. I was a biology and education major; Dr. Thomas W. Turner was one of my mentors. Dr. Turner had been a colleague of Ernest Just. He was also a founder of the Catholic Interracial Association, and his feisty fighting influenced me. But the person who most influenced me was Allison Davis who was then a young English instructor. This black scholar had taken a master's degree in English literature from Harvard. Despite being near the top of his class, Harvard could not help him find work teaching at a white institution. This was just not done in those days. Sterling Brown, Davis's black contemporary in English at Harvard, went on to Virginia Theological Seminary. Then, later, Brown went to Howard University for the same reason that the most talented black scholars ended up at black institutions and, in particular, at Howard. The segregation of American university faculties was the main reason. Here was an illustrious group: sociologist E. Franklin Frazier, political scientist Ralph Bunche, Doxey Wilkerson in education, Eric Williams in history, and Alain Locke in philosophy. Allison Davis addressed the question of academic elitism in "The Negro Deserts His People," *Plain Talk Magazine* (1929), and called for dedication to the needs of the South. In 1931, the year I graduated from Hampton, Davis wished to become more relevant to Afro-American needs. He left English and Hampton and went back to Harvard to begin studies in social anthropology. He worked with W. Lloyd Warner at Harvard and spent a year in London with Malinowski. His shift in academic interests influenced my decision to move from biology to the social sciences.

During my senior year at Hampton, Allison Davis was invited to teach at the Quaker school, Pendle Hill, in Wallingford, Pennsylvania, outside Philadelphia. But he was "retooling" as an anthropologist. He recommended me instead. I was offered a scholarship in exchange for working with the Joint Committee on Race Relations of the Society of Friends. I gave speeches and participated in a variety of peace and antiracism organizational activities. On one project, the Peace Caravans, a friend of mine and I went down south as far as Tuskegee collecting signatures along the way to be sent to the First World Disarmament Conference in Geneva in 1932—that was a risky venture. It was at Pendle Hill that I first heard Reinhold Niebuhr speak. This is when I read his important *Moral Man and Immoral Society: A Study in Ethics and Politics* (1932), with a chapter suggesting nonviolent civil disobedience for Negro Americans.

There was great interest in the Gandhi movement at Pendle Hill; Gandhi had sent one of his followers to lecture to us in 1931. It was the head of Pendle Hill who founded the Fellowship of Reconciliation out of which the Congress of Racial Equality (CORE) eventually emerged. When you look closely at the history of peace and antiracism activities in this country Gandhi's influence on us predated his influence on Dr. Martin Luther King. In fact, an Indian student is now doing research that suggests that Afro-

Americans through their press were well aware of Gandhi and the nonviolent movement and its tactics decades before King's adoption of Gandhism. I also read Reinhold Niebuhr's *Reflections on the End of an Era* (1934) during this period and was greatly impressed by his call for fundamental structural reforms of American society.

After my year at Pendle Hill I taught science at the Quaker-run Christianburg Normal Industrial Institute in the mountains of Virginia. The western part of Virginia could not afford to run segregated schools in each county. Black children were simply told to go to white schools for their elementary education. For high school, several counties contracted with the Quakers to run a boarding school for blacks. As a consequence, the black students were getting a private boarding-school education at the state's expense—another irony of segregation. The first irony was Quaker support for such a solution to keep schools segregated. But even under those circumstances my experience with racial segregation, no matter how mild, was to me a daily affront and was barely tolerable. I welcomed a letter from Allison Davis who was then in England. He was about to return to the United States to begin anthropological fieldwork in Mississippi and asked me to assist in various ways. This was my initial entry into the field of social anthropology.

The Deep South

In 1935 Allison Davis joined the faculty at Dillard University in New Orleans as a base from which he could conduct research in Mississippi. It was Davis's objective to use anthropological techniques to find out the facts—how is Jim Crow organized and what motivates it? Then, as he said, "We shall destroy the system." Davis's motives and objectives were very different from those of his mentor, William Lloyd Warner. This is a point that is not discussed in Warner's methodological note to *Black Metropolis* (1945). Warner conceptualized the Deep South project several years earlier than the northern study while he was working on his Yankee City series. Warner wanted to study an American community by using the same participant observational techniques one would use to study a nonliterate society. Warner's theoretical focus was similar to that of Radcliffe-Brown, with emphasis on social structure rather than the traditional anthropological focus on cultural practices, institutions, and artifacts. Warner was interested in how you could chart people's movements across class lines. Well into the writing of his second volume he realized that no one had really conceptualized the southern racial situation with structural concepts. So the idea of *Deep South* was born.

Warner observed that southerners were primarily concerned with blacks as an endogamous group, insisting that each race be separated from the other in family and associational relations. Warner felt that this was consistent with a minimal definition of caste, where all institutional expectations and interpersonal interactions were organized by a "color line." What was intrinsically American about each caste was that social class subdivided them. The sanctions were secular rather than religious, as in India. This caste analysis was the theoretical perspective within which Allison Davis and I were identified as fieldworkers. In order to conduct the research even the black and white researchers were not able to associate with each other.

In fact, Davis had briefly worked with Warner in Newburyport, Massachusetts (Yankee City), in the small black section of town. Davis's manuscript, which should have been a part of the Yankee City series, was never published. There were others interested in the social class aspect of research on black communities. E. Franklin Frazier, for instance, had such a study in mind when he wrote *Black Bourgeoisie* (1957).

The research for *Deep South* was done by having a white couple (Burleigh Gardner and his wife) live in the white community and a black couple (Allison Davis and his wife) live in the black community. Their objective was to learn how people in each community defined their position in relation to others—who was "higher" and "lower" than they and why? By doing "evaluative participation" at the top and bottom of a society, you could find out where the collective understanding of social boundaries was. It was these divisions within a community that Warner called "social classes." Furthermore, the lines between groups were marked by "symbolic placement"—each group identified themselves by their automobiles, dress, speech, and so on. (See the first volume of the Yankee City series for Warner's methodological discussion, *The Social Life of a Modem Community* [1941].) Warner was also concerned with how indigenous class and caste lines were maintained. By the third year of the project, Allison Davis and his wife were identified with the black upper class in town and, therefore, did not have access to the black lower class. It was my job to move into the black lower-class community and do that part of the ethnography on the bars, juke-houses, shouting churches, and general lower-class areas. This gave me an experience in dealing with the bottom strata of society that stayed with me in research for *Black Metropolis* and in British race relations.

The Deep South research was not begun simply because William Lloyd Warner was interested in doing it. His attention and that of others were called to the South by the Scottsboro case and the Communist involvement generally in the South. There was general acknowledgment that little was really known in the North about the Deep South and the potential for other Scottsboro cases. The Deep South research was funded by the Rosenwald Fund and the Harvard Graduate School of Business Administration, which was interested in how costly it was to maintain segregation. There was another research team from Yale in the same area under John Dollard whose efforts resulted in *Caste and Class in a Southern Town* (1937) and Hortense Powermaker's *After Freedom* (1939).

Clearly the location and timing of these projects were no coincidence. The Communists were very active throughout the South. Concepts of "class" and theories of the role of the economic factor in social change were being widely discussed. These researchers made it clear that the social class they were discussing was different from the economic solidarity espoused by Marxists. When I went to the University of Chicago I found William Ogburn insisting that there was no resemblance between his culture lag theory and Marxian observations about changes in the social superstructure that were responding to changes in the base. Professor Warner points out in one of the Yankee City volumes that the idea of social class having any relation to the means of production is irrelevant in the United States.

The University of Chicago

When the Deep South project ended, my intent was to go and work for the Southern Tenant Farmers Union as an organizer. Their interracial cooperative cotton farm in Mississippi had impressed me greatly. But Allison Davis persuaded me to apply for another Rosenwald Fellowship, this time to study anthropology at the University of Chicago. Davis also wanted me to continue working with him in analyzing the *Deep South* notes. It was 1937 in the middle of the Great Depression. Roosevelt's New Deal made it possible for William Lloyd Warner to get a WPA grant to support graduate students' fieldwork for *Yankee City*. When he moved his base to Chicago, his students with WPA aid worked with Horace Cayton to build a data bank.

I joined the project and conducted research on a subject of interest to me. I prepared a mimeographed monograph, of which about five hundred copies were circulated: *Churches and Voluntary Associations in the Chicago Negro Community* (1940). This monograph has a number of hand-colored maps, since WPA rules would not authorize printing them, and now sells as a collector's item. A number of Ph.D. dissertations were produced from the data bank. Initially, there was no intention of using the material for any major publications. Later we decided to write *Black Metropolis*.

The WPA grant paid salaries but not rent for the research project. Cayton managed to get rent money from local numbers racketeers, referred to in *Black Metropolis* as "shadies." Cayton developed strong rapport with them. My participant-observation specialty was with the "lower class." At first, the numbers syndicate on the southside of Chicago was composed of ten blacks and one Italian. Later an Italian group took it away from the blacks. Cayton estimated that during the depression the numbers business had the largest payroll in Bronzeville. The running of the research project is described in detail in Cayton's autobiography, *Long Old Road* (1965). Working on this project was an important contribution to my graduate training in social anthropology at Chicago. This experience further confirmed my belief in the possibility of rapid change in American race relations.

In the late 1930s it was not odd for me to live in the ghetto participating in the life of the lower-class segment of the community. My not-too-well-educated associates felt that they were helping an upwardly mobile "brother" trying to save money. In 1939 eleven people were writing theses and dissertations from the data bank. At this point, Warner and Cayton decided that a book should come from the project. They both asked me to apply for another Rosenwald Fellowship in order to write the first draft. At first, I was more interested in finishing the work for my degree, but I postponed that goal. My focus had been on the black churches and on the lower class, and Cayton's on the shadies and upper strata of Chicago.

You will find a methodological note in *Black Metropolis* by Professor Warner, where he describes the research on *Black Metropolis* as a continuation of *Deep South*. To Warner, both the North and South met the requirements for a minimal definition of a caste-ranked social stratum with endogamy as a cardinal rule. Louis Wirth disagreed, as did Horace Cayton, with the idea of calling the interracial situation in the North "caste." To them the North is characterized by the social structure of an urban setting, fluid, not fixed.

Also we could not use Warner's techniques of evaluative participation strategy in stratifying individuals in Chicago. The population was too large. And Bronzeville was far too complex to understand as a whole through participation. This was only possible in small towns such as Natchez, Mississippi, or Newburyport, Massachusetts. So we focused in Chicago on using club and church memberships, studying a sample of them to determine class dividing lines, with census categories as a check. What some sociologists call "status inconsistency" was apparent. Social status was not dependent on occupation, education, or income. What determined status and participation was lifestyle, with occupation, income, and education determining the limits. Education was the most important of these three criteria, in relation to lifestyles.

Meanwhile, Robert Redfield was becoming a major influence on my work in a department that had been dominated by Radcliffe-Brown's functionalist theory. However, the influence of Radcliffe-Brown's variety of British social anthropology is apparent in *Black Metropolis.* The emphasis was on social structure, not on culture—much to Melville Herskovits's dismay. I was very much interested in black church rituals and the style and content of sermons. There are stock phrases and common elements in prayers. Very little of this sort of behavior was used in *Black Metropolis.* You will find more interesting analyses of sermons in Joseph Washington's *Black Religion: The Negro and Christianity in the United States* (1984). Nor is there discussion in *Black Metropolis* of black folklore, the blues, or gospel music (which, incidentally, started in Chicago at Reverend Dorsey's Pilgrim Baptist Church shortly before I began doing research). *Black Metropolis* has other shortcomings. Our selection of material for presentation is biased toward the middle class. There was nothing in the book that took note of and assessed the "disrespectable" behavior within the middle class—for instance, the "blue movies" of the male subculture of clubs and fraternities. The sexual activities of the lower classes are not handled with "kid gloves." Another major weakness is that *Black Metropolis* lacks adequate statistical sampling procedures such as those in Helen and Robert Lynd's *Middletown: A Study in Contemporary American Culture* (1929). For instance, the representativeness of many of the generalizations might legitimately be called into question. Our only defense is that our own participant observation, forty years ago, made *Black Metropolis,* to some extent, an "inside view."

Like *Deep South, Black Metropolis* was not written simply out of academic interest in the black community. There was a great deal of general concern about the black condition during the depression and the early years of the Second World War. Marxists were using Jim Crow in the South and the condition of the ghettos in the North as very effective propaganda against the United States both at home and abroad. During the war years, the potential for black disloyalty and disruption was a very real threat. The foundations and the New Deal government sponsored research in the hope that it would help in decision making. At the same time that Cayton and I were at work on *Black Metropolis,* the important Gunnar Myrdal project was under way, which resulted in *An American Dilemma: The Negro Problem and Modern Democracy* (1944). The Carnegie Foundation had hoped to lend credibility to the research it sponsored and to actually minimize bias by having it directed by a Swedish social scientist, Professor Gunnar Myrdal.

E. Franklin Frazier was passed over as director because of his new emphasis on the global implications of race relations and because of his conflict with Melville Herskovits over the African cultural survivals question. It was decided that the way to utilize black scholars was to ask each to do a working paper. I did one on black voluntary associations and churches in the North with Allison Davis preparing one on the South. Oliver Cromwell Cox would have no part of the project. Ralph Bunche did one on black political leadership. When Gunnar Myrdal had to leave the country because of the war, Arnold Rose took over the project, but Ralph Bunche did some of the most important tasks in preparing two volumes for the press. Ironically, Myrdal did not publish Bunche's paper. It has been thought by some that Bunche's *World View of Race* (1936) had made him a project liability, since he concluded that pamphlet with the statement that racial conflict would only end after a "great class war" breaks out around the world.

The great concern about race in the United States would not have occurred had not the Left made race relations a key part of their critique of American institutions. After the Scottsboro case, race relations in the United States ceased being an isolated domestic issue and became an international embarrassment. It was defined as a flaw in the United States identity as a progressive democracy. The need to counter this image was partly expressed by the willingness of foundations to fund research into domestic race relations. The Rosenwald Fund supported *Deep South* and *Black Metropolis*. The Carnegie Foundation supported *An American Dilemma*. The American Council on Education supported Allison Davis and John Dollard's *Children of Bondage* (1946) as well as E. Franklin Frazier's *Negro Youth at the Crossways* (1967), Charles Johnson's *Growing Up in the Black Belt* (1941), Ira De A. Reid's *In a Minor Key* (1940), and W. Lloyd Warner, Buford H. Junker, and Walter A. Adams's *Color and Human Nature* (1941). The American Council on Education funded a series of studies on white youth as well.

There were other reasons, too, why the 1930s was so productive of books and articles about Afro-Americans. There was an informal coalition between major black leaders, many union leaders, and the Communist Party U.S.A., which was protected by the New Deal. For example, John L. Lewis, who was a Republican, depended on the Communists to organize where management was particularly recalcitrant about recognizing unions. But as soon as the CIO was well established, Lewis expelled twelve unions because of their alleged Communist leadership.

A number of conservative black college presidents quietly protected black radicals on their faculties. Mordecai Johnson, for instance, the president of Howard University, managed to fend off white federal legislators, who controlled Howard's budget, from engaging in a witch-hunt on his campus. Howard's faculty was a virtual center of activity for black Left intellectuals during the depression years. John Hope invited W. E. B. Du Bois, the most prominent of black radicals, to be on his faculty at Atlanta University after the NAACP became dissatisfied with him. He was fully aware of the opposition this would cause among trustees and donors at a time when the university was hard pressed for financial support, but he was loyal to Du Bois. The president of a little black college in Texas once said to a radical faculty member, "I hear you are publishing articles and poems in a magazine up there in New York run by people called 'Trotskyites.' You keep publishing up there, but not down here. These crackers ain't ever heard of a Trotskyite." In a previous period, covert support that made it possible for the NAACP and other organizations to successfully investigate lynchings in the Deep South came from none other than Booker T. Washington. This protection of radicals, left-wing and other, became a part of the academic tradition, breached only when severe pressure came from southern legislators.

The white Left on college campuses who played such a crucial role in internationalizing domestic race relations did not have white conservatives as administrators to run interference for them. An example is the case of Bernhard J. Stern, the assistant editor of *The Encyclopedia of the Social Sciences.* Stern wrote a book on Lewis Morgan, the anthropologist whose work on the family was used by Frederick Engels to write *The Origin of the Family, Private Property, and the State.* Despite Stern's distinguished scholarship, he was a virtual nonperson at Columbia University, "frozen" at the lecturer level. Randolph Bourne, who was important in the early days of the *New Republic,* was fired from Columbia. Gene Weitfish, a less-prestigious colleague who coauthored *Races of Mankind* (1953) with Ruth Benedict was the object of a federal witch-hunt when their pamphlet on race was used to combat racism in the army during the Second World War. She was fired. The white Left gave important support to the Southern Negro Youth Congress and the National Negro Congress led by A. Philip Randolph. It is forgotten that E. Franklin Frazier and Ralph Bunche played important roles in the National Negro Congress movement when A. Philip Randolph was president.

The role that the Left played in making race an important issue and in supporting black organizations needs to be reassessed. The older view is questionable that Afro-Americans were cynically "used" by West Indian and white Communists to advance their own cause and agendas. There was a lot more to the relation; each side was trying to use the other. Harold

Cruse popularized the view of left-wing perfidy in *Crisis of the Negro Intellectual* (1967). A more accurate appraisal is apparent in *The Narrative of Hosea Hudson: His Life as a Negro Communist in the South* (ed. Nell Painter, 1979) and in Mark Naison's *Communists in Harlem during the Depression* (1983). The close working relation between the Left and black intellectuals unraveled rapidly in 1941. The Communist Party U.S.A. initially refused to take sides in the Second World War due to the Soviet agreement with the Nazi leaders that neither would attack the other. The United States was clearly committed to aiding Britain and the European nations. A. Philip Randolph of the National Negro Congress (NNC), who was not a Communist, resigned as president of the United Front organization. NNC executive board member Ralph Bunche wrote the draft for the Republican Party's statement on the Negro for the 1940 elections.

The period of the holistic studies of community was over as well. Evaluating and monitoring change became more important to social scientists than understanding the internal structure of community.

The Postwar Years

The depression years showed us that profound change in American race relations was possible. Anthropologist William Lloyd Warner was impressed, however, by the extent to which rigid caste in the southern boundaries was maintained. Allison Davis and I, on the other hand, were impressed by just the opposite—the extent to which whites and blacks ignored caste codes—in unions and in some churches. (For examples of how the codes were often violated see Charles Johnson's *Patterns of Negro Segregation* [1943].) Change was even more pronounced in Chicago where the CIO was organizing the packinghouses and steel mills. Some of the most popular labor leaders who were effective in mobilizing Italian and Polish workers were black. There were daily events that were at variance with scholars' traditional view that William Graham Sumner's gradualism was the most appropriate form of social change—"slow change in the folk-ways."

Robert E. Park's theory of "a race relations cycle" was questioned, and Marx's idea that workers of the world would unite seemed justified. While Allison Davis and Warner had been instrumental in starting me on an academic career in anthropology, sociologists Louis Wirth and Everett Hughes had a greater influence on me during this period. They were taking activist positions in the Chicago struggles against racial discrimination. Amid the excitement surrounding interracial cooperation, I remember a warning from an old and uneducated black preacher in the South. He told me,

"Wait until the white brothers get the wrinkles out of their bellies, young man." After the war ended, the euphoria diminished, disappearing even in the CIO unions. The radicalism of the 1930s and the internationalization of racial politics of the 1940s led a number of scholars, including me, to greater interest in the subordinate condition and circumstances of black people internationally. The prospects of postwar national independence in Africa reinforced this interest in Africa and the diaspora, especially in Latin America and the Caribbean.

It was very clear to us by the end of the war that, if the federal government in the United States stood firmly behind the social objective of equality for Negroes, fundamental change could be brought about. During the war many of us saw ordinary whites in the South for the first time acting outside their "normal" caste context. It was particularly striking to see southern whites interacting with blacks as peers in nonunion situations. What made the difference was the weight of the government and military situations. However, protest was necessary to keep up the momentum.

But then, in 1943, I was given choices—be drafted to fight in a war that I opposed, go to jail, or volunteer for the Maritime Service to serve aboard its only integrated ship. I volunteered and here is where I saw change at firsthand. We were assigned bunks alphabetically and not by race. The fact that we all had to depend on one another in order to survive at sea made black and white crew members peers regardless of race. We saw that racial barriers did not have to be a permanent part of the nation's social mores, changed only by time and social evolution. Racial barriers were situational and could be changed purposefully and directly.

The idea that purposeful change was possible and that change would occur went deep into black postwar expectations. In a way, the expectations that served as a backdrop for activism and massive support for the civil rights movement in Montgomery in 1954 came out of the war years. McCarthyism and the Cold War only delayed this activism and eliminated what might have been well-organized support from the Left for the movement.

After doing my Ph.D. research in the British Isles and teaching in Liberia between 1945 and 1954, I became involved with the Southwest Hyde Park (Chicago) Association. By then, I was less inclined to study race relations in the abstract or race relations in which I was directly involved. We were struggling against the University of Chicago's efforts to control and maintain racial segregation in the community. This experience taught me a lot about institutional racism and denial. "Denial" was an important part of the strategy to maintain segregation in Hyde Park. Ironically, the argument in the 1950s was that race was of declining significance. It is also ironic that the past chair of the university's sociology department is William Wilson, author of *The Declining Significance of Race: Blacks and Changing American Institutions (1978)*—the most recent articulation of denial. The chair in the 1950s was Philip Hauser, and the department's emphasis on demographics was very useful in "saving" the neighborhood for the university. There is a chapter on this community struggle in Peter Rossi and Robert Dentler's *Politics of Urban Renewal* (1961).

In 1958 I left for Ghana. I was in Ghana as chair and professor of sociology at the University of Ghana from September 1958 to February 1961. While I was in Africa, the classic Frazier-Herskovits debate was put into perspective for me. I would now agree with Melville Herskovits that there has been a conditional maintenance at Africanisms in the New World. Initially Herskovits did not see this. Not until he had returned from Surinam in the early 1920s did he see African retentions in the United States. He held that there were reinterpretations, a few syncretisms, and retentions. He also believed that each major cultural group had a focus. For New World Africans their cultural focus was around religion and was most readily expressed through music and dance. Herskovits claimed that Cayton and I had suppressed evidence of Africanisms in Chicago church behaviors and that Pentecostal behavior was an "obvious" case of an African retention. It was in this emphasis on "locus" that Herskovits was led astray. By the time he wrote *The Myth of the Negro Past* (1958) he was sensitive to the more subtle and significant manifestations of Africanisms such as body movement, worldview, and family traditions rather than to specific concrete cultural forms.

In contrast to the Herskovits position, E. Franklin Frazier and I initially believed that rural southern folkways had replaced Africanisms. We argued that in social class and rural isolation, blacks were culturally no different from whites. After Frazier had spent time in Brazil he modified his view and acknowledged that there were still Africanisms among blacks in the United States. What the overseas experience had shown us both was that the basic structure of African societies was not organized around the conjugal unit. The center of family life was the lineage, usually of one parent only. In these cases, the African extended families were worship units for ancestor veneration and the maintenance of ancestor shrines. The destruction of African family ties in slavery weakened the basic religious unit and substituted elements of Christianity. Men having multiple conjugal relations was a reinterpretation, especially in the Latin countries. There was the practice of marriage "in the church" and then there was marriage "in the community." In black communities in both North and South America there have not been clear sanctions against extramarital relations. (See Frazier's "The Negro Family in Bahia," *American Sociological Review* 7, no. 4 [August 1942]: 465–78.)

The reason why Africanisms are more tenuous in North America is because of the thoroughness of Protestant insistence on eliminating all evidence of what they called "heathenism." Also Africans were a smaller proportion of the population than in a country like Brazil or on Caribbean islands. Blacks in colonial North America had more exposure to European culture. In the Catholic Latin countries slaves were encouraged to retain some elements of their culture and to reinterpret religious and family traditions. For example, in Brazil, urban slaves were not only allowed but also encouraged to set up voluntary associations under the auspices of a specific saint. Anthropologist Roger Bastide has given us a magnificent analysis in his book *The African Religions of Brazil* (1978).

One value of comparative studies is the insight they give us of the different ways in which race is defined. For example, Brazilian scholars describe race relations in the United States as "the prejudice of blood." Regardless of social status, skin color, or anything else, you are "black" if one of your parents or grandparents is so classified. In contrast, Latin race relations are based on "prejudice of mark." Color rather than "blood" is the basis of ascribed racial status. Some Brazilians insist that if you are wealthy or highly educated, you can enjoy the privilege of white status. But in reality, even money does not completely "whiten." All the Latin countries, including Brazil, draw distinctions at the extreme top and bottom of society—whites and blacks. What Stanford's Carl Degler (*Neither Black nor White: Slavery and Race Relations in Brazil and the United States* [1970]) calls "the mulatto escape hatch" is the key to understanding what it means to say education or money "whitens." Mixed blood individuals, not blacks, can reach the "top."

Latins are willing to call variations of racial mixtures "white," whereas this is not the case in North America. The larger numbers of Africans brought into Latin America and the inability to maintain rigid control over them were important reasons for this difference. For example, there were forty thousand Africans in Mexico City when Jamestown was founded. The result in the Latin countries is a tripartite system of race relations. Whites are at the top; mixed bloods (mestizos and mulattoes) are in the middle; and blacks are at the bottom of society. This is certainly the case in Brazil. It is also true on some non-Latin Caribbean islands such as Jamaica, where colored intermediaries between blacks and whites are referred to as "brown," or as Jamaicans phrase it, "red." "Shade of color" is highly relevant. Haiti is the only exception to the Caribbean tripartite system. The French whites were driven out, so mulattoes and blacks have fought for power. An important student of Caribbean societies suggests that in time there will be racial homogeneity. (See H. Hoetink's *Caribbean Race Relations: A Study of Two Variants* [1967].) What stands in the way of this eventual homogeneity are social class differences where whites and coloreds are slowing the pace of miscegenation. For the long run, Hoetink is probably correct. There are many poverty-stricken whites in the slums of S~o Paulo and Rio living right next to blacks. They are being "Africanized" and have little reason to defend the racial status quo.

Some significant work has been done on African culture in the Caribbean. Franklin Knight wrote *Slave Society in Cuba during the Nineteenth Century* (1970) followed by *The African Dimension in Latin American Societies* (1974). In Cuba slavery was ended in 1885, but by then 70 percent of slaves were free. Many of these were mulattoes. Ibos and Yorubas were being brought into the country as late as 1885. This meant that African culture in Cuba was vigorous just two generations ago. The Trinidadian musicologist Jacob Elder did work on the preservation of African social structure, *Song Games from Trinidad and Tobago* (1965) and *From Congo Drum to Steelband* (1969). Michael G. Smith, a Yale anthropologist, studied the Hausa in Africa and the continuation of African (Ibo and Yoruba) cultural forms in the New World. *Culture, Race, and Class in the Commonwealth Caribbean* (1984) was the result. He also wrote *Dark Puritan* (1963) about a cult leader in Grenada who drew on Africanisms within the population.

George Simpson of Oberlin wrote about Jamaican religious movements. Much of his work appeared in the journal *Social and Economic Studies* published in Jamaica. John Rickford at Stanford is doing important work on Africanisms in language. Several French scholars have studied the diaspora. Their collected work can be found in *Les Afro-Americains, Memoires de l'institut Francais d'Afrique Noire* (IFAN) no. 27 (Dakar, Senegal, 1952): 11–101. Then there is Joseph Harris's edited volume *Global Dimensions of the African Diaspora* (1982), which contains a number of significant papers. There are relatively few anthropological studies on West Indian cultures carried out by West Indians. Until very recently West Indian scholars focused on economic and political studies, a priority in developing nations. Governments and economies needed to be established, while local cultures were primarily associated with poverty and backwardness—a class bias. There is now a growing appreciation for the complexity and richness of local Caribbean cultures.

These studies of African peoples spread across the New World have shown the variability of African retentions. The work done to date gives us only a glimpse of what exists. Several more generations of scholars have more than enough work waiting for them in uncovering additional reinterpretations, syncretisms, and retentions of African cultural elements in the diaspora. When we look back on the Frazier and Herskovits debate and consider what we have learned since then, there is an Afro-American culture. But in comparison to African American cultures in Latin America and the Caribbean, Africanisms in the U.S. Afro-American culture are far more attenuated. Also in comparison to other core cultures in the New World, the North American culture has been influenced the least by Africanisms. The impact of Africanisms on the larger American culture is another area that is largely unexamined except in music. Herskovits had a rating scale on Africanisms with the bush Negroes of South America at the top and urban blacks in North America at the bottom. (See Herskovits, ed., *The New World Negro: Selected Papers in Afroamerican Studies* [1966].) He was correct in having U.S. Afro-American culture at the bottom and the urban United States at the very bottom. Overall, the cultural differences between Afro-Americans and white ethnic Americans is much less than the differences between white ethnics and Japanese Americans, Chinese Americans, or Jewish Americans.

The Current Period

It has been a long struggle within anthropology to move away from physical and biological classifications of race. In the 1940s most anthropologists began to insist that what were considered racial differences were really cultural. Some anthropologists suggested that we simply drop race as a concept, substituting ethnicity as a more useful one. (See Ashley Montagu, *Man's Most Dangerous Myth: The Fallacy of Race* [1974].)

Until very recently there were anthropologists who believed in the existence of a "Hamitic" race in Africa. They held that the Hamites were a cattle-breeding, light-skinned people who conquered ancient African Negroes and brought a higher civilization to the African continent. I challenged this view in 1958 with "Destroy the Hamitic Myth" in *Presence Africaine.* A person who did pioneer work to destroy this myth was Joseph Greenberg, then at Columbia, now at Stanford. He demonstrated in the *Southwestern Journal of Anthropology* that there never was a Hamitic language. If there was no language, there were no people.

But the Hamitic myth was only an introduction to the work that is now under way. Until 1970 the issues of race and culture were largely the province of scholars. The 1930s was the last time there was popular interest in race and culture, due then to racist theories emanating from Hitler's Germany. But the black studies movement changed that. Black students became new readers. They asked serious questions and were motivated by personal interests in identity. At the same time, some black scholars had declared the beginning of a new era—see Joyce Ladner's edited work *The Death of White Sociology* (1973). The critiques of traditional scholarship and the university curriculum as Eurocentric were particularly pointed. There was a new interest and openness to understanding the African experience outside the United States and an understandable exasperation at not knowing just what Afro-American culture was—like Herskovits's initial enthusiasm. I was one of the very few scholars of my generation to head an Afro-American studies program (at Stanford) in the early and stormy years of the formation of black studies. I had to rethink my work and direction.

Amid the new interest in the African diaspora, I had just finished a still-unpublished book, "Africa and the Black Diaspora: Impact of Africa on the New World" (1970). At the same time, Cheikh Anta Diop's *African Origin of Civilization: Myth or Reality* (1974) was emerging as a central challenge to the Western view of the role of Africa in world history. Diop's research challenged the view that the ancient Egyptians were a mixed race and that the Egyptian high civilization came out of the Middle East. Diop's thesis is that the early Egyptians were indigenous Africans—a "Negro" people—and that their high civilization was a refinement of existing African cultures, not a European or Middle Eastern importation. Diop insisted that his thesis could be proven if the Egyptian government would allow the testing of mummies in the Egyptian museums for amounts of melanin in the skin. However, Arab scholars have resisted Diop's work because by implication it makes them invaders of Egypt. Diop's work also follows after the very popular work of Howard University professor Chancellor Williams, *The Destruction of Black Civilization* (1971). Williams's work gives us a sense of the gravity of what a West Indian professor, George James, called "stolen legacy" in his book by the same name (1954) and British classicist Martin Bernal reveals in his book *Black Athena: The Afroasiatic Roots of Classical Civilization* (1987).

The emerging studies of the African diaspora and the corrective of ancient Egyptian history represent a formidable challenge to current American and European views. An important Western misconception was reflected in Carl Degler's *Neither Black nor White.* This excellent study is marred by Degler's contention that racial prejudice is natural and that it was normal for light-skinned people to look down on dark-skinned peoples. Degler has also privately criticized Frank Snowden's claim in

Blacks in Antiquity: Ethiopians in the Greco-Roman Experience (1970) that the ancient Greeks were not prejudiced against Ethiopians. Degler believed that Snowden should have known better. Degler's view is not simply his own. It is affirmed at length by social psychologist Kenneth Gergen in his essay "The Significance of Skin Color in Human Relations," *Daedalus* (spring 1967). This view of the superiority of light skin over dark skin runs through much current European and British scholarship on virtually all aspects of European contact and relations with the African world from ancient Egypt through the modern African diaspora. Sometimes it is a subtle assumption; occasionally it is explicit. It seemed to me that the view articulated by Degler and Gergen was an appropriate point from which to begin critical comparative studies. The question of the universality of prejudice against dark-skinned people should be examined in this fashion.

I began such critical comparative studies right after finishing "Africa and the Black Diaspora." The trail of enquiry led from the New World back through the Old. Bastide had pointed out some very significant developments in Brazil where poor whites participated in ceremonies of synchronized African and Catholic worship. In this sense there was a declining significance of color and race but not of Africanity. In this context the question arises as to how African cultural elements as well as "blackness" (phenotype) function in different places in the New World. This called for basic conceptual clarification: racism, color prejudice, and slavery are three very different elements in human experience. Slavery is the oldest and does not necessarily have any reference to color. At some points in history many different racial groups have been slaves and slavers. In contrast, racism is relatively recent, if we define racism as a system of belief avowing that groups of people are thought to be either superior or inferior based on heredity, sometimes symbolized by a distinctive phenotype. Specifically, a racist system assumes that all people in positions of power should be drawn from the superior group with those who are inferior being excluded from consideration.

If racism is recent, then racial slavery is also recent, where the distinction between the master and the slave is based on race. The Aryan myth is one such form of racism. The Nazis' distinction between themselves and Jews has as its counterpart the Hamitic myth—wherever you find light-skinned people in Africa with features of Caucasian people, they are superior to Negroes. I contend that these racist myths are recent, having developed since the eighteenth century. What has been difficult about the attempt to trace the origins of racism is its constant confusion with color prejudice, which has a much older history that is distinct from racism. I asked the question,

"Have sub-Saharan Africans been viewed universally as inferior in the realms of aesthetics, status allocation, erotic appeal, and mystical/religious attributes?" By exploring this question I found that societies prior to the eighteenth century, including those in Europe, reveal all sorts of inconsistencies. Color prejudice certainly existed in the Old World in various degrees, but it did not in itself fix a group's position in relation to power. *Othello* is a good example. Color prejudice toward Othello was expressed, yet he was recognized as having high status. Here is where I would be critical of Frank Snowden's book *Before Color Prejudice: The Ancient View of Blacks* (1983). He did not draw a distinction between color prejudice and racism. A more appropriate title for his book would be *Before Racism.* He discusses attitudes toward black people in antiquity, and there was some color prejudice.

There are many examples of color prejudice in the Old World, but it is in the New World after the sixteenth century that color prejudice, slavery, and racism become intertwined. It is in the African diaspora that color prejudice begins to be used to justify slavery. Racism as a systematic justification and belief develops later (in the eighteenth century) to justify both color prejudice and slavery. In Europe from at least the eleventh through the fifteenth centuries, blacks held high status in the religious symbol system until the expansion overseas began. Evidence would include almost three hundred Madonnas in France and the veneration of Saint Maurice. Four towns in the Alps are named Saint Moritz after the black military saint who was martyred in Roman times. E. H. P. Baudet states in his *Paradise on Earth: Some Thoughts on European Images of Non-European Man* (1965) that blacks were virtually canonized prior to the sixteenth century. This respect and veneration were not carried into the New World where slavery had to be justified. The only black saint venerated in the Americas is Martin de Porres of Peru, the saint of the poor and dogs. His counterpart in Europe, Saint Benedict the Moor, became the head of his monastery in Sicily. Nothing like this happened to Martin de Porres. Saint Benedict could be tolerated. He gave up his high position for the kitchen.

Charles Verlinden's studies in *The Beginnings of Modern Colonization* (1970) are very important in verifying the recent origins of racial slavery. Before 1500 white slaves from the Black Sea area were held in slavery throughout southern Europe and on Crete and Cyprus. When the Turks took Constantinople in 1453, the European Mediterranean nations began to look elsewhere for slaves. Prisoners of war from North Africa were replaced gradually by blacks from below the Sahara desert. The sugar complex—including African slaves—was brought to the Americas by Spanish and Portuguese settlers. Even after African slavery had been an established fact for more than a hundred years, racism had not clearly come into existence. In fact, theories of racism developed in the seventeenth and eighteenth centuries as adjuncts to nationalist European conflicts. (See Theophile Simar, *Etude Critique sur la Fondation de la Doctrine des Races au 18e et Son Expansion au 19e Siècle* [1922].) Racism (the doctrine of ascribed superiority and inferiority) was first applied by the French upper class to the peasantry and later by the English aristocrats to the English urban lower class. Eventually, European nations were thought of as "races." The initial rationale for European racism began as a defense of nationalist and class superiority. These ideas embedded in European cultures were not applied to blacks until African slavery had to be defended against early abolitionist attacks in the eighteenth and nineteenth centuries.

The racism applied to blacks was at first in the form of a religious defense (sons of Ham whom Noah cursed), which evolved into a pseudoscientific defense (defective genes). What was being defended was the basis of class privilege and who would hold wealth and social control. Here is when history, back to the Egyptians, had to be rewritten to justify current and future superiority—the evidence is quite clear. (See George Fredrickson's *Black Image in the White Mind: The Debate on Afro-American Character and Destiny, 1817–1914* [1971].) An example is furnished by the authors of an early classic in "scientific" racism, the founders of the American School of Ethnology. They were very pleased that their book sold well in the slave South. That book was *Types of Mankind* (1854) by Josiah C. Nott and George R. Gliddon. But the most vicious attacks against blacks did not come from writers such as George Fitzhugh, who wrote *Sociology for the South* (1854). They came, rather, from northerners defending the position of new European immigrants who were competing with increasing numbers of former slaves and their children for jobs and housing.

Abraham Lincoln told a group of abolitionists that if he freed the slaves, he would lose all his (white) troops. Four million freed slaves would go North and fight the Irish— far more than those who had come by way of the Underground Railroad. After Irish workers in New York City rioted against blacks in 1863, the policy of recruiting black soldiers was accelerated. (See James McPherson, *Marching toward Freedom: Blacks in the Civil War, 1861–1865* [1968].) Fredrickson reminds us that along with the emancipation of slaves in the District of Columbia, Congress passed a bill to fund emigration of freed Negroes to Haiti, Nicaragua, and the Congo.

After the Civil War and general emancipation, blacks and abolitionists were no longer a threat to upper-class white privilege in the South. Instead freed blacks were a threat to two other groups who kept racism going—the new unions in the North defending petit bourgeois white immigrant privileges and upwardly mobile poor whites in the South. C. Vann Woodward presents the career of Tom Watson, the politician and populist leader, as a good example. He was initially an antiracist and defended blacks from lynching, but once he began to perceive blacks as a threat to upwardly mobile poor whites, he became violently antiblack.

For the past century and a half racism has been applied to blacks: first as a defense of slavery, later as justification for continued black subordination, and then to give white labor a competitive advantage for privilege and status. Racism is purposeful—it eliminates competition. Racism was first employed by the French upper class, continues to be class-bound, and was not used against blacks until the later stages of slavery in the United States. Racism is not an expected and natural event across all peoples and times. We might conclude that racism can be eliminated in the future.

Future Challenges

Racism across all times and peoples is based on myths that include the Aryan myth and the Hamitic myth. A number of scholars are in the process of exposing it. Martin Bernal's *Black Athena* is an important contribution, showing, as it does, how classical history was rewritten and distorted in the past century in order to justify continued derogation of blacks. Once we can get beyond racism and its denial, the task for the scholarly community will be to correct the omissions and distortions about black societies in the New and Old Worlds—ancient, recent, and contemporary. This will be an exciting task and challenge. Volume 1 of my *Black Folk Here and There* (1987) is just such a beginning. In the first chapter on the Nile Valley civilizations, there is a challenge to other investigators to critically examine the counterracist theses. Also Chancellor Williams's miscegenation thesis about Egypt's fall needs to be further studied. Diop's characterizations of African and European civilizations need modifying, and Yosef Ben-Jachannan's work in religion needs critical analysis. These authors are for the most part factually accurate, but are their interpretations of these historic periods accurate?

We have to take care that we do not read back the present into the past and continue distorting the human record. Based on the three periods of work reflected in my journey as a scholar, there are a series of research topics that I hope will be pursued. They are in addition to points already discussed in this review.

1. An analysis of the new type of social system that is replacing caste in the American South.
2. To what extent have southern whites been acculturated into black (Afro-American) culture? Such work would have to be done institution by institution and be sensitive to cultural and situational factors. Investigators might begin in sports and music. What are the implications of white acculturation of black culture?
3. There is need for a comparative study of race relations using samples from three settings: integrated high schools in the South, integrated southern colleges (private and public), and integration in historically black colleges in the South. What are the impacts of stereotyping in each situation on the black and white students' sense of self- and cultural identity?
4. A reexamination of the "culture of poverty" theory with reference to current urban Afro-American communities and the so-called urban underclass. This will require renewed study of the internal dynamics and cultures of communities.
5. A comparison of black and white racial and cultural relations in a sample of small towns selected by region. This information is needed to contrast with generalizations about black-white relations based on large urban settings.
6. A comparative study of inner city riots in the United States with riots in London and Liverpool. Were the objectives of American and British rioters different? Were the dynamics leading up to the riots the same? Were the reactions of the authorities any different?
7. A comparative analysis of changes in values, leadership, and group formation and cohesiveness among Afro-Americans during and after, roughly, 1974. Our current circumstances reflect a very different era than the historic periods before the mid-1970s. What were the forces that produced and now sustain these changes?
8. What has been the impact of the increasing number of Asians in the population on black-white relations in the United States and in the western states particularly?
9. There is a need for a reexamination of Melville Herskovits's "intensity scale" of African retentions, reinterpretations, and syncretisms.
10. There is a great need for "Middletown" type studies of Caribbean and Brazilian peasant communities. We need to know the range and types of Africanisms still existing and what impact (if any) modernism has had on African indigenous culture and community in the New World.

11. A comparison of differential values and patterns of interaction between blacks and East Indians in four locations: Trinidad, the Cooperative Republic of Guyana, the Natal province of South Africa, and Kenya.
12. The role of Ghana in southern African liberation struggles during the Nkrumah regime.
13. A critical examination of the implications of the "Negritude" concept for social action in Africa and the diaspora. This concept is still strong in West Africa and is used as a counter to Communism.
14. An analysis of the U.S. Joint Committee of Recovery in the 1930s depression and the subsequent careers of its members. This group was largely responsible for implementing programs that headed off major conflict.
15. An objective assessment of the period of collaboration between Afro-American leaders and the Communist Party U.S.A. during the 1930s. Most recent information suggests that a reassessment of this relation is due.
16. A translation of *Al-Jahiz: Boast of the Blacks* from Arabic is needed along with a critical review of Western responses to this work.

Some individual work has been done on issues related to the topics above, but each topic deserves more focused attention. Throughout, my work has been motivated by curiosity and indignation rather than anger and harsh experiences. My career has been atypical partially due to coming from a bicultural family. Also I never saw a ghetto until I was twenty-one. In a way I have been an outsider from the upper South looking into the Deep South and northern ghettos. Mississippi was more of a culture shock for me than West Africa. (See "Reflections on Anthropology and the Black Experience," *Anthropology and Education Quarterly* 9, no. 2 [summer 1978]: 85–102.)

Finally, my contributions have not been in mainstream anthropology, but rather in area studies and peripheral theoretical questions. Oliver Cox and C. L. R. James were the only black social scientists of my generation who dealt with "mainline" problems such as the overall impact of capitalism on all whom it had touched and on sociological theory. Black scholars such as myself have been more empirical—concerned with documenting our specific conditions and the circumstances of our oppression. But our struggle against racism and its distortion of the African and European past and present has brought us to a crucial point. In order to eliminate racism and better understand ourselves we will have to deal with and correct the mainline scholarship that has been produced in the past two centuries.

6

Blending Scholarship with Public Service

Robert C. Weaver

I have had a career as both a scholar and a public servant that began in the 1930s with the New Deal. I know what government can do when there is the political will to act. I have seen it and have been a part of it. I have also been a contributor to the scholarship on housing, labor, and ethnicity. More recently, my attention has focused on the neoconservatives who have been misleading us in race relations. Their impact is much greater today than we realize and reflects the current political agenda of withdrawing government from its constitutional mandate of providing for the common good and general welfare of the nation.[1]

But regardless of whether a scholar is a neoconservative, liberal, or radical, a common trend has developed over the years and is particularly apparent in the literature on ethnicity. We have gone from one extreme early in this century—that black people have no redeeming features—to the other extreme: if the saints were in our midst, they would not be good enough because we have such high expectations of everyone in the race. None among us should fall prey to drugs, poor school achievement, or any of the other crises we are in. Much of the public debate on these issues is more indignant and shocking than useful. I think it is important not to overemphasize or romanticize who we are or to ignore our diversity. This means recognizing that increasing numbers of us are living in and responding to an extraordinarily unsupportive human condition. Any people in our circumstances and with as few choices would respond in much the same way.

The way that young inner city black males are categorically viewed reflects this disjoining of expectations and their real social context. In all this, I have taken a very strong stand against people who have a single idea about the cause and solution that overshadows everything else. There is still a tendency among social scientists to try to find out what the cause is when there is no one cause but a whole series of them. An example is the recent statement by an influential university president that the large number of female heads of black families was due to the failure of antipoverty programs. It is absurd to say that this one factor is the cause of something as complex as the increase in female-headed households, and it is inaccurate to say that the antipoverty programs have failed.

I had received my bachelor of science degree cum laude from Harvard College in the class of 1929. Two years later I completed the residence requirements, passed the general examination for the Ph.D., and received my master's degree. In the fall I taught at A&T College in Greensboro, North Carolina. The following fall I returned to Cambridge and began work on my dissertation. Up to this point my parents had financed my higher education, as they had that of my brother who was four years ahead of me in school. The university gave me an Austin Scholarship that covered my tuition, and I saved half my yearly salary, expecting it to cover my other expenses for the academic year 1932–33. Largely for financial reasons, I elected to write on a subject that utilized library materials rather than one calling for the collection of data by survey. I completed my thesis by late June and my Ph.D. requirements by July 1933. The heart of the thesis, with an introduction by the author, was the lead article in the Franklin Lectures.[2] This publication's advisory board was made up of two Harvard professors and one from Boston University.

I am now eighty-one years old and do not write or speak with the same energy or ease that I had when I was twenty-one. My forty-eight years of scholarship and public service began when I finished my doctorate at Harvard in the summer of 1933. While at Harvard I was a friend and roommate of John Preston Davis who had also graduated from the Washington, D.C., black Dunbar High School and was graduating from the law school. We had a number of bull sessions and much of the time talked about the New Deal. We were very concerned because none of the major national Negro organizations appeared to be doing much about black participation in it.

We thought that Negro labor should be represented in the public policy debates in Washington because the government was setting up codes on minimum wages. So we decided to get involved and established the Negro Industrial League. Privately, we held that John P. Davis was the "Negro" and I was the "Industrial League." With a lot of energy and no funds, the two of us went to Washington in the summer of 1935. We met a retired black man named Robert Pelham, who had been in the federal government for years. He had a news release center where he gave us free office space and a typewriter. We got enough money for a secretary and began appearing at hearings of the National Recovery Administration (NRA).

We were something of an oddity at these hearings: first, no one expected us; second, we were literate; and finally, we were contentious. Charles Lawrence, in his dissertation at Columbia, wrote that we were "ubiquitous," as we reappeared at a series of code hearings. I generally wrote the testimony and John presented it. Sometimes we switched. We did not get a lot out of the NRA, but we did get across to the media that blacks were not receiving attention in the New Deal hearings on minimum wages. It was not our conscious intent to call attention to ourselves but, looking back on our subsequent careers, it did help. By the end of the summer we had a little money from the NAACP and a few small pledges from black churches.

Launching a Career

I really wanted to get into the New Deal, for it intrigued me very much. The Roosevelt administration's first adviser on Negro affairs was Clark Foreman, an emancipated white southerner who did his graduate work at Columbia. Secretary Harold Ickes had been given a hard time from blacks for hiring a white adviser, so I was hired as an associate adviser and eventually replaced Foreman. My work was very much in line with my interests as an undergraduate when I had written an honors thesis on the movement of the textile industry from New England to the South.

So in the late fall of 1933 I was working in the Department of the Interior and the Public Works Administration (PWA). Harold Ickes was the head of both. There were a lot of requests for loans and grants coming in, a lot of important issues were under review, and I had access to material that no one else had. At the same time I was also working informally at Howard University with a group who were peers of my older brother. They were first-class producers and in the following decades turned out to be some of the most prominent Afro-American scholars in letters, law, and social sciences. This gave me the opportunity to associate with very able and productive people. So when I eventually got more involved with the faculty at Howard, I already knew them. Sterling Brown was part of this group. The *Journal of Negro Education* published scholarly papers on social and economic issues that came out of this group, as did *Phylon* at Atlanta University. Until these two journals were founded, we had no national scholarly journals. All we had were *Crisis* magazine, *Opportunity*, and occasional magazines that no one had ever heard of. At least in *Crisis* you could use a style where articles could be annotated.

The New Deal was very controversial. Older blacks were still Republicans from head to foot and claimed that the New Deal could not work because the best white folks were not behind it. I had a job involving, among others, the PWA school and PWA housing programs. I was twenty-six years old at the time and went to see the secretary, asking to be a consultant for the housing division. I wanted to get involved in the first public housing program. In my meeting with Secretary Ickes, who administered housing in the PWA, he asked me, "Young man, what do you know about housing?" "Very little," I replied. He responded, "None of the other so-and-sos know much about it either. You'll do fine."

Working in the housing division of the PWA led me into administrative activities, and I realized it was necessary to keep a very careful record of what was being done. No one was keeping records of what was being done in public housing and the impact it had on black Americans. Only national summary level statistics were published, and these could not be utilized to better administer local programs. I had a number of concerns. First of all, I wanted to see if blacks got a fair proportion of housing units. This was accomplished from the beginning of the program. Second, I was interested in seeing that they got a fair proportion of the important jobs, building and managing the nation's first public housing.

By monitoring local level statistics we were able to put selective pressure on federal projects. One of our first achievements was to get virtually all the established black architects to design housing projects. Paul Williams and Hilyard Robinson had designed a project in Washington, Langston Terrace, which won all sorts of honors. John Wilson codesigned a project in Harlem. McKissick and McKissick did a project in Nashville and also had a construction company. We were able to get a lot of additional blacks into the building trades because I had worked out a formula that involved prima facie evidence of lack of racial discrimination on each and every federal public housing building project. This formula was the forerunner of affirmative action. We effectively used quantitative data in the late 1930s.

Our policy of having individual projects show prima facie evidence of lack of racial discrimination was amazing in several ways. First, it worked. Second, it worked in the North where labor unions dominated and were often closed to blacks. And it worked in the South where racial segregation was still the law and custom. Our policy was effective in two racially disparate arenas because our policy administration was backed with the political will to make it work.

The initial federal public housing program was very different from anything we have now. It was conceived, operated, managed, and owned by the federal government, and therefore, the federal government could not escape responsibility for it. So when blacks came in and said they could not get jobs or skilled work on building projects, I got Bill Hastie, a Harvard friend who was then an assistant solicitor in the Department of the Interior, to set up a legal basis for prima facie evidence of lack of discrimination.[3] With the legal background provided, I had to get data on black participation. I took local census data and then asked some organization, usually the local Urban League, to do a survey among blacks. By the 1930s blacks had been largely pushed out of the construction industry, and the few blacks remaining were in small construction and repair work.

The most obvious problem was that blacks did not have the skills to work on large, concrete and steel-framed high-rise structures that became typical of public housing in large cities. You had to know how to make forms for concrete; the black carpenter had little or no experience. Then there were all the new technical developments, such as central heating, electrical installation, and sheet metal work. Few blacks were trained in any of these new crafts. How were we to get around these problems?

I did three things. First, I went to the head of the Bureau of Labor Statistics, who was a friend of mine, and asked him to work with the unions. It was our objective to make them either admit blacks to the unions or give them temporary work permits so they could work on our projects. I would look at the supply of labor in the census and set the expected percentage of black hires for each project a little below the census figures. We had to have a way of putting teeth into our expected results for each project. My second action was to get the payrolls of every project in my office. My staff and I would go through them, designating each salary by race. In this way, we could see how many black males had been working. Finally, we would get payroll-by-payroll records because the union or the project managers could lay off one black man one week and put another on the next week. Thus identifying the color of workers was not enough. There would have been no continuity if we had not monitored progress as we did. Through early PWA housing projects we put $2.5 million in wages into the pockets of skilled black workers. Our policies and follow-up, as well as PWA cooperation, brought them into the jobs, got them some training and experience they did not have before, and kept them from starving.

Finally, not all the pressure for change was centralized in Washington. The PWA insisted that each development had an advisory committee, often with some black members. These committees were very important, as they gave us a sense of what the local issues were and enabled us to individualize the implementation of federal policy for each city.

It was a legal opinion that ended direct federal control of local public housing. The federal government could not use eminent domain to take over private land for public housing, only the city or state governments could do so since power to designate land for federal building resided in the state. The federal housing program was decentralized and local housing authorities were formed to plan the projects, hire the architects and construction firms, and then operate the projects. We pressed for the appointment of blacks on local housing authorities and had a modicum of success. The early precedents, however, soon became more widely prevalent.

The federal public housing program began in 1934, and the legislation enacted in 1937 led to the formation of local housing authorities. The decentralized authorities in each major city went into action in 1938. On the basis of having had nonwhite representation on the federal local advisory committees, Nathan Straus, the administrator of public housing during this transition, strongly urged that blacks should be represented on the new local authorities. There had been excellent people on the first advisory committees, and their effectiveness became a precedent for blacks' serving on local authorities. When we selected the first housing managers, they too were excellent people. We had a black man directing an important housing project near Atlanta University, and we made certain that his salary was substantially equal to white managers in the South. The idea of Negroes directing something was, of course, not agreeable to everyone.

From the federal housing program, I went into federal programs in the defense and war production industries. War production was different from housing because to get things done quickly and on time was crucial. The number and complexity of products also made administration very difficult. Army people were running production in some instances, and they had some sense of equity, but not if it was going to delay the war effort. Training blacks to work in war production would take time and we simply did not have it. Also Franklin Roosevelt was certainly not an aggressive person in race relations; when he was in Georgia, he had no trouble accepting the race situation there. A few people in his administration, however, were struck by issues of equity. Two of them had been my bosses, Ickes and Straus, and another was Aubrey Williams, the director of the National Youth Administration, which became the major source of training blacks for war industrial employment.

In war production, as in the federal housing program, I conducted formal surveys as part of my work. I would also sit up at night writing articles to report what was going on. Working for racial equity in war production presented a new challenge. In the First World War there was great need for unskilled labor, but in 1939 war production required trained workers—semi- and single-skilled labor. Because armaments were so much more sophisticated, blacks would have to be trained in order to get such work. The most logical black candidates for this training were the young and those in "traditional" work—janitors, cleaners, and other unskilled laborers. The problems were twofold: the first was to establish opportunities for blacks to be trained, and the second was to motivate black candidates to go through the training. I could tell them that there was a job at the end of training, but they would not believe me. Concurrently, the black press would occasionally accuse me of painting too rosy a picture, as getting a fair break with regard to work was counter to their experiences. They would ask, who did I think I was . . . Moses? And certainly, I could not convince them that I was Moses. When you tell a man that he will get a job in "the great by-and-by," he will not believe it; we had been given empty promises for generations. The great by-and-by came after you died. Fortunately, we had help in convincing some black workers to undergo job training. The Urban League and the NAACP were most helpful, and the National Youth Administration proved to be crucial. The training branch of the Office of Education was of little help, partly because of its ties with the unions.

Writing While in Public Service

What has concerned me in all my administrative roles was how to describe racial discrimination and then prove that it exists. Clearly, the average man working or trying to get work knows what he is experiencing when he is being discriminated against. Yet no individual is in a position to prove that his experience of discrimination is any more than his own. (I used to tell E. Franklin Frazier, author of the classic *Black Bourgeoisie* [1957], that he was writing about his family and, in particular, his wife and not about all middle-class blacks.) The description and proof must come from within the organization, and the solution has to be tailored to fit the specific organization and circumstance. But description, proof, and appropriate solutions are not sufficient alone, as whatever action taken to address racial discrimination in the organization must be backed by leadership, which has to have the will to seek change.

My concern for describing, proving, and seeking appropriate solutions to racial discrimination has been at the core of my writing over the decades. Given the administrative nature of my government posts, I did most of my writing at night. My wife was in academe, so she understood the importance of this. Also we did not have to attend all the social events: in fact, I was quasi antisocial in the cities where we lived and preferred small groups of people who were doing things rather than competing in conspicuous consumption.

Other scholars have influenced anyone who is committed to scholarship; the early work of W. E. B. Du Bois, particularly *The Philadelphia Negro: A Social Study* (1899), had the deepest influence on me. That a single man carried out the study and presented the number of insights in it is astounding. The other influences were Charles Houston and later Bill Hastie who were both deans at Howard University Law School. They led activities to undermine racial segregation in schools and are responsible for much of the background work that led up to the 1954 Supreme Court ruling outlawing racial segregation in education. The great book by Richard Kluger *Simple Justice* (1976) was written about their efforts and contains short biographies of them.

I have very clear memories of how we would sit around at Howard trying to figure out how we were going to bring down racial segregation. Thurgood Marshall was there, shifting with ease from folk humor to serious legal discourse, and Sterling Brown would offer delightful interludes with his poetry. Charley Houston was already developing the groundwork for challenging legal segregation, and by doing so, demonstrated not only his mastery of the law but also the talents of a great strategist.[4] While we fought for legal desegregation, we were not naive about what it would bring. This was a very exciting group, which was acting and working on new ideas, and pushing very hard for change.

At the close of 1944 I left the federal government and went to Chicago to become the executive director of Mayor Edward Joseph Kelly's newly created Committee on Race Relations. The research and articles I had undertaken and written earlier led to the publication of my first book, *Negro Labor: A National Problem* (1946). The research I soon undertook at the American Council on Race Relations after resigning from the City of Chicago job led to my second book, *The Negro Ghetto* (1948). In part, it drew on my memorandum on the economic and social aspects of race-restrictive housing covenants for the use of lawyers engaged in litigation against such covenants before the Supreme Court.[5]

The early successes of public housing earned it a reputation for reshaping its occupants into self-reliant and healthy citizens. What was overlooked was that those involved had been previously upwardly mobile. These were temporarily low-income, recipients due to the mass unemployment that was prevalent in the 1930s and well into the following decade until war production began to ease the situation. As times got better, many of the carefully screened and selected occupants moved out. This was accelerated in 1945 when the administration in Washington ordered removal of all over-income tenants, many of whom would gladly have paid higher rents for their comfortable accommodation and thereby continued to provide stability for the projects.

Increasingly in the 1950s a growing proportion of public housing tenants were recruited from those who were already the victims of poverty, and they brought their problems with them, which the new physical environment failed to eradicate. Soon three-fifths of public housing tenants were on low fixed incomes; almost half the nonelderly occupants were part of broken families, and three out of ten were without an earner in the family. It soon became clear that housing alone could not and would not prove to be an antidote to the despair of poverty. Public housing, once seen as the cure, quickly became the cause, and it was considered an undesirable institution. The program reacted by stressing housing for the elderly who were not prone to acts of violence, delinquency, and similar antisocial behavior.

Other circumstances had adverse impacts. In 1969 the Brooke Amendment required that no tenant pay more than 25 percent of his income for rent in public housing. While designed to protect low-income residents, it had an adverse impact on the projects by reducing the financial capacity of management to maintain property during a period of increasing maintenance and operation costs. The deficit became so large that Congress urged the Public Housing Administration to request larger annual contributions and doubled the amount asked by the administration.

There was, however, another factor in the situation. The structures that provided shelter were sometimes thirty or more years old. Large-scale maintenance had been delayed, and many buildings had developed structural defects. Finally, in the late 1970s funds for renovation were approved, but local authorities often used them to cover operating deficiencies that continued to increase. Properties continued to decline; some were boarded up and others demolished.

The Reagan administration evidenced the most pronounced antipathy toward public housing, placing a two-year moratorium on construction of new units and a one-year partial moratorium on modernization of existing public housing in the 1986 fiscal budget. These developments caused some housing authorities to close and demolish unit, because they could not afford to run them. Pruit Igoe, built during the Eisenhower years in St. Louis, is a good example.

The term "black underclass" is widely used but subject to criticism because some feel that it implies that the victims are to blame and exonerates or minimizes the impact of economic, political, and social factors. This is accentuated when the term is used in tandem with the concept of ghetto culture. For me, the urban underclass is isolated from mainstream culture and the economy of the city (although a segment derives high income from the underground economy). Generally the majority lack education, are illiterate, and have very little labor exposure or expertise. They are people who, for the most part, do not have jobs now and have little or no prospect of jobs in the future. Those termed the underclass basically are concentrated in large cities, and in today's economy a large proportion of their labor has become superfluous.

Interestingly, the evolution of this segment of the population was recognized before the currency of the term "underclass." For example, as early as 1971 reputable social scientists published articles such as "The City as Sandbox," "The City as Reservation," and "The Inner City in the Post-Industrial Era." Additional titles included "The Central Cities as Storage Bins for People Who Have No Productive Roles in the Market Economy." In 1981 I wrote: "Continuing poverty . . . , especially among the youth, amidst general affluence is a threat to our economic, social, and political system. Youth and many others who share their poverty, joblessness, and lack of legitimate opportunities are prone to enter the street life of hustling. Alienated from society, they have little or no vested interest in it or its economic and social institutions. Events in England in the summer of 1981 dramatically demonstrated this."[6]

Prospects for Change

The only bright prospect is that, given the nation's current demographics, in the coming generation there is going to be a labor shortage. The nation will be forced to train and hire blacks and other discriminated-against groups if our economy is to continue to grow. This is an important opportunity if there is the political will to take advantage of it. Of course, the nation may decide not to bring economically marginal American blacks back into the mainstream. The nation may instead decide to bring in foreigners who have not developed American high expectations for wages and benefits.

Whatever is done to address the racial question in the coming years, more, not less, government involvement will be required. There is a case in point. What if wealthy industrialists put their money where their mouths are with individual uplift projects? The man who was giving a graduation address to a group of young black and Puerto Rican children threw aside his prepared notes and said that any one of them who finished high school and went to college would receive a full scholarship from him. Clearly this motivated the young people and many of them have responded. Now others are doing the same thing. Certainly they are correct in not giving their money directly to the schools. These are good gestures, but what they are doing is not enough to make a difference for the vast majority of poor black and Latino children. To do this on any reasonable scale will require government involvement.

The success of this philanthropist was based largely on his breaking down of the young people's sense that they were worthless and no one cared. Some young people, especially black males, graduate from high school and cannot read or write. Why? They do not believe, even if there are any jobs out there, that they can get them. The main thing we can do to change their expectations and those of their peers is to offer them jobs. Do not say, "There may be jobs. . . ." Give those who are already qualified jobs and let them be models to all the others of what can be done. Black kids are convinced that they cannot get meaningful jobs, and they are correct for the most part. Back in 1962 on Charter Day at Howard University I said the tragedy of racial discrimination is that it is a barrier to success and sometimes an excuse for failure.

We should also learn about our heritage—but we must be very careful that in destroying the myths that held us in bondage we do not create greater myths that carry our heritage beyond what it really is. This gives some black academics the opportunity to make outrageous claims.

But whatever we do for ourselves and no matter how many well-intentioned individuals act on their own to correct some of the inequity in the United States, there will be no substitute for resolute government action. There is no other entity mandated by our Constitution that is morally responsible for administering justice and seeing that the common good is achieved and maintained. No organization except government has had or can have in the future a great enough impact to improve the plight of people who have been and continue to be discriminated against because of their race. If we care to go back and look at our successful attempts at economic and social change, and there are some impressive ones, there are enough models to show what can be done. But we have to keep one thing in mind: no matter how strategic and how effective an action plan, if it is not backed up with political will, the effort's impact will be, at best, temporary.

NOTES

1. Weaver, "Black Americans and Neoconservatism," 79–81.
2. Weaver, "The High Wage Theory of Prosperity," 3–43, 88–99.
3. Ware.
4. McNeil.
5. Weaver, *The Negro Ghetto.*
6. Weaver, "Black Americans and Neoconservatism," 93.

REFERENCES AND FURTHER READING

Du Bois, W. E. B. *The Philadelphia Negro.* 1899. Reprint, with a new introduction by Herbert Aptheker, Millwood, N.Y.: Kraus-Thomson Organization, 1973.

Frazier, Franklin E. *Black Bourgeoisie.* New York: Free Press, 1957.

Kluger, Richard. *Simple Justice: The History of Brown v. Board of Education and Black America's Struggle for Equality.* New York: Knopf, 1976.

McNeil, Genna Rae. *Groundwork: Charles Hamilton Houston and the Struggle for Civil Rights.* Philadelphia: University of Philadelphia Press, 1983.

Ware, Gilbert. *William Hastie: Grace under Pressure.* New York: Oxford University Press, 1984.

Weaver, Robert C. "The High Wage Theory of Prosperity." Franklin Lectures, New Hampshire, June 1935.

———. "The Impact of Ethnicity upon Urban America." In *Ethnic Relations in America,* ed. Lance Liebman. Englewood Cliffs, N.J.: Prentice-Hall, 1982.

———. *The Negro Ghetto.* New York: Harcourt, 1948.

———. *Negro Labor, a National Problem.* New York: Harcourt Brace, 1946.

7

Pursuing Fieldwork in African American Communities

Some Personal Reflections of Hylan Lewis

My first merry-go-round was a revolving bookcase at home. From a very early age I read most of what I could get my hands on. I voraciously read dime novels on American life. One series of early library withdrawals was by Henry Altshuler on American Indians. I also read my older sister's magazines, including *True Stories.* While in elementary school I sold and read *Crisis* and *Opportunity.* Charles S. Johnson edited the latter. In college I read W. E. B. Du Bois. His *Souls of Black Folks* (1902) left a lasting impression on me. Charles S. Johnson's *Negro in American Civilization* (1930) and his writings on the Negro in Chicago also influenced my early thinking. The content and examples of Charles Johnson's books were not all that was impressive to me: Johnson was also a graduate of Virginia Union, my alma mater. He was among other graduates of Virginia Union who established an important tradition that included Abram Harris (Sterling D. Spero and Harris, *The Black Worker: A Study of the Negro and the Labor Movement* [1931]), Charles Thompson (founder and editor of the *Journal of Negro Education*), Chandler Owens (trade unionist and editor of *Messenger*), and Eugene Jones (influential head of the National Urban League). I was very lucky to have had a group of professor-mentors at Virginia Union; notable were Rayford Logan, Henry McGuinn, Arthur P. Davis, Elizabeth Johnson, and Joshua B. Simpson. They were forerunners of my graduate professor-mentors at the University of Chicago, who included Ernest Burgess, Everett Hughes, Louis Wirth, William Ogburn, Herbert Blumer, and Paul Douglas.

I grew up in Washington, D.C., during interesting times. There was a Negro community that included a large complement of professionals and many government workers. Many of these residents were very diligent in defending black rights. One of the more important institutions was Dunbar High School. It was a jewel of the community; its faculty could have easily been compared to that of a small college. Those who taught at Dunbar were notably among the most-accomplished and best-educated blacks in the community. A large proportion of the teachers had degrees from Williams, Smith, Vassar, Amherst, Harvard, and other elite colleges and universities; and they were largely at Dunbar due to racial segregation. This was the only place such accomplished persons could teach.

My elementary school teachers were among the best-educated people; they also demonstrated care about all of us. They were very interested in what we were doing, and they were among my first and most enduring models. Because of them, I felt rather proud and good about myself, and I did not feel much of the bitterness and harshness that normally went with the structure and invidiousness of racial segregation. I remember the local ice cream company distributed blotters that featured black historical personages on them. There were also calendars with black businesses and churches on them extolling the virtues of black men and women and historical events. All this was underscored by the fact that my father and other members of the family knew and talked about significant contemporary features such as judges, editors, the recorder of deeds, the superintendent of Division 13 (the Negro school district), direct descendants of Frederick Douglass, and various political figures.

My days in Virginia, including public high school in Hampton and college at Virginia Union in Richmond, did much to open the world for me beyond the early Washington days. Even though Union High School in Hampton was unaccredited during my stay there, it remains an important set of imprinting experiences for me for many reasons. These reasons include the fact that I had an extraordinarily effective core group of teachers that included Jessie Wyette, the Richmond sisters, James Ivey, and Y. H. Thomas—the principal who was something of a Renaissance man. I was encouraged to do many satisfying and creative things. These included founding and editing the school paper, being a prize winner in statewide oratorical contests, acting in a variety of school plays, being much in demand for declarations and speeches, being an honor student, and tutoring schoolmates.

At Virginia Union I did some of the things I had done in high school. The feats of the debating teams were a central part of school tradition, and I was a proud member of the debating team. Many prominent alumni were college debaters about whom I learned from "Pat" McGuinn, the coach. He also introduced me to sociology and economics. He was one of my extraordinary teachers, along with Rayford Logan in history and political science, Elizabeth Johnson in English, Joshua Simpson in philosophy, and Arthur P. Davis in literature.

While in college, I was interested in a number of things, such as the Richmond Tobacco Workers Strike of 1931. I helped James Jackson, a schoolmate at Virginia Union, write his first speech in support of the striking workers. Jackson became an activist in the Communist Party U.S.A. and later was among the well-known persons prosecuted and jailed. The Social Science Research Council (SSRC) sponsored a special fellowship program for southern college seniors. At the initiation of Charles S. Johnson, an influential member of the council, I applied for and received the fellowship that permitted me to go to the University of Chicago. At the same time, Eugene Jones offered me a position at the National Urban League; I chose the fellowship. There were three SSRC fellows at Chicago—Sarah Alice Mayfield, a white student from Birmingham Southern; Estelle Hill from Fisk University; and me. The scholarship was extraordinary by today's standards. It was only one thousand dollars, but it covered full tuition and provided a living allowance for food and travel in those depression days. I could get food and lodging for twenty dollars a month. We were able to live well and not interrupt our studies with financial concerns.

The period from 1932 to1933 was a very good time to be at the University of Chicago. My classmates included Oliver Cox (*Caste, Class, and Race: A Study in Social Dynamics* [1948]), Horace Cayton (St. Clair Drake and Cayton, *Black Metropolis: A Study of Negro Life in a Northern City* [1945]), Edward Shils (*Tradition* [1981]; *The Academic Ethic* [1984]; and other works with Talcott Parsons), and Joseph Lohman, to name a few. Besides extraordinarily talented peers, I had important and good relationships with professors who included William Ogburn (*Social Change with Respect to Culture and Original Nature* [1922]) who was important in enabling my passage through graduate school. Herbert Blumer was an important teacher and mentor, as were Everett Hughes and Louis Wirth. In a special kind of way, I learned a lot from Ellsworth Faris because of the way his mind worked. My minor at the university was in economics—mainly labor and collective bargaining—with Harry Millis and Paul Douglas among others.

In 1933 I went to work at Howard University as an assistant in the economics department under Abram Harris. Initially, I did the statistical work on his *Negro as Capitalist: A Study of Banking and Business among American Negroes* (1936) for thirty dollars per month. In 1935 I became a full-time teaching assistant and taught statistics. This was before E. Franklin Frazier came to Howard from Fisk University to revitalize the sociology department. When Professor Frazier arrived, I shifted my teaching over to sociology with W. O. Brown and took over Frazier's classes when he was called to New York City to study Harlem after the riot in 1937. Frazier and I were active, along with Doxie Wilkerson, in the Howard chapter of the American Federation of Teachers. I was the union's legislative representative. To give you a sense of the times, which were marked by significant anti-Communist and red-baiting, like all government workers, faculty at Howard had to sign statements saying that we were not members of the Communist Party in order to receive paychecks.

Blackways of Kent

In 1939 after an unsuccessful attempt in the prior year, I was awarded a Rosenwald Fellowship to continue my studies at the University of Chicago. By 1941 and World War II, I had all my requirements for the Ph.D. completed except the dissertation. During the war, I worked in Washington in the Office of War Information. At the end of the war, I became aware of the private foundations that worked with government officials to plan postwar centers for social science at Harvard, Chicago, the University of California, and Cornell University. One dimension of this development was the offering of a special scholarship for people who had worked in government. I applied as a way to fund my thesis research but did not get it. My impression was that I did not have the benefit of a sponsor among those who were planning this new national research agenda; furthermore, I suspect that my research topic, the minority intellectual, was not of interest or was not described as effectively as it might have been.

I left Washington in 1945 to teach at Hampton Institute (now University). Two years later, I got a telephone call from John Gillin, professor of anthropology at the University of North Carolina, who asked to come see me to discuss a project he was directing. He had funding to do a study of different southern regions. He was looking for a Negro student to do fieldwork in the southern Piedmont area. After a warm conversation about communities and fieldwork research, I volunteered to join his team of graduate students so that I could do my own research. I also took the project because there was a challenge. Could I follow the rules and do something significant? I had done fieldwork before in Washington; Chicago; Richmond, Virginia; Alabama; and Mississippi but this project had some very special challenges.

A hands-on quality characterized community research in the 1930s and 1940s. Researchers took sufficient time to understand communities and the people in them. Experienced social science investigators felt compelled to do fieldwork themselves and not to rely solely on junior research assistants. Continuities and comparisons were the usual way; ideas, concepts, and techniques derived from fieldwork in one study were frequently explored in other communities. Although I had training in economics, history, and statistics, much of my training and research was in the tradition of community studies; so it was not out of character for me to do fieldwork again. It was after a year of fieldwork in a small South Carolina town in the Piedmont that I wrote *Blackways of Kent* (1955).

This community-based, participant observation study was undertaken after the classic community studies of the 1940s and 1930s. I was once asked what did I expect to find that was not already described in, for example, Allison Davis, Burleigh Gardner, and Mary Gardner's *Deep South* (1941) or John Dollard's *Caste and Class in a Southern Town* (1937). Part of the answer was in the doing of it at that time, in seeing how these small-town communities were changing during the pivotal post–World War II years. My findings were not earth shaking. The palpable humanity of the people and the complexity of their lives as described in this study emphasizes that the people of Kent were not means and ends for the student; and by no means were they just statistics.

A question that puzzled me was, was there any such thing as a distinct culture in the southern communities I did fieldwork in? Another question was, were there distinct ways of communications between the black communities that I studied? The community I studied reflected all the changes in the national culture that was in rapid transition in the postwar years. If there had been other community-based field studies along with mine in other black and white communities, I think these transitions would have been more apparent. We might have anticipated the present era and better understood the background to changes in these communities in the 1960s. *Blackways of Kent* was an exercise in people's ability to adapt, cope, and change. The study was not a Deep South or a black metropolis. Its claims are relatively modest. It showed that the organic solidity of community existed but was increasingly under siege in the middle 1950s.

Transitions in Community

I have returned to a number of communities in which I have lived and studied and have not yet been able to fully capture a way to indicate how they have changed. A major problem is perspective. Everything seems much smaller. This may be a function of growing older. But what is important is the nature of the kinds of person-to-person cues available to someone who "navigates" through the community as a stranger. Such cues just do not seem to be there anymore. So if you are looking to get a clear sense of the community, there is little to draw on. Instead, I have felt disorientation and have wondered how much of this is due to memory loss. I have to keep my limitations in mind as I comment about what changes I think have happened.

Because there have been very few in-depth community studies since the Second World War, there is very little in the literature to help us understand how American communities have changed in the past generation. Essential work would include William Wilson's research and publications. These studies have been done largely in the face of the more impersonal and technically driven trends in social research. Not only have communities changed but also the people who have studied communities have changed, along with the research methods they employ. The priorities and politics of research have changed as much as communities, if not more, and should be a topic of study in themselves.

Recently, a group of city planners visited with me. What they wanted was knowledge about the "quality of life" for the so-called underclass. What they were really asking for was a miracle—there is no way that question can be adequately answered without extensive and long-term fieldwork. So what I did was walk the streets of upper Harlem to get tentative answers to their questions. Overall, the sense of community that existed in the 1940s has continued but in a very limited sense. The thing that struck me during my walks through Harlem was that no one looked at me or acknowledged my presence. In addition, I did not observe others in the streets being acknowledged, and clearly these were people who lived there. This was certainly a kind of fragmentation of human contact and a self-containment in one's own world. What is apparent from the lack of social contact on the streets is different from the older references to social fragmentation in the ghetto.

The appearance of fragmentation creates a problem not only of how outsiders see the community but also of how people within the community see themselves. People in the community are not likely to experience much social integration in day-to-day interactions. There is little centering of social life; nevertheless, there is something human and interactive going on. An indication was apparent in signs posted all over the community announcing that a neighborhood group was planned. What does one make of this? Whom did they represent, and how could they be representative of such fragmented social worlds? Even long-term residents seem transient to one another. Since there is so little to work with, what I perceived might be retrospective falsification, but then it might not.

Whether I accurately perceived the sense of community in Harlem or not, there has been drastic change in the demographics of black communities since the 1940s. The number of people has increased dramatically, especially the number of young people. There is much more movement of households from residence to residence, and the kinds of expectations people have of their turf have changed. This does not mean that the communities of the 1940s were idyllic. They had their problems. But they did not seem as threatening as they do now.

Then and now, young people have a certain need of elements of adventure. What is missing today is what Everett Hughes called "safe venture." In my youth, we were venturesome, and lucky, and protected by others and by certain kinds of tolerance. What kids do today is almost ipso facto delinquent and safe ventures has become seen as a medley of threatening acts. What the new experiences of young people reflect is that the quality of life has changed as well as the quantity of life-behaviors (something we do not talk about) in regard to the options people have and the consequences of these options.

E. Franklin Frazier, Charles Johnson, St. Clair Drake, all of us who did community-based fieldwork, were asking in the 1940s what was going on in black communities. Look at Frazier's term "communities of destruction" used to refer to black urban communities of the 1930s. Frazier meant that black communities destroyed the social fabric. These communities are certainly more deadly now than in the 1930s. Communities today are much more frightening. The pace of life is a lot different. There seem to be many more young adults, and they are meaner. My friends used to express concern about my safety because the neighborhoods I would go into were so dangerous. Fieldwork was easier in the 1930s and 1940s because the limits of what you could do and say were clear. Now even the most experienced field researcher cannot be certain.

I am confused and dissatisfied with many of the treatments and presumed studies of class. The ground shifts so much—are we talking about status, lifestyle, occupations, or the "bourgeoisie"? If you stick to a definition that looks at occupations, then certainly there have been changes because of occupational differentiation as well as changes in the style of life. I would concur with Drake and Cayton's notion that social class among blacks is as much about behavior and lifestyle as it is about money. But now there is a big difference that has not been accounted for in how we view black social class. The guy working for minimum wage is competing with workers in other parts of the world, not simply ethnic whites on the other side of town. The wage and social class possibilities now seem unlimited with the internationalization of economics. We are really approaching the global village and with racial inequality still intact.

There was a time when you knew everyone in your community. The community was compact. The options and range of things to do, to be, and to own were limited. However, the disposition to make distinctions and to recognize status differences was certainly there. These distinctions and differences were manifested in style and closeness to presumed power and authority. So, for example, in the black community of Richmond, Virginia, in the 1920s and 1930s the headwaiter at the Jefferson Hotel was black. He had no more than a high school education. The same applied for the messenger at the bank. But then, they could be arbiters within black society. This is what happens when you are locked out of options and opportunities to be upwardly mobile outside of the community. To be somebody did not have the same basis then as today. The calculus has changed.

Today who would care about the headwaiter? As the meaning of occupational and educational achievement has changed, our images and statistical evidence become more misleading. The white and black middle classes appear to be converging, when, in fact, the convergence is only in ideology and politics. There is another paradox of black life. Along one dimension young black people are more race conscious in recognizing barriers, but they are less able to handle them than the older generation. But along a second dimension they are less race conscious because of the things they take for granted—for what they can and cannot do.

Transitions in Research

We no longer have the partial dominance of the Chicago School of Sociology that set the tone and style of research for an era when the community was a central research focal point. The significance of the Chicago School was not its ecological theories but rather its insistence that research be based on direct fieldwork. The people who worked within the Chicago framework were significant in their own right. It would be very difficult to find a St. Clair Drake or an Allison Davis today or an E. Franklin Frazier. These were men who had the interest, who were challenged and took true pleasure in doing good fieldwork—spending time in the community. Studies today are much more instrumental and more political than they were in the 1940s. Ethnographic studies are something that one becomes engaged with because what you can learn from people in their real-life settings is rich and endless. Now, you study in order to do something explicit, or to prove a hypothesis, or to do something for the marketplaces that is characteristically done by business or government or foundations.

Contemporary researchers consider the prewar black community studies, in general, and the Chicago School, in particular, to be outdated. But ironically the core ideas of both sets of studies are still being used in contemporary studies. Much of what has been done in the past two decades is redundant and has a textbook quality. When I think back to the communities upon which *Deep South, Black Metropolis,* and *Blackways of Kent* were based, there was energy, creativity, and complexity in all aspects of social life. Certainly, communities today are at least as interesting as they were fifty years ago, but you would never know that from contemporary social scientific writings.

A problem is how can anthropologists and ethnographers carry over the holistic sense of "Plainville, USA" to today's massive urban communities? The prewar macroimpression of community may no longer be possible in large urban communities. But it is still possible to understand community as it is lived locally and seen from the microsocial perspective. These kinds of community studies can be done today on a limited scale. There is a need for a revisit to the Deep South, Chicago's South Side, Harlem, and all the other cities where ethnography was done. I would like to see them all revisited with no more than a three-person team. These new field studies need to be creative works reflecting the present in its own right. They would have to be not only fieldwork studies but also studies in the sociology of knowledge, given the complexities of perception and perspectives both within communities and among researchers. Another indispensable part of the new research would be good writing. The essay form is the most effective way to communicate, not the kind of technical social scientific jargon we see so much of now.

Macroeconomic explanations of urban development and transition are important advancements of the Chicago model. But a macroperspective could not explain how and why the Chicago riots of 1922 occurred. Charles Johnson had to study this from a microlevel and through extensive fieldwork. The writings of Robert Park and Ernest Burgess were touched by reality by virtue of the fieldwork represented in the community studies of the Chicago School. Frazier's work on the Negro family reflected the times; it was influenced by the Chicago School and based on fieldwork. If Frazier had been a student at Columbia University, his community and institutional studies would have been quite different.

When earlier work on the community is compared with contemporary research, there are changes in language, concepts, approaches, and constructs. But changes that have come about have not been developed fully. As a result the older, prewar concepts of community have not been succeeded by newer ideas nor have they been discredited. But they are used in part because research, since the 1960s, has been dominated by a more utilitarian use of technique and knowledge. Utilitarian research has been a result of the union of academic interests with those of government, foundations, and publishers. Very few academics talk about the role of publishers in all this. The role of publishers is heavier and more insidious then we think. Herbert Blumer said it best: "all race relations studies are policy studies." Another way of putting it is that all students and scholars are political men and women at the same time. One of the problems for the serious scholar who wants to study community in depth is working through utilitarian minefields.

William Wilson's "Black Underclass"

Several books have been written by William J. Wilson and heavily promoted (*The Declining Significance of Race: Blacks and Changing American Institutions* [1978]; *The Truly Disadvantaged: The Inner City, the Underclass, and Public Policy* [1987]). The group of people Wilson describes does not differ from St. Clair Drake and Horace Cayton's "shadies" or William Lloyd Warner's "lower-lower class." James Bashirs at Queens College (New York City) says, as you begin to look at these notions of an underclass, you have to look at the old structural analysis of Robert Park and Ernest Burgess. You have to factor in the concept of caste. In each of these ideas of the underclass, the people are seen as pariahs—but no one wants to say that. It runs against the grain of our culture and beliefs about opportunity in America.

We get the concepts in our research that we want and deserve, whether it is Richard Cloward's notion of delinquency, Oscar Lewis's culture of poverty, or Wilson's declining significance of race and the black underclass. These are, in fact, much like slogans and statements about our times, rather than apt descriptions of real people. These loaded ideas are quick characterizations that lead by necessity to assigning blame. This point is very clear when you look at the way these ideas are used. What does one do with members of an outcast group—or someone who is beyond the pale? If you listen to the ways in which the concept of the underclass is used, you hear a phrase that is used in so many ways as a grab bag and catchall for American society's outcast and various pariahs.

Lacking adequate studies of communities, we tend to settle on such a notion as the "underclass" because it is quick and simple. Such concepts as the culture of poverty, which was effectively critiqued by Charles Valentine (*Culture and Poverty: Critique and Counter-Proposals* [1968]) and numerous others, keep coming back in different forms. Blaming the victims lost the battle in the 1960s but won the war by 1990. When you trace the conceptions of the "ghetto" forward to the present, you recognize the social need for concepts such as the culture of poverty and the black underclass. The function of such concepts is to account for a mixed bag of pariahs and to justify both their isolation and exclusion and the reasons why so little will be done to eliminate the need for such a class of people.

In a sense the popular press has been more to the point. *Time* magazine had a cover story in August 1977 entitled "The Unreachable." Underclass is a term long used in class-ridden Europe, notably applied by the Swedish economist Gunnar Myrdal. The *Time* article pointed out that the "American underclass" has become a rather common description of people who seem to be stuck permanently at the bottom of the economy and removed from the American dream. The concept accents the intergenerational character of the underclass and its permanence. They are consigned to the heap. These are people who are totally disaffected with the system and have given up looking for jobs. When you talk about the underclass, you are talking about people who are not in the class system at all.

Finally, the concept of the black underclass can be put into a real-life context. What if I went up to the Bradhurst area of Harlem and started asking where is the "underclass"? I would clearly be crazy. The fact that I cannot go to Harlem and find a self-identified underclass points to who needs and uses the term and for what purpose. People in Harlem, who hear you asking for the underclass, should be aware of who you are and what you are about to do to them. They might have a much better sense of who they are, why they are in the condition they are in, and what they would like to be called. If I approached you with some foreign term that was inaccurate and going to stigmatize you, you would run like hell, or certainly be defensive. The alternative would be for me to be open, to learn from the people I want to understand, and to establish their trust. Research does something not only to subjects of the research but also to the researcher as well.

The Ghetto

More must be said about the term "ghetto" because it is older than the concepts of the culture of poverty and of the black underclass, but it has a similar history. The term is used variously to identify whole sets of urban people and their institutions—blacks, Puerto Ricans, Mexicans, the poor, and the lower class. The ghetto also refers to identifiable boundaries—Harlem, Watts, Roxbury, Chinatown—in order to mark off these areas because they meet certain socioeconomic criteria such as incidences of poverty, deteriorated housing, and pariah-like peoples with undesirable and misunderstood norms, values, and mind-states.

The frequent practice of equating ghetto with an entire community encourages the tendency to apply generalized concepts and theories to everyone who lives in that area. The ghetto should be seen as delimited parts of the larger community. The term "ghetto" was first applied to the black urban experience as a metaphor drawing on the early modern experience of Jews in Europe and the early immigrant communities of New York. Louis Wirth's influential 1928 study *The Ghetto* gives the following description: "The ghetto owes its existence not to legal enactments, but to the fact that it meets a need and performs a social function. The ghetto, in short, is one of the so-called 'natural areas' of the city" (Wirth 1928).

It is interesting that before the 1940s, none of the studies of the "Negro" included in the influential and prestigious community studies of the University of Chicago applied this term to the urban experience of blacks. Neither the term "ghetto" nor Wirth's meaning of the term appears in E. Franklin Frazier's *Negro Family in Chicago* (1932) or *The Negro Family in the United States* (1939). The term "ghetto" as applied to the black urban experience may first have been used by Robert Weaver (*Negro Ghetto* [1948]). St. Clair Drake and Horace Cayton, in their *Black Metropolis* (1945), used "black ghetto" to refer to the involuntary segregation and exploitative aspects of the all-Negro Chicago community. "Black ghetto" had a negative meaning and was used in contrast to "Bronzeville," which denoted the more pleasant and benign aspects of the segregated black community. It is fair to say that the term "ghetto" did not receive its popular, public, and social science acceptance and usage until the mid-1960s, after the publication of Kenneth Clark's *Dark Ghetto* (1965). It is no coincidence that Clark's book was subtitled *Dilemmas of Social Power.*

The point of departure for *Dark Ghetto* was *Youth in the Ghetto: A Study of the Consequence of Powerlessness and a Blueprint for Change* (1964). This was the report of the planning stage of Harlem Youth Opportunities Unlimited (HARYOU), financed by the Kennedy administration's Presidential Committee on Juvenile Delinquency and the mayor of the City of New York. While the HARYOU document emphasized the plight of youth in Harlem, *Dark Ghetto* concentrated on the problems of ghetto communities everywhere and with all its inhabitants.

"Ghetto" is still one of the most loaded concepts in the social sciences. The term has become even more politicized as ghetto entities became associated with the racial confrontations and riots in the 1960s. Depending upon ideology, and political and economic interests, the fact and idea of the ghetto can be viewed as positive, promising, and to be preserved; it can also be viewed as pathological, infesting, and to be disposed of. Since 1970 I have run across several characterizations of the ghetto in social science literature. In these descriptions, one can simply replace the term "ghetto" with "underclass"—it would have virtually the same meaning and effect.

The term "ghettos of opportunity" has been used to characterize central city neighborhoods when European immigrants occupied them. They provided maximal access to jobs in an early period when expanding industrial opportunities were more centralized. Many of these neighborhoods are now occupied by blacks, Puerto Ricans, and Chicanos—new immigrants fulfilling the same labor functions. These same neighborhoods can now be characterized as "ghettos of hardship" because of inordinately high unemployment rates and less access to jobs, especially high-paying jobs. The ghetto of hardships is in large part a function of decentralization of industry in the United States. "Gilded ghetto" has come into vogue to mean something very different from those narrow enclaves of wealth in America's depressed downtown. Urban renewal and, more recently, black capitalism reflected the argument that the ghetto is primarily an undeveloped area. It is one that requires a face-lift and economic development from within. The "dispersed ghetto," or ghetto dispersion, is offered as an alternative to the gilded ghetto. It reflects the argument that, if it is residential segregation that isolates the poor from high paying suburban jobs, then the solution lies in a dispersion of the segregated minority throughout suburbia. "Infectious ghetto" is a phrase used by the economist Nils Hansen (*Intermediate-Size Cities as Growth Centers,* 1971) in arguing that ghetto economic development is crucially dependent upon the development of rural areas, especially in the South. Surplus farm and rural nonfarm labor should be encouraged to migrate to intermediate-size cities. This would provide relief to the surplus labor problem in both secondary urban and rural markets.

When I was doing the study *Blackways of Kent,* Robert Redfield, the distinguished anthropologist, asked me what was I going to find that John Dollard had not? His question suggests that there is a shallow limit to what people have to show us or to tell us about their reality. Because of the self-imposed limits social scientists put on themselves, I bank a lot on the novelists, the poets, and the essayists to provide insights. Social scientists are so narrow and the technology takes us away from the reality. William James said that if you miss the meaning, you miss it all. So much of social science misses the meaning. Social scientists may get a meaning, but it has very little to do with the people being described. What we are groping for now is the meaning of the underclass. Is it something permanent, alienated, alien, consigned to the dung heap of society? If that is what the underclass means, it is a hell of a meaning. We are writing off people and not because of their own shortcomings. William Wilson brought to bear a whole group of ideas and put them together about a people who are "isolated." But whose isolation is it?

The Politics of Research

World War II had a lot to do with changing the technology, sponsorship, image, and perspectives of all research, not only the social sciences. It became a heady thing for the academician to pick up his briefcase, go to Washington, D.C., on Thursday or Friday, come back to class on Monday and talk about having met with some important person. With the new sponsorship came technologies where you now have to have a staff of specialists. Much early research was a type of cottage industry where you had a wife and occasionally one or two others as assistants or associates. The bureaucratization of research has changed that. With the politicizing of knowledge in the postwar period has come sometimes uneasy unions between the sciences, politicians, administrators, the business community, and foundations.

Social scientific research is no longer a cottage industry; it is a bureaucratic production. It now involves a variety of people who must have managerial and synthesizing skills. The trend toward bureaucratic social science became apparent with Samuel Stouffer and his associates at the Pentagon during World War II and afterward. He was able to invent and adapt technological and organizational forays. He and his peers became adept in ways to manage, get money, and combine academics with policy. This kind of enterprise goes back to the Hoover days when William Ogburn, the University of Chicago sociologist, set up the first use of statistical measures and indicators to get a sense of the nation's development and direction.

The "new" sciences became very apparent by the early 1960s with the War on Delinquency and then the War on Poverty. The multimillionaire businessman and former governor of New York, Nelson Rockefeller, showed how to use money and power to manipulate opinion and knowledge. But it was President John Kennedy who brought all the bright young boys to government, including Moynihan and others who joined the government partly to manipulate the wheels of power. Among their manipulations were the results of the War on Delinquency, which was sometimes poor science but good public policy. An administration came to power that sought to galvanize opinion for social change. They used slogans, but these slogans had to be backed with the elements and trappings of science. So the War on Delinquency was this great admix of "let us do something about delinquency," while at the same time it did little or nothing about the underlying conditions that caused delinquency. Such a contradiction could not be built on really good and effective research. The War on Delinquency set a precedence; so when Lyndon Johnson came into office, the "social change" alliance of government officials and academicians created a new slogan, "the War on Poverty."

It is no coincidence that by the 1980s the slogans were discarded and condemned by the same people who created them. The fact is that the 1960s liberals are the 1980s neoconservatives. They are often one and the same people. In retrospect, they were never serious about real social change. They used the social sciences to justify their slogans and then turned around and charged that the "programs" were not working! And they certainly did not blame themselves.

Look at the slogans—War on Delinquency, the various notions of the ghetto, the culture of poverty, and the culturally deprived. We are truly dealing with an enterprise where the slogan is the only message. If we identify a group of people who live in a certain area by some trait, what do we know about them? We know nothing that we did not believe already. And what do we do about their plight? The answer is nothing that we did not already plan to do. So we say the cause of their plight is an interaction among social structure, behavior, culture, and psychological states. All this means is that we simply do not know who these people really are and often why they are in the state that they are in. And once more, we do not plan to do anything to really change their condition. The claims are circular because the bureaucratic social scientists do not distinguish between the chicken and the egg.

The 1960s and Black Families

Not everyone who was involved in the War on Poverty was uninterested in serious social change. There were those who believed in the capacity of government to mobilize people, resources, expectations, and ideas, who believed they could make a real difference in history. The failure of the "wars" was in the great expectations and to a major extent because of the effective pressures leveled against the programs by many interest groups that were threatened by them. So many of the War on Poverty programs were starved because there were serious attempts to do exactly what they were supposed to do. The early HARYOU in New York City was one example of those serious attempts. The early HARYOU and several other local programs can be seen as more serious than the politicians and some academicians wanted.

A challenge to daring scholars would be to do detailed and thorough studies of the leading actors of the War on Poverty. It would be interesting to look at the histories, careers, and utterances of people like Nathan Glazer, Daniel Moynihan, and William Kristol. Look at some of the later actors in the 1930s and 1940s, including a few who joined the Young Communist League. Many of these people thought that they were on the cutting edge of social change. We underestimate the role that ego plays in the proprietorship of ideas and people. Ideology may be much less important than ego. The perception of one of the causes of failure of the War on Poverty was related to the writings and utterances of officials like Assistant Secretary of Labor Moynihan who was congratulated by many for bringing the plight of the black family to public attention.

In 1964 Daniel Moynihan visited me while he was in Washington. He invited me to lunch, where he described the Negro family study that had circulated in government circles before it was published. There were extensive discussions of its content and how it was to be used. I was doing a study of black family at about the same time with Elizabeth Herzog. Our study was a matter of concern since our findings might not have supported the Moynihan agenda. On another occasion, during the preliminary work on Johnson's White House Conference on the Negro Family, Moynihan and Glazer came to see me. They were friendly and probing and wanted to see what Betsy Herzog and I were doing in our preparations. Later Edward Banfield at Harvard University called me at Moynihan's suggestion. I considered their concerns and interests as being mainly political. Moynihan never did fieldwork where he actually dealt with black families. Real bases for insight or accuracy and scientifically defensible results were not the point of the Moynihan Report *(The Negro Family: The Case for National Action* [1965]). It was intended to be a political statement to justify specific government actions with respect to a whole category of citizens about whom we knew very little.

There was a danger then as there is now of seriousness. The content of much of politically motivated social and behavioral scientific products is neither better nor more accurate than what is produced by novelists, poets, and clowns. The most important policy statements in the past twenty years have been witnessed by a familiar situation wherein data have come after the pronouncements or were not seen as initially relevant. Too often, the main motivations have been promotion to higher ranks, ego enhancement, and control of information, not primarily to really get good knowledge. But as long as we have a few loose cannons in each generation, such as St. Clair Drake and C. L. R. James, there will be good knowledge that is grounded, accurate, and sensitive to the realities of the people who are being studied.

Research Topics

One of the most obvious lines of investigation for the study of contemporary black urban community should be related to marginality. Many urban blacks conduct social relations with one another as well as with white Americans as marginal persons. Large urban centers today show a fragmentation of community unimagined thirty years ago. In order to do the contemporary scene justice, we need to rethink the concept of marginality. What Richard Wright and Ralph Ellison showed us was not simply some fictional portrayal—certainly it was not new. Marginality need not be negative. So many people, especially minorities, have survived on the edges of society by manipulating their marginal identities. This is where Ellison was so perceptive when he wrote about life "underground."

Some investigator might begin by looking at the literature from the early 1960s on the mass society. What students of mass society saw was a society that was essentially middle class and white. This is what Louis Wirth called "the taken for granted." They took for granted that the things blacks did not take for granted were not relevant or did not matter. In their discussion of fragmentation, blacks were excluded; whenever it comes to looking at blacks more than superficially, there is a lack of interest. One reason is because Americans become concerned with things once they are made afraid of them such as crime, the black male, and drugs. Americans are ignorant of most things that do not threaten them.

Ironically, marginality used to be thought of as something intellectuals experienced, but now marginality—even exclusion and invisibility—are seen as a way of life for a large number of people in our society. In this context, the Chicago fieldwork imperative is useful but it should not be used to explore the old version of the concept of marginality. A more current visualization of marginality that more closely fits reality will have to be developed and come to the fore. There is indeed a withering away of old ideas and senses of what an urban community should look like. Whatever it is to be replaced by, marginality is an intrinsic part of the new visibility. The urban experience for most black Americans is so compartmentalized that it is beyond the alienation literature. It will be crucial to find out how much of this new marginality is occurring in Mississippi and how much of it is occurring in New York, Chicago, and California.

What kind of researchers will do the sort of work that I have sketched and suggested? Are there any St. Clair Drakes who will go into an urban community today? One of the effects of current studies is that they also contribute to marginality by objectifying social reality and emphasizing the exotic, the different, and the outsider. We might get around this problem by accenting the dialectical aspect of our concepts. At the same time we talk about the underclass, let's also talk about the "overclass." At the same time we talk about the culturally disadvantaged, let's talk about the culturally advantaged. If there is a culture of poverty, there must also be a culture of wealth and so on. We will not get the full understanding without some way of systematically correcting politically motivated concepts that isolate and misrepresent people.

I would also like to see role reversals in race and community research. Have white investigators do fieldwork in black communities; have black investigators do fieldwork in white communities. Let's see if they uncover the same sort of insights we already think we know or knew about these racial and culturally distinct communities. Role reversal would really become interesting if it were also done with reversals in social class settings. Have middle-class black investigators study lower- or upper-class white communities; have white middle-class conservative investigators study lower-class black communities. If each team stayed long enough, they might find out something about themselves and the community that neither they nor we knew about or had even thought about.

Negroes and blacks have affected the ongoing culture and style of the nation from the beginning. We need to investigate these influences, in which case, there are several distinct goals—to understand the culture and how it has influenced the larger culture, and then to understand how it has persisted. Melville Herskovits and E. Franklin Frazier are to be honored for debating the presence and persistence of African ways in contemporary society. In today's climate, can we or need we live with all three perspectives, that African cultural influences have influenced society, have persisted, and have changed?

Do we use Negro, black, Afro-American, or African American? I hesitate to concede this country to white folks, and if we are to be African Americans, then I want to call them European Americans. Again there is a political aspect to this research. Manning Marable in "African-American or Black: The Politics of Culture" *(Black Scholar)* points out that it does not matter whether we call ourselves black, African Americans, or Negroes. What we call ourselves is less important that how we relate to each other and whether or not we create a positive self-awareness and culture integrity for our children. Part of that identity will always be grounded in images of Africa; however an equal or larger part of this identity must be determined by the continued struggle for democratic freedoms in this country. I embrace the proactive part of this identity, although, I was born colored, grew up Negro, became black, and now I am on the verge of becoming African American. I did not have anything to do with any of these changes.

A third line of cultural research should deal with the presence, absence, extent, and context of continuing black self-hatred. Racial segregation helped to create one type or dimension of black self-hatred; this point was an important element underscored in the evidence that led to *Brown vs. Board of Education* in 1954; and this led to ending legal racial segregation. Yet has not de facto segregation helped to create the conditions for a new black self-hatred as a counterpoint to racial pride? I am not suggesting that we continue to produce and support overstatements such as those in Abran Kardiner and L. Ovesey's *Mark of Oppression* (1951) or William Grier and Price Cobbs's *Black Rage* (1968). We are more complex than that. There is a bit of Nat Turner in all of us; and there is also a bit of Sambo too. We have the disposition and the ability to be angry, to be mad, to assimilate, and to wear masks; this is all there. None of these dispositions is exclusive, and each calls attention to very serious issues.

A fourth line of investigation calls for a return to looking at the American South. I am not convinced that we fully understand race relations and community in the "New" South. There have been major changes there since the civil rights struggle of the 1960s. What has happened? We need to do another study such as *Deep South*. Closely related to changes in the South is a fifth line of investigation, the historically black colleges and universities. These need to be examined in terms of the new national realities. Their roles in black community life have been and continue to be critical. Blacks are not "book" people, but we do have expectations and a culture around learning and education—we know very little about this aspect of our collective ways of doing things and of thinking. What happens now that Williams College (historically white) and Morehouse college (historically black), for example, want the same black students? What does this mean for racial identity in black communities for black individuals who did not go to a historically black school? Morehouse, Spelman, Lincoln, Fisk, and Virginia Union do not mean the same things to young people today that they meant thirty years ago.

The Middle Class

In the 1930s and 1940s we had our "block boys"; there were men of all ages on the streets: they were today's equivalent of the "underclass." They were fewer in numbers, and there was more social distance between them and the middle class. Today, in public places, the middle class has a lot more contact with the so-called underclass than it did before 1960. The "block boys" stayed in their neighborhood and in specific areas, but now they tend to be all over. These men are far more numerous today and are much more threatening. The presence of our current out-of-the-class-system population stands in sharp contrast to the black middle class. Their closeness to each other makes the contrast all the more apparent.

The closeness of the black out-of-the-class-system and the middle class might also be the reason for so much current emphasis on role models as a solution. There is virtually no strong evidence that members of the middle class—whoever they might be—are or can be role models for the "underclass." My sister's classmates and teachers at Dunbar High School in the 1920s and 1930s did not serve as role models for the young men who hung out on the street corners in southwest Washington, D.C. Prewar black communities were not idyllic times for role models. Giving young people role models, because that is what we thought worked in the prior generation, may be based on generalities that are not true. This whole issue of role models needs to be studied. Also what worked thirty years ago may not work today. This is a different time and a different generation.

The discussion of role models brings me to E. Franklin Frazier's classic on the middle class, *Black Bourgeoisie* (1962). The book was based on lectures he gave in France. I talked with him about it frequently. It was an essay in the tradition of the French essayists—this type of communication is what Frazier was after. The essay was written for a French audience and was to be general in treatment and meaning, not social scientific in the narrow sense. It was colored by Frazier's own wry and bemused view of the foibles of friends, colleagues, and card-playing Washingtonian "society" people. But this confluence of this kind of people can be found anywhere in the country and among all groups. Frazier described people who were parochial and cosmopolitan—very contradictory. One of the compliments paid to Frazier was from a Jewish businessman who had read his book and said with a small smile, "Why you are talking about us."

The significance of *The Black Bourgeoisie* is how it helps readers to reflect on themselves and their forebears. It was not meant to be a rigorous social scientific work, and it should not be taken that way. Also the book described a time very different from the present. There would be a very important place for work like *The Black Bourgeoisie* if we further recognized the essay form in the social sciences. Then there would not be this tendency to decry a well-written essay for not being scientific. What successfully passes today as social scientific research is often more in the way of good writing in the humanities. I for one would encourage the use of history and literature in providing clarity to what is happening out there, and make more use of the essay form. Essay means "to try"—and we need to try more!

Being a Scholar: The Personal Price

The reality is that race is everywhere in the American context. Race makes a difference because it is there in every aspect of our lives, regardless of our status. A black scholar may choose to say that it is declining or that it is no longer the basis of group inequality. But there is no way this same scholar can be treated or thought of in some particular way apart from his race. Even if he is accepted by his white colleagues and wins awards, race is a factor. Some are rewarded and become black tokens, but most are subjected to mistreatment at some time, in some settings. It is no news that many black scholars even today are not extended real opportunities to achieve, and probably most are invidiously and automatically identified by skin color or heritage.

If they could have their cake and eat it too, many blacks would take this: to be white and black. If I walk into a restaurant with several other black men, we can take for granted that we will be treated in an isolating and uneasy way. We can predict where we will often be seated—near the kitchen. Scholars who ignore or who no longer understand this fact of life must live very odd sorts of personal lives. Clearly, they spend very little time with other blacks and in public.

Many of the older generation of distinguished black scholars in the social sciences—including Charles Johnson, E. Franklin Frazier, Ira De A. Reid, Abram Harris, Ralph Bunche, and St. Clair Drake—rarely had real mentors. Certainly there were people in many cases who appeared to be mentored externally in relations with senior white scholars, but on the inside of these "mentor" relations we were likely to be very much on our own. There was a real loneliness in the lives of the older generation of accomplished black men and women. One way I think this took form was in the fact that they had very few children; these might be thought of as potential burdens or potential hostages.

There is a little book by a Brazilian novelist who looked at this loneliness of mixed-race men in the Brazilian context, Machado de Assis, *Epitaph of a Small Winner* (1952). It's a novel about a world traveler, a man who does much of everything before he finally dies. The epitaph is that in all his accomplishments he had no children. This suggests the cost and by-product of achievement for many. In the case of our older, more distinguished scholars, they were bucking the system; they fought the battles of reputations and won but at a major price.

A study of the lives of prewar black scholars with international reputations could be very interesting. The cohort of young men and women who went to Harvard, Amherst, and Williams before World War II would make an interesting study as would their families and children. Look at the relations they had with the black communities of Cambridge and especially unknown landladies. What personal baggage did they pick up and discard and when? What personal price did these extraordinarily bright and accomplished men pay? They did well in part because they were very aware of people, who sometimes wondered if they could do the work. So they not only did the work, they overdid it. J. Saunders Redding, the English literature expert, told me that as a student he was embarrassed once in class for not being prepared. He said he would never let that happen again; and it never did. Men and women such as Redding had to be conditioned for loneliness and extraordinary discipline. It was very clear to them that "you travel and you travel light" in terms of the emotional and personal burdens you can carry.

For one example, Frazier's wife took care of the home and the image making and respected Frazier for what he did by giving him the time and circumstances to work. Very frequently the wives of such men were upwardly mobile, the daughters of respectable families, headed by ministers, or principals, or at least persons who were college graduates. While women generally supported their husband's work before World War II, a study of the family lives of these men might find a very different story. Did these wives get jobs; did they want to work? Every time these men moved from college to college did their wives willingly go? Did they support the husband's career and put their own aside?

Then, there were the stresses and strains of having children who could not defend themselves as well as their accomplished parents. These were very heavy burdens to carry while taking advantage of rare opportunities and having repeatedly to demonstrate abilities. To get those rare opportunities and to demonstrate what one could do was extraordinarily important for this generation. If you look at the wives of these men—Frazier,

Johnson, Abram Harris, Weaver, and Bunche—this impression becomes very apparent. Incidentally, few of my senior colleagues at Howard University before the war had children, especially those who had achieved international reputations.

I think it is possible to develop a more humane society in which we reduce the extent of marginality many people are now experiencing. I have great faith in the resourcefulness of mankind while being aware of the limits and weaknesses. When all else seems to fail, affirming life just might make a real difference. One asks what is and what will be the quality of life for the coming generations of daughters and sons. There must be the disposition to forge ahead and do the very best one can. In this context, there must be recognition of the limitations of planning and the rational aspects of living. Creativity, ideas, and innovations can make important differences. Until we are willing to deal with the great imbalance in the distribution of wealth, we will not be able to create enough good jobs to employ and support the poor and emphasize underwriting the continuity that maintains a middle class.

At this point one might want to ask what meanings and conclusions can be gleaned from these episodic and sometimes rambling comments about aspects of my life and career. There would be questions about some of the things I might have learned about the people and communities in which they and I have lived and worked. When I am faced with these kinds of questions, there comes to mind an image that is two generations old: it is of a rather grizzled plantation worker I met in the Mississippi Delta. In all seriousness, he said: "Mr. Lewis, there is three things in life you got to know about to get along; there's a 'Nigger,' a 'Peckerwood,' and a mule; and I knows all three." This reminds me of an exchange I had with a professional colleague; he asked me, "What keeps you going?" My immediate answer was: "three things—momentum, laughter, and friends!"

In my mind, these vignettes go far to characterize in indelible and positive ways most people I came to know in the communities in which I did field studies. Like them, I have had—and sometimes still have—widely ranging experiences of injustice, discrimination, mistreatment, and abuse, mainly involving race, but also sometimes involving class, and now increasingly age. I know the meaning of anger, bitterness, hurt, and the urge and behavior of retaliation—of getting even and even triumphing. I have never considered myself a saint, nor would I want to be. But the most important thing in all this for me and for the thousands of "Woody Lloyds" in the myriad of communities I have known is that I have never thought of myself as a victim. Nor will he and I ever allow ourselves to be victims in our minds and concepts of self. One of my many friends in the black community of Kent in the southern Piedmont some fifty years ago said it best: "It ain't your fault how much education you get. It ain't your fault if you didn't go to school. The only thing your fault is how you treats people." How people treat themselves against the background of how they are treated in the larger society is the story of *The Blackways of Kent* and a basic problem in the study of any subculture.

8

An Architect of Social Change

Kenneth B. Clark

Dr. Kenneth B. Clark's and Dr. Mamie Phipps Clark's studies of the effects of racial segregation on African Americans' self-concept and educational outcomes were used in the 1954 U.S. Supreme Court decision *Brown vs. Board of Education* to outlaw racial segregation in public schools. Kenneth Clark also developed HARYOU (Harlem Youth Opportunities Unlimited) in the 1960s, the first program to address the effects of urban racial segregation on African American young people. Dr. Kenneth Clark has been one of the nation's foremost proponents of racial desegregation and has written and lectured extensively on race relations.

Early Influences

Dr. Francis Cecil Sumner, chairman of the psychology department at Howard University during the 1930s, was the specific influence on my becoming a psychologist. Dr. Alain Locke in philosophy was another important influence.[1] My academic interests were in social psychology, literature, and philosophy. I cannot say that there were any specific readings that influenced me. I read widely and all of it had an impression on me. The things that I read were all integrated into my mind. After receiving my bachelor's degree, I remained at Howard to complete a master's degree in psychology and was encouraged by Sumner and Locke to go on for the doctorate. I applied to Cornell and Columbia—two universities with distinguished psychology departments. Cornell declined my application. The letter stated that I would be "uncomfortable with their program"—not for academic reasons but rather because of my race. I guess they thought they were doing me a favor. I will never forget it. Fortunately, Columbia's psychology department did not see it that way. I was admitted, and the late Otto Klineberg became my major adviser.

I experienced no barriers in my work as a graduate student at Columbia in the 1930s. My professors were very supportive and influential in my work. I may have been the first black to get a Ph.D. from Columbia in psychology. Under Otto Klineberg's mentorship I continued my interest in social psychology and developed an interest in social relations, race, and social problems.[2] We worked very closely together.

All of my time was not spent at Columbia. I worked downtown as a part-time research assistant of sorts with the New York Urban League. Eventually I completed a dissertation that reflected my interest in literature back at Howard University and my work in social psychology with Otto Klineberg at Columbia.[3]

A major personal influence on my academic success at Howard and Columbia and subsequent work was my mother. I grew up in New York City in a residential area overlooking Harlem. Both my parents were born in Jamaica and grew up in Panama. My mother left Panama for the United States and took my sister and me to New York City. My father stayed behind in Panama. My mother was very clear about wanting a better life and always insisted on being objective and factual. I always remember her wanting me to study and understand the world around me. My mother never returned to Panama. For years my father wrote to me and talked about my mother's virtues—all of which I already knew. I visited him once in Jamaica when I was about ten or twelve years old. He had a white-collar job with one of the steamship companies and was very proud of himself. But I was not at all impressed by him. When I returned to New York, I told my mother that I was not impressed, and she was not surprised.

The Doll Research

Professor Klineberg introduced me to Gunnar Myrdal while I was a graduate student. Myrdal hired me as a research assistant to work with him on *An American Dilemma: The Negro Problem and Modern Democracy* (1944). I worked closely with Gunnar Myrdal and Arnold Rose; it was a very rewarding experience. Myrdal and I had a friendly relationship. When he returned to the United States after the Second World War, we talked about working together, but we never got around to it. While I was his student, Professor Klineberg also introduced me to Robert Carter, an associate of Thurgood Marshall, who was later appointed to the U.S. Supreme Court.[4] I had not met Carter before Klineberg referred me to him. Apparently, Bob told Thurgood about the work my wife and I were doing on African American self-image, and Thurgood encouraged him to continue his involvement with me. Thurgood Marshall was associated with a number of people at Howard University, and Ralph Bunche was someone we both knew. I knew Ralph Bunche throughout his career, from his Howard University professorship to his work with the United Nations. Eventually I was called upon to testify and provide evidence of the negative effects of racial segregation in a number of court cases that resulted in the Brown decision. I was involved at the trial level of cases in South Carolina, Virginia, and Delaware. My wife, Mamie, was also a psychologist;[5] she joined us for the case in Virginia. But we were not directly involved at the trial level in the Kansas case that subsequently went to the Supreme Court. Working on these cases was an intense experience. Everyone involved worked very closely together and in the process became very friendly. This was when I met Marshall and worked with William Hastie.

When I completed my work at Columbia, I envisioned doing research in social interaction, race, and self-image. My dissertation had nothing to do with the law; in fact, it was not even tied to racial self-image. I had no idea that our involvement with Thurgood Marshall and those NAACP cases would lead to a Supreme Court decision that would set the stage for the most important challenge to racial segregation in the twentieth century. Mamie's and my interests were strictly academic. We did our work on black self-image not because of an interest in the law but because of our interest in psychology and race. One thing we did at that time was to apply our academic work by founding Northside Center for Child Development in New York City. This was primarily my wife's interest. She initiated it, and I worked very closely with her in running the center and developing its various programs. I should point out that it was at Northside that I did the interviews with young African American children that isolated the detrimental effect of racial segregation on them. Thurgood Marshall later used these interviews as evidence in *Brown vs. Board of Education.*

When the Supreme Court made its decision, I was teaching my class at City College, City University of New York. My secretary rushed to the class to tell me. Shortly afterward, I got a telephone call from Thurgood Marshall. We were all very happy and delighted with the victory. Thurgood invited a group of us to dinner at a downtown New York hotel. It was a celebration, but it was also a planning meeting to decide our next moves. Soon after, I met with Thurgood in his office and he said to me, "Kenneth, this is positive, but it is just the beginning. We have a lot of work to do from this point on." He was very pensive. That was the first time I had heard him take this position—that the decision was not the end. It would only open up avenues for racial advancement in the United States.

One of the most dramatic pieces of evidence of the negative effects of racial segregation on African Americans cited in the 1954 Supreme Court case was our "doll studies." Black youngsters were shown anatomically correct dolls with white and brown skin colors. I asked the children if they saw themselves in the dolls and, if so, to describe themselves. I also asked them what they thought of themselves with reference to color. By using the white and brown dolls for comparison and as self-identifiers, the children articulated their sense of self-image regarding race and color. For the most part their reactions were negative. The majority of them preferred the white dolls and rejected the brown dolls. They tended to describe themselves through the dolls as ugly, unattractive, inferior to whites, and expressed a desire to be lighter in color. I contend that this would not have been their reaction if they had grown up in a racially balanced environment where they could see the positive and negative sides of people of all colors and races. These children were reflecting a perceived negative and inferior environment based on race, coded by skin color. I published advice to parents on child development and race in *Prejudice and Your Child* (1963).

For years this doll evidence and interpretation of the evidence stood as a classic measure of the psychological effect of racial segregation on African American youth. Then in 1971 this interview technique was replicated by the psychologist Judith Porter, who gave the evidence another interpretation.[6] She too found that young black children reacted negatively to questions about themselves as seen through the dolls. They preferred the white dolls and rejected the brown dolls. She asserted that part of the young people's negative reaction was toward the dolls themselves. It was unusual for black children to have anatomically correct and colored dolls until very recently. In each case, the children's reaction regarding their self-image was confounded by the children's reaction to dolls they were unfamiliar with and probably frightened of. Porter asserted that if they had been used to playing with anatomically correct and same-color dolls, their reactions to questions about their self-concept might have been quite different.

I did not respond to Judith Porter and others who reinterpreted the doll study's evidence of blacks' negative self-image. We used the dolls as indications of what these young people thought about themselves, not the dolls. It was very clear to me in the interviews that I had with the young people that they were talking about themselves, not about the dolls. The dolls were used as a convenient way for the children to talk with me about their feelings. The dolls were not isolated in the children's mind or in mine. Judith Porter and other critics did not seem to understand this important point. There is no way for Porter or anyone else to explain away, through the dolls, the young people's personal reference to themselves in terms of self-rejection. I do not think that Porter and others read our full reports on file at the Library of Congress very well.

Dark Ghetto

In our work at Northside, Mamie and I were involved with young African American people and their parents. By 1960 conditions in Harlem were deteriorating rapidly. The condition of housing was getting worse; the schools were failing; and rising unemployment was displacing families and undercutting community life. De facto racial segregation was taken for granted while its de jure form was being outlawed and protested against in the South. Black people were consigned to the ghetto, and its negative impacts were present everywhere. The effect of being ghettoized was especially evident in the problems of the young people Mamie and I worked with. We felt that it was very important that we do something to address these conditions. To communicate our concerns, we launched a major study of these conditions and made recommendations for improvements.

The task before us was not simply academic. To make changes would require influencing public policy. Government would have to address the problem of de facto racial segregation and its effects in the North. It was vitally important that racial integration begin at all levels of education.[7] By this time I was especially concerned with segregated education and race relations in the North. My academic interests and desire to effect change led to developing a plan to address the needs of the Harlem community and its young people. The result was HARYOU. (See *Youth in the Ghetto: A Study of the Consequences of Powerlessness and a Blueprint for Change* [1964].) The justification and rationale for programmatic change was presented in *Dark Ghetto: Dilemmas of Social Power* (1965) for which Gunnar Myrdal wrote the foreword.

Apparently, the late congressman Adam Clayton Powell Jr. and his staff had read an early draft of *Dark Ghetto*. For some time before *Dark Ghetto* was published, Congressman Powell had tried to get Mamie and me involved with him. He was very close to the Kennedys, and they wanted me to get closer to him. We were not interested in associating with Powell and kept our distance. We were much more interested in academic and psychological social problems than we were in politics, especially after *Dark Ghetto* was published. One of the reasons was because Powell tried to take over the HARYOU community programs. He wanted to control Mamie and me as well as the programs and to take credit for the programs and their positive work. Powell, like virtually all the other politicians we encountered, appeared to do things primarily out of self-interest.

The only politician we respected and got close to was the former Manhattan Democratic Party leader, the late J. Raymond Jones.[8] Mamie and I agreed with Jones that politicians in general, and black politicians in particular, could do a lot more than they did to improve race relations. Jones was something of an idealist. He did not have his hand out all of the time. He seemed fiercely independent. This is partly why he was always in conflict with Adam Powell. Jones said what he thought, and white people had to respect him for that. Adam would have liked Jones to be a partner with him. I respected Jones for his integrity, but I did not respect Adam Powell. There was nothing idealistic or altruistic toward the community in Adam Powell. Unlike many politicians, he was not really detrimental, but he was not the positive force he could have been. But one does have to give Adam credit for two things. First, he had a distinguished congressional record; he was effective there. Second, he was well known and approved of locally. I do not think that we have had another Adam Powell.

You might note that there is no sequel to *Dark Ghetto*. The problems of racial segregation and its effects are worse today than they were in 1960. Then, there was some embarrassment in the government over racial segregation and a desire to do something about it. But today, neither blacks nor whites question it, find it unjust, or are willing to do something about its negative effects in education, housing, or the quality of life for whites and blacks alike. There is no lack of ideas about what needs to be done.[9] A sequel to *Dark Ghetto* would be useful if there were interest and a will to act. But there has been a lack of both for some time.

Reflections

I am no longer an optimist. If you look at the facts, segregation is worse in the North now than it was before 1970. In fact, black children are no better off educationally than they were then. The irony is that there are better educational situations in the South for blacks now than in the North. When we now add to poor education the terrible conditions among blacks in housing, employment, and health in both the North and South, there is little reason for optimism. When I worked with educators and government officials during the 1970s through the Metropolitan Applied Research Corporation (MARC), I could see the willingness to take action waning and a new acceptance of the inferior place of black people in American life.[10]

In retrospect, there is a factor I, as a behavioral scientist, would emphasize if I had to do it all over again and knew what I know now. I would have looked much more deeply at the racism that is deeply ingrained and a very disturbing reality in American life, affecting both blacks and whites. It affects every institution and everything we do. I would hit this point a lot harder. Without looking squarely at racism, *Dark Ghetto* seems naively optimistic, an exercise in wishful thinking.

I think Malcolm X was closer to anticipating our current condition than the other major figures of the 1960s. I interviewed Malcolm X,[11] and he and I also talked frequently. The perspective Malcolm had on Adam Powell was not far from my own. Malcolm was a fascinating man who blended realism with idealism. He did not attempt to influence my work or the shaping of HARYOU, as did Adam Powell. He knew what I was doing and respected my academic interests. I used to invite him up to my classes where the students responded very positively toward him. I respected him and knew something then about Malcolm that is not well known. His thinking was independent of the Muslims long before his split with them. They did not influence him as much as some believed.

My lack of optimism about the present puts me closer to James Baldwin's perspective. He was not optimistic about the possibility that white America might see that they were the cause of the so-called race problem and that it was detrimental to them as well as to blacks. Mamie and I invited Baldwin to our home, and he was very clear on his feelings about the racial dilemma in the United States and who was responsible for it. On the other hand, Martin Luther King Jr., whom I also interviewed and spoke candidly with, was genuinely idealistic and optimistic about the future of the United States. Martin Luther King Jr. really believed that race relations in the United States would eventually take a positive path and that blacks would reject hostilities. He really believed it. He was genuine in his belief that blacks would have to educate whites. The only anxiety I could detect was over the pace of change. He believed that the United States had some positive potential toward race. But U.S. involvement in the Vietnam War troubled him deeply. He was opposed to it. War disturbed him.

Malcolm X, James Baldwin, and Martin Luther King Jr. went against the tide of public opinion. They caused many to rethink their beliefs about themselves and their relations to others. All three improved the United States in some way. But in doing so they were a threat, and two of the three were killed because of that threat. To be black is bad enough, but to be outspoken may be even worse. A personal experience illustrates this point.

Not many people know that I collaborated with Talcott Parsons in editing *The Negro American* (1966). This was Parsons's one and only venture into race relations. I do not know who suggested me to him or why he decided to collaborate with me. I certainly did not initiate the project with Parsons. We worked well with one another, freely exchanging opinions and information. It was a real collaborative relation that was not like the experiences of others with Parsons. In the end, we were each pleased with the final product. He was involved in planning a race relations institute or department at Harvard. Though I am the only African American scholar that he published with, he did not involve me in the planning. He knew that there was no point in doing so. Harvard would accept only a prominent black scholar who was not outspoken. Any black who is independent and outspoken is unacceptable and a threat. Parsons knew that my independence, my willingness to speak out, my views on race, and my uncompromising advocacy of racial integration would not be acceptable at Harvard. So even among scholars where free expression and enquiry are valued, racial attitudes make a difference.

Areas of Future Enquiry

I consider my best work to be *Dark Ghetto* and *Pathos of Power* (1974). If I had to select between the two, it would be *Pathos of Power.* When I look back on it, I can see why *Pathos* was not as well accepted. It was a personal and philosophical statement. The limits of both books would be the basis upon which I would want to see scholarly work done in the future. First, I would want to see more critical studies of the political process. I did only one brief project with politicians while with MARC.[12] If I were younger, I would look very closely at the contributions of black politicians to improving the conditions of blacks in the United States. My concern is that their numbers have increased but their contributions have not. Certainly they have not had the same impact for their black constituencies that Irish and other white ethnic politicians have had for theirs. The question is, why have black politicians not had the same beneficial effects? The more of them there are, the better the condition of blacks should be. In reality, it appears the more we have, the worse our condition.

I spent a lot of time over the years informally looking at black politicians. I could not escape analyzing them. The reason I did not write about them was that I did not think they were interesting. Most of them strike me as being more concerned with their own careers than with improving the conditions of their people. None of them are moving forcefully on the problems of race. My critical attitudes toward politicians and the political process are probably why I have never been asked to serve in any political capacity. Even when I was on the New York State Board of Regents, I would argue with fellow regents on matters of educational principle and never sought their approval or support for what I did. I would always say what I thought.

A second major area of enquiry that I would like to know more about is the history and basis of hostilities among European ethnic groups and how these hostilities have influenced American race relations. White ethnics do not like each other, either in the United States or in Europe. But here in the United States, they have blacks to be united against. I would like to know more about that. I would like to know how they handle that problem among themselves and among their children. Their reaction to black people is not just over competition for jobs, having to pay taxes for alleged social services for blacks, or a genuine belief in black inferiority. There is something more fundamental. I look at the ethnic hostilities and potential hostilities among northern whites and realize that they are lucky to have blacks. This to me is a very important problem, but no one seems to be paying any attention to it. This is clearly an area of great denial among northern white ethnics. I feel sorry for them because of their ignorance and pathos. I am now certain that their hostility toward blacks comes all the way from their European cultural roots.

A third area of enquiry is that of hostilities among blacks based on skin color. Blacks deny its existence and importance, but it is there. Light-skinned blacks are generally more highly thought of than darker-skinned blacks, just as was the case early in this century. Self-hatred and intragroup discrimination based on color exists and affects all black-on-black relations both in and outside families. You can still find black women having more positive reactions to lighter-skinned peers in comparison to those who are darker. Black men are not as overt about it, but consciousness of color and valuing lighter-skinned members is there among them as well.

A final area is about what I now assert. I talk about what our schools have been doing to white children. It is not enough to talk about how schools destroy black children. They are increasingly failing white children as well. It is clear now that you cannot oppress one group without also psychologically and socially injuring the advantaged group. If change will come, it will not be primarily motivated toward helping only black children. It will have to come out of enlightened self-interest.

NOTES

1. Locke.
2. Klineberg and Clark, *Characteristics of the American Negro* and *Negro Intelligence and Selective Migration.*
3. Ibid., "Some Factors Influencing the Remembering of Prose Material."
4. Bland; Davis.
5. M. Clark.
6. Porter.
7. K. Clark, *The Negro Student at Integrated Colleges.*
8. Walter.
9. K. Clark and Hopkins, *A Possible Reality* and *A Relevant War against Poverty.*
10. K. Clark, *The Educationally Deprived* and *The Pathos of Power.*
11. Ibid., *The Negro Protest.*
12. K. Clark, Bond, and Hatcher, *The Black Man in American Politics.*

REFERENCES

Bland, Randell. *Private Pressure on Public Law.* Port Washington: Kennikat Press, 1973.

Bunche, Ralph. *An African-American in South Africa. Athens:* Ohio University Press, 1938.

———. *The Political Status of the Negro in the Age of FDR.* Chicago: University of Chicago Press, 1973.

———. *A World View of Race.* Washington, D.C.: Associates in Negro Folk Education, 1936.

Carter, Robert, et al. *Equality.* New York: Pantheon, 1965.

Clark, Kenneth B. *Dark Ghetto.* New York: Harper and Row, 1965.

———. *The Educationally Deprived: The Potential for Change.* New York: MARC, 1972.

———. *The Negro Protest: James Baldwin, Malcolm X, Martin Luther King Talk with Kenneth B. Clark.* Boston: Beacon, 1963.

———. *The Negro Student at Integrated Colleges.* New York: National Service and Fund for Negro Students, 1963.

———. *The Pathos of Power.* New York: Harper and Row, 1974.

———. *Prejudice and Your Child.* Boston: Beacon, 1963.

Clark, Kenneth B., and Jeannette Hopkins. *A Possible Reality: A Design for the Attainment of High Academic Achievement for Inner City Students.* New York: Emerson Hall, 1972.

———. *A Relevant War against Poverty: A Study of Community Action Programs and Observable Social Change.* New York: Harper and Row, 1969.

Clark, Kenneth, Julian Bond, and Richard Hatcher. *The Black Man in American Politics: Three Views.* Washington, D.C.: MARC, 1969.

Clark, M. P. "Changes in Primary Mental Abilities with Age." *Archives of Psychology* (1944): 291.

Davis, Michael. *Thurgood Marshall: Warrior at the Bar.* New York: Carol Publishing, 1992.

Klineberg, 0., and K. Clark. *Characteristics of the American Negro.* New York: Harper and Row, 1944.

———. *Negro Intelligence and Selective Migration.* New York: Columbia University Press, 1935.

———. "Some Factors Influencing the Remembering of Prose Material." *Archives of Psychology* (1940): 253.

Locke, Alain. *Negro Art: Past and Present.* Washington, D.C.: Associates in Negro Folk Education, 1936.

———. *When Peoples Meet: A Study in Race and Culture Contacts.* New York: Hinds, Hayden and Eldredge, 1946.

Myrdal, Gunnar. *An American Dilemma: The Negro Problem and Modern Democracy.* New York: Harper and Brothers, 1944.

Parsons, Talcott, and K. Clark, eds.. *The Negro American.* Boston: Houghton, Mifflin, 1966.

Porter, Judith. *Black Child, White Child: The Development of Racial Attitudes.* Cambridge: Harvard University Press, 1971.

Walter, John C. *The Harlem Fox: J. Raymond Jones and Tammany, 1920–1970.* Albany: State University of New York Press, 1989.

9

Personal Reflections on W. E. B. Du Bois

The Person, Scholar, and Activist

HERBERT APTHEKER and FAY APTHEKER

There are some very good biographies of Dr. Du Bois that outline in great detail the life of this extraordinary man. One should read volume 1 of David Lewis's *W. E. B. Du Bois (Biography of a Race, 1868–1919* [1993]); Manning Marable's *W. E. B. Du Bois: Black Radical Democrat* (1986); Herbert Aptheker's *Literary Legacy of W. E. B. Du Bois* (1989); and Arnold Rampersad's *Art and Imagination of W. E. B. Du Bois* (1976). And then, of course, there is Dr. Du Bois's autobiography—*The Autobiography of W. E. B. Du Bois: A Soliloquy on Viewing My Life from the Last Decade of Its First Century* (1968). This essay is not intended as a substitute for any of these works. It is an attempt to answer some essential questions that emerge out of a careful reading of the Du Bois biographies and autobiography. His later years are especially important to look at. Who was W. E. B. Du Bois as a person; how did he produce such extraordinary work; why did he work so hard and so long; what were his goals and intentions; why did he return to the NAACP a second time and why did he eventually leave; how did he attain his physical longevity; why did the U.S. government persecute him; and did he really give up on the United States when he left the country? In responding to these questions, Fay and I draw from our personal knowledge of Dr. Du Bois and from four decades of immersion in editing the Du Bois works. There are also a few points that the biographers missed that will give the reader a good sense of the man.

I first met Dr. Du Bois in the spring of 1945. He had a small office at the National Association for the Advancement of Colored People's (NAACP) headquarters on 41st Street and Fifth Avenue across the street from the New York Public Library's main building. He was director of special research and was kind enough to offer a corner of his already cramped office to me to work on my *Documentary History of the Negro People in the United States,* vols. 1–2 (1951). Dr. Du Bois frequently complained about his lack of space to the NAACP president, Walter White, but it was to no avail. My family and I became very close to Dr. Du Bois and his wife, Shirley Graham Du Bois. We frequently spent time with him; we admired him; and it was an honor for me to see to it that his later works were published. Dr. Du Bois was a father to me, and Shirley Graham Du Bois told others that he regarded me as a son. He was one of the greatest figures of this century, and it has been a privilege to have spent the past four decades editing his work and making certain that his extraordinary contributions are available for all to read. Our reflections on W. E. B. Du Bois are based both on the written record and on Fay's and my memories of our many occasions with him.

The Early Years

Du Bois was especially devoted to his mother, Mary Du Bois, and during his early years in Great Barrington, Massachusetts, he could not be separated from her. They were very poor, but he never felt impoverished. He used to help out by performing various chores for the neighbors, such as delivering newspapers and coal. His friends consisted primarily of other black children who lived in the area. He spoke of playing with them in the hills, of sledding in the winter, and of generally having a very happy childhood. His father had left the family quite early. Du Bois did not know his father, but he knew that his father was a Civil War veteran. His father left the family in Great Barrington for some unknown reason. Du Bois suspected that it might have been because he had difficulty finding work. Great Barrington was a predominantly white town with a small black community there and in the surrounding villages. Opportunities for work were very limited. Some years later he was incensed that Arna Wendell Bontemps wrote that he was illegitimate. Dr. Du Bois told Dr. Bontemps that his mother and father were indeed married.

We knew very little else about his family. He had a grandfather, Alexander Du Bois, who lived in New Bedford, Massachusetts, whom he occasionally visited. Apparently, his grandfather was very stern and went to great lengths to affirm his worth as a man, not simply as a Negro. He was also a real taskmaster, whom the young Du Bois came to appreciate. On one of his trips to visit his grandfather, when he was about fourteen years old, he went to the Connecticut state capitol in Hartford. He took great pride in signing the visitors book. He was so excited about signing that he wrote to his mother and told her that by signing this book "his name would last." I believe that Du Bois's grandfather was buried in the Yale University Cemetery during the late 1880s. It came up in conversation with Dr. Du Bois in reference to a debate as to whether or not a black man should be buried there. Dr. Du Bois also had a half-brother of whom he was not aware until the Great Depression. This alleged half-brother was destitute, and a social service agency tried to get Dr. Du Bois to take financial responsibility for him. I remember that Du Bois was irate over this matter, refused to make payments, and was very troubled by it.

Du Bois's extraordinary talents were apparent early in his schooling. It was uncommon for a black child to complete elementary school and go on to the local high school. He was the only black student in the high school and was at the head of his class. At the age of fifteen he wrote local newspaper articles, some of which appeared in T. Thomas Fortune's *New York Globe.* He also wrote some articles for the *Springfield (Mass.) Daily Republican.* He was very conscious of his abilities early in his life. The whole town knew of his abilities, especially when he graduated from high school as their youngest graduate and with high honors.

There was another extraordinary event in young Du Bois's early years. The people in the town, both black and white, got together and raised money so that he could go to college. Several people were responsible for this—his mother, who died shortly after he graduated from high school; Frank Hosmer, the high school principal; Edward Van Lennep, superintendent of the Congregational church's Sunday schools; and the Reverend C. C. Painter, a retired federal Indian agent and former pastor of several Congregational churches.[1] Mary Du Bois had been a member of the local Congregational church and had undoubtedly approached Frank Hosmer. She was also a member of a new African Methodist Episcopal Zion church in Great Barrington.

But even with Du Bois's extraordinary talent and the backing of the town and several prominent citizens, racism was not absent from his life. The reality of race became very clear to him as a teen. Young Du Bois loved to dance and went to his first high school dance expecting to enjoy himself. The girls used to have dance cards on which the names of prospective dance partners were written. Since he was the only black student in the school, he was also the only black student at this dance. So he went to a white student and asked her to dance. She refused. He did not press the matter, but he knew that she refused because of his race. After graduation from high school, Du Bois wanted to go to Harvard University. But despite his obvious talent, Reverend Painter dismissed young Du Bois's interest in

Harvard and insisted that his place was at Fisk University in Nashville, Tennessee, among his own kind. Since Reverend Painter and his churches were providing most of the money for Will Du Bois's college education, his decision stood. Du Bois did not object. While he wanted to go to Harvard, he also wanted to be in the company of other black people. Fisk would give him that opportunity.

The Student Years

Du Bois arrived in Nashville in the fall of 1885. He described Fisk as a small college built after the New England tradition, where Latin, Greek, mathematics, and history were taught. There were then twenty-five students in the college department; the school was very small and had very good teachers. At Fisk, one went to bed at 10:00 P.M. sharp. Du Bois was to maintain this practice as a lifelong habit to which he partly attributed his longevity. Here as in Great Barrington, Du Bois was a leading student. He wrote again for the newspaper, the *Fisk Herald,* and became an active member of the larger Nashville black community as he had been in Great Barrington. His professors recognized his talent, but his strong interest in the community and in the average and generally uneducated blacks went against his professors' advice. This interest found expression in his service as a summer school teacher in the Tennessee countryside. He plunged into this new activity, which would expose him to his people. He also went to dances in Nashville against which his classmates and teachers had warned him; and he had his first sexual experience during one of his teaching summers with his landlady, who seduced him. He spoke in amazement many years afterward of the beauty of black women at Fisk.

Two incidents during his years at Fisk had a profound and long-lasting effect on him. In the first, he agreed to manage a small glee club that would make money during the latter part of August with singing engagements in the Midwest. In order to get there and support themselves the club members had to work as waiters at a summer resort hotel at Lake Minnetonka, Minnesota. The job exposed Du Bois to the worst of white bourgeois culture—husbands with their girl friends, lavish spending, women looking for sexual encounters, waiters competing with one another by clowning for guests, and having to steal food so they could get enough to eat. At some point during this time, he was robbed of a great deal of money. I did not get clarification from Dr. Du Bois whether this was his money or the choir's money. Whatever the case, it was a traumatic experience for him. The second incident occurred during a visit to Nashville. He was walking downtown, dressed as usual in a suit, when he accidentally bumped into a white woman. He immediately apologized; the woman turned, saw that he was black, and slapped him.[2] Du Bois never forgot this, and despite his involvement in the community, he never went into Nashville again during his student years.

It was at Fisk that Du Bois decided to always present himself in his manner and speech as very correct and proper—a model gentleman. This was part of a deliberate image that he decided to convey early in his college years. He was determined to show all others, white and black, that a black man could be refined and cultured, and could enjoy all the high and noble things of life. So he endeavored to be just the opposite of the accepted black stereotype, which was subservient, unkempt, and without good taste. For the rest of his life he was always immaculately dressed and sensitive to his public image. This attention to image pervaded everything he did.

Du Bois finally got to Harvard. His professors at Fisk recommended him. He was admitted as a junior and was given a fellowship of $250. He deliberately lived off-campus in a rooming house. This is significant because most of the white students lived on campus in a series of halls with distinct dining clubs. Du Bois intentionally limited his involvement at Harvard to his studies after his glee club application was turned down. And as before, he found social support and encouragement in the Boston black community and wrote with several other students for the *Boston Courant,* a black weekly. I suspect that he found black women in Boston to be among the more progressive members of the community—his friendship with St. Pierre Ruffin, a national leader of the black women's club movement and editor of the *Courant,* was an indication of this.[3] Du Bois's lifelong support of women's equity and political enfranchisement is a point seriously underestimated by Du Bois biographers—it was evident as far back as Great Barrington, but it took formal expression during his Harvard years. As others have pointed out, by his Boston years Du Bois was very clear about his long-term goals for improving the political and social conditions and relative position of African Americans in the United States and of playing a leadership role in this improvement.

Despite Du Bois's reticence as to social involvement with whites at Harvard, he had very good and close relations with several faculty members who were his mentors. They were Albert Bushnell Hart in history, and George Santayana and William James in philosophy. In fact, Du Bois was very impressed with William James, was a guest in the home of Dr. and Mrs. James, and for a while thought that he would be a philosopher. But financial considerations changed his mind. At Harvard after receiving his bachelor's degree and while working on his master's degree, he gave a paper at the 1891 meeting of the American Historical Association. The paper was titled "Suppression of the African Slave Trade." It was very unusual for a black person to be allowed to present a paper at this time. There were substantial written comments on Du Bois's paper from the professors present. Shortly after this presentation, he completed his master's degree.

Du Bois wanted to study abroad. This was something that he had wanted to do while at Fisk, but there, he had neither the money nor the opportunity. At Harvard it was the practice after completing a master's degree for the best students to go to Europe for their doctoral degrees. Former U.S. president Rutherford B. Hayes was a member of a Harvard Board and was quoted as saying with regard to overseas fellowship funds that the money was always given to white students because no Negro was capable. Du Bois wrote an angry letter to Hayes. To his surprise, Hayes met with Du Bois in New York and agreed to provide financial support for his trip to Germany from the Slater Fund for the Education of Negroes. After his meeting with Hayes, Du Bois celebrated by walking down Fifth Avenue in New York; he saw an expensive shirt in a shop window and bought it—he had to be dressed appropriately in Europe.

Berlin was important to him; he loved his studies and did very well at Friedrich Wilhelm University. Because his money was so limited, he kept very strict financial accounts, which became a lifelong habit. Also his best male friend while in Europe was a Jewish student from Poland. They took a trip together where a hotel manager agreed to give Du Bois a room but not his Jewish friend. Du Bois was amazed at this reversal of what one expected in the United States. He refused to stay at that hotel. Du Bois and his friend continued to correspond after he left Germany. In Germany Du Bois also met the sociologist Max Weber who, later in Du Bois's career, visited him in Atlanta. Weber wanted to have Du Bois's *Souls of Black Folks: Essays and Sketches* (1903) translated into German, but the project was never done, probably because of World War I. But despite doing well academically, Du Bois did not get his Ph.D. from Friedrich Wilhelm University. The faculty refused to give him an early oral examination, and the Slater Fund refused to provide additional funds. He believed that he deserved the doctorate and was very disappointed.

Du Bois came home in debt and without a Ph.D., but he had learned a great lesson—that racism against black people in the United States was not an innate condition or natural disposition among European peoples. He saw it then as a peculiarly American phenomenon. He was all the more determined to devote his career to challenging racism. On his twenty-fifth birthday he recorded in his diary that he pledged to make a difference in the world. By then all the necessary experiences and training were in place for him to begin his extraordinary career. At this point the only thing missing was an ideal, a goal, and an alternative to the social system as he knew it. He knew about Karl Marx and had attended local meetings of the German Social Democratic party, but he was not a socialist when he came back from Germany. But he was on his way toward defining his own sense of socialism.

Early Career and Family

After returning from Europe, Du Bois began his teaching career as an instructor of Latin and Greek at Wilberforce College in Xenia, Ohio. He wanted to teach more but they would not let him. His attire and obvious lack of religious piety were of great concern to the college's religious administration. Meanwhile, he worked on his Harvard dissertation, "The Suppression of the African Slave Trade, 1638–1870." He was awarded a Ph.D. in 1895, and his dissertation became volume 1 in the Harvard Historical Series. While in Ohio, Du Bois married. He was physically a very handsome man. Women were attracted to him. He welcomed them, loved every bit of it, had no hang-ups with women, and had great respect for them. His first wife was Nina Gomer Du Bois. A student at Wilberforce, she was from an Iowa farm background. She was also biracial—her father was a black carpenter and her mother was German.

Du Bois's abrupt marriage and outspoken views further alienated him from the Wilberforce administration; he knew that it would not be long before they terminated his appointment. When he was recruited by the University of Pennsylvania to do a study of the Negro community of Philadelphia, he seized the opportunity. He went to Philadelphia with his young bride and baby. They moved into the Seventh Ward, the study site, and lived over a cafeteria. Du Bois worked around the clock for one and half years studying everything that was available on the Seventh Ward. He personally interviewed five thousand individuals and paid particular attention to their migration patterns from the South and how they managed financially amid extreme poverty in Philadelphia. Meanwhile, his wife, Nina, suffered. Living in a city for the first time and taking care of their first child was an ordeal. Du Bois's salary did not put them much above the condition of others in the community. This is when Du Bois wrote his classic *Philadelphia Negro* (1899), which was the first urban sociological study ever done in the United States. He began urban sociology, as it is known today; he had no model, no theories, and no established methodologies on which to base his work. Du Bois stated modestly sometime in the 1950s, "I made this study of the Philadelphia Negro, which is even recognized today as a good sort of social study and has been very widely used."

The Philadelphia Negro was an extraordinary study and was recognized as such shortly after publication. With Du Bois's training, published Harvard thesis, and now a major work, the major universities should have recruited him. But this was the 1890s when the plight of black people in the United States and in many other parts of the world was becoming more desperate. The only place Du Bois could get a university position was in a black college. Given his scholarly and personal interests in black people, he went after such an appointment. This time it was at Atlanta University, which was somewhat more enlightened and tolerant of Du Bois's liberal religious views and his willingness to speak out. Atlanta University also wanted Du Bois because the university was interested in doing a series of conference studies on the plight of black people in cities—Dr. Du Bois was eminently qualified. Dr. Du Bois was appointed as professor of history and economics in 1897 and was soon on his way toward producing another series of vitally important studies.

In Atlanta tragedy struck soon after he and his family were settled. Their first child, Burghardt Gomer Du Bois, who was only eighteen months old, died of sewage pollution from Atlanta's water system. He was buried in Great Barrington. Nina Gomer Du Bois was as unhappy in Atlanta as she had been in Philadelphia, and the loss of their son was a devastating blow. Dr. Du Bois told me that his wife never recovered from this loss and was quite depressed thereafter. The loss of his son sensitized Du Bois and gave him a sense of the spiritual meaning that so many other blacks around him depended upon. In addition, Atlanta was becoming increasingly dangerous as the iron curtain of Jim Crow descended on the South. In anticipation of a race riot against blacks, the Du Bois's had a secret hiding place in their house for their daughter, Yolanda, in case their home was attacked. While Du Bois was away doing research in Alabama for the federal government, his family had to use it in 1906 during a major uprising. Fortunately, the rioters did not harm Mrs. Du Bois, the baby, or the house on the Atlanta University campus. Dr. Du Bois caught the first train back. He sat with his shotgun on the porch for hours just in case the rioters came back. Shortly afterward, he moved his family to Baltimore.

What many Du Bois scholars are not aware of is the extent to which Du Bois conducted studies for the federal government. Besides his better-known Atlanta University conference studies, he did extensive fieldwork on sharecropping in Alabama and Virginia. This was very dangerous work. He risked his life many times interviewing sharecroppers at night in fields, at crossroads, and at informants' homes. As a result, few people knew the South as well as Du Bois. He knew its heart and soul. Since these were contracted studies, they were turned over to the government and were not published. Some years later, Dr. Du Bois came to the conclusion that his work was not being used by the government to better the plight of black sharecroppers. So he went to the Labor Department to get them. What he found out was that most of the results of his years of work, and what were undoubtedly the most important and extensive studies of sharecropping ever done, had been destroyed. They did not even offer to give the studies back to him or to give them to a library or archive, which was then the practice. The studies that survived, such as *The Negroes of Farmville, Virginia: A Social Study* (1898), *The Negro in the Black Belt: Some Social Sketches* (1899), and others were only a fraction of his work. He told me that the Labor Department analysts thought the studies were too critical, too detailed, too real, and amounted to a condemnation of the South. This was one of the most devastating events in Du Bois's professional career—for years afterward, he did not even want to talk about it.

The Labor Department was not the only agency that found Du Bois's work threatening. In time, as at Wilberforce College, Du Bois's work and his willingness to be outspoken, got him in hot water repeatedly with the Atlanta University administration. He was simply too radical. But lack of funding did not prevent him from completing an extraordinary series of studies. He did the entire Atlanta University studies over fourteen years on less than five thousand dollars per year. In addition, he wrote *The Souls of Black Folks: Essays and Sketches* (1903), *John Brown* (1909), and edited conference works, *The Negro in Business* (1899), *The College-Bred Negro* (1900), *The Negro Common School* (1901), *The Negro Artisan* (1902), *The Negro Church* (1903), *Some Notes on Negro Crime, Particularly in Georgia* (1904), and *The Health and Physique of the Negro American* (1906). Wealthy donors refused to contribute to the university because of his presence and his prominence in criticizing Booker T. Washington. He was concerned that he was an embarrassment to Atlanta University, which he loved, and was costing this struggling institution money they desperately needed.

Dr. Du Bois's experiences doing research in the community and his criticism of Booker T. Washington, the most prominent black power broker and accommodationist in the early Jim Crow period, affected Du Bois's political thinking. By 1907 he realized that there was an alternative to Jim Crow racial segregation and economic exploitation. He considered himself a socialist and said so. But Du Bois's criticism of American racism was not limited to domestic affairs. His magazine and newspaper writing while in Atlanta made this very clear. Ever since his years in Europe, Du Bois had paid particular attention to the international scope of racial oppression. By 1902 he was aware of the atrocities committed by the U.S. Army in the Philippines. He knew of the Anti-Imperialist League as early as 1899. The league was headed by Moorfield Storey, who later played a prominent role in the founding of the National Association for the Advancement of Colored People (NAACP). Du Bois showed pictures of the atrocities committed by American troops in the Philippines in his classroom. This is also the time when Du Bois met the prominent anthropologist Franz Boas, who came to speak in Atlanta. Boas had been working his way intellectually toward exposing the racial myth of innate white superiority, but he was not fully there yet. It was Du Bois's growing sense that the world could be changed for the better, his determination to make that change for the better happen, and the increasing isolation and struggle to hold on to his academic position that prompted Du Bois to leave Atlanta. He resigned from Atlanta University in 1910 to join the newly founded NAACP.

Early Activism

The first decade of the twentieth century was decisive in the growth of Du Bois's political perspective. A series of developments during this time showed a progressive radicalization of Du Bois's thoughts. In 1900 at the first pan-African conference, Du Bois wrote the appeal to the world. But this was not an anti-imperialist statement. Rather, it was a liberal appeal for decency toward the colonies—he argued that it was in the best interest of all concerned that the major colonial powers treat their colonial nations humanely, that colonialism eventually be ended, and that the educated African make plans for this transition. He was not a radical at that time. At first he was even mildly supportive of Booker T. Washington. Only as Washington became the power broker for powerful industrial interests and failed to use his influence to oppose Jim Crow did Du Bois become concerned. And then, Du Bois focused mainly on Washington's potentially abusive business practices. There were others who were much more critical of Washington; for example, Ida B. Wells-Barnett and Monroe Trotter were critical of Du Bois for his moderate views toward Washington.[4]

Booker T. Washington's apologetic leadership and service as a power broker in the face of worsening racial oppression radicalized many, including Du Bois. This was the decade (1900–1910) when the iron curtain of racism and de jure segregation was established in the South—in very much the same fashion that open racism is being reinstitutionalized in the United States today. This was the Bloody Decade when close to eight hundred lynchings occurred and the South passed its Jim Crow legislation. In these critical regressive years Du Bois traveled throughout Alabama, Virginia, and Georgia interviewing sharecroppers and ordinary black folks whose lives and livelihoods were being crushed. He was in the rural countryside doing increasingly covert and dangerous interviews as the rapes, night riding, and lynchings intensified. By the end of the decade his field experiences had radicalized him and alienated him from the accommodationist leadership of Booker T. Washington.

As the first decade of the new century passed, the publication of *The Souls of Black Folks* pushed an increasingly radical Du Bois into a position of national leadership. A key chapter in this book is "On Booker T. Washington and Others." This is a slightly revised version of "The Religion of the Negro" published in *New World* magazine (Boston) in 1900. *The Souls of Black Folks* was a best-seller and pushed Du Bois's relatively mild but pointed critique of Booker T. Washington into wide circulation and prominence. So when one considers the combination of factors—increasing racism, Du Bois's emerging radicalism, his prominence after *Souls,* and his personal ambition to improve the condition of the race—leaving Atlanta University and his future leadership in the formation of the Niagara Movement and of the NAACP could have been predicted.

The Niagara Movement was to be an alternative to Booker T. Washington's organization and agenda. Like Du Bois its members were college-educated, professional black men who advocated civil rights for blacks, enforcement of laws against lynching, and access for blacks to a liberal arts education as a foundation for work in the trades and the professions. But given Du Bois's academic, publication, and research commitments, and his disposition as a scholar, leadership was not one of his strengths. Booker T. Washington's Tuskegee Machine campaign against the movement and its smear tactics nearly destroyed the Niagara Movement. Washington's opposition was also directly responsible for taking over a number of black community newspapers that were initially sympathetic to Du Bois's criticism of Washington and for the unemployment of a number of Niagara movement members.[5]

While the Niagara Movement was struggling for its survival, a white reform group, called the Constitution League, headed by John Milholland, had fallen out with Booker T. Washington. They had been supporters of Washington, but their criticism of the Roosevelt administration's mass dishonorable discharge of black troops after the Brownsville, Texas, riot put the league at odds with both President Roosevelt and Booker T. Washington. Du Bois knew Milholland well. It was Milholland who paid for Du Bois to go to London in 1910 to challenge and debate Booker T. Washington. Milholland's daughter, Inez, was a lawyer, a radical, and one of the white women who helped found the NAACP. She died in her thirties. Du Bois's and Milholland's friendship led to the joining of the black Niagara Movement and the white Constitution League and the formation of the National Association for the Advancement of Colored People in 1909.

But it took more than Du Bois's and Milholland's friendship to get the NAACP started. The decisive event was the 1908 Springfield, Illinois, riot where a number of black men were lynched. William English Walling, a socialist and cofounder of the NAACP, called for white liberals to build a new social movement. In 1909 the first NAACP convention was held in New York City with both blacks and whites in attendance. Much of the historical writing about the early founding of the NAACP portrays its white cofounders as sort of liberal reformers. Many were a lot more than that. They were, in fact, socialists and radicals in their day. George Frazier Miller, a black minister from Brooklyn, was a socialist. By this time Du Bois also called himself a socialist, though he did not clearly define what he meant by it. Among the white NAACP founders was Mary White Ovington, a leftist socialist. The most "moderate" of these white founders was Oswald Garrison Villard, who was not a socialist and not nearly as radical as his grandfather, William Lloyd Garrison. He, like Milholland, was an early supporter of Booker T. Washington but had become quite critical of the Tuskegee Machine's excesses.

The philosophy, goals, potential, and strategies of the NAACP's founders, are not those of the organization we know today. Then the NAACP stood for the international advancement of "colored people." This is not just African Americans. It was to include Filipinos, Native Americans, and Puerto Ricans as well. This was stated quite explicitly at the founding of the NAACP. I am afraid the current leadership has forgotten that. They did not call themselves "colored" because it was a high-class thing to do or because they were snobbish or wanted to deny who they were. They meant just that—"colored peoples." The first president of the NAACP was the white radical Moorfield Storey. Storey was also the first president of the Anti-Imperialist League of the United States. His interests prior to the NAACP included the liberation of the Philippines from the United States and ending the genocide committed in this country against Native Americans. Du Bois was a member of the league and, while he was in Atlanta, wrote to

Storey congratulating him on his work. The pictures Du Bois showed to his classes of the atrocities of U.S. troops in the Philippines were gotten from Moorfield Storey.

If anyone has any doubts about the radical roots and persons behind the NAACP, they should read the *New York Times* article on the founding of the NAACP to see how frightened many were of the organization and its founders. A black radical group that advocated racial equity could be ignored and then would have to struggle to survive assaults from Booker T. Washington, as was the case of the Niagara Movement. A white radical group would be too distant from the problem and would lack credibility. However, black and white radicals together would be beyond Booker T. Washington's control, could potentially have access to the black rank and file, could have credibility as advocates and spokespeople on the race issue as it affected whites and blacks, and could have access to the white general public. An interracial radical organization would also be a living testimony that racism is unnecessary and not something innate in either blacks or whites. Ironically, those in the white establishment were not the only ones troubled with the idea and reality of a radical interracial organization. The black radical Ida B. Wells-Barnett quit the NAACP because she felt there were too many white people involved. The black radical newspaper editor Monroe Trotter refused to be part of the NAACP for the same reason.

Many people think of Du Bois as only concerned with and a leader of blacks. Many also divide his life and thinking according to their own sharp division between domestic and foreign affairs. This is not accurate. His outrage over events in the South and equally shocking events overseas was connected as far back as his student days in Berlin. He saw the connections between oppression here and overseas. Others who were as international in their perspective as Du Bois founded the NAACP. This was the perfect vehicle for Du Bois's activism. And his leadership in the pan-African movement was not something apart from his involvement in a globally defined NAACP and the British Labour Party. The early NAACP radicals supported his pan-Africanism. Remember that it was John Milholland (an NAACP founder) who made it possible for Du Bois to debate Booker T. Washington in London in 1910—something that was beyond the resources of the Niagara movement.

Dr. Du Bois was not the only black activist who believed in the need for a pan-African movement. This was a dream of black anticolonial activists in the Caribbean, in Africa, and in the United States. Martin Delany and Robert Campbell had a pan-Africanism implied in their back-to-Africa efforts in the 1860s. Marcus Garvey and George Padmore called for a pan-

Africanism as well, as did Monroe Trotter. Dr. Du Bois's importance to this dream is that he brought to the table his bridging of white and black radicals who could see the domestic "race problem" as part of a larger blueprint, which included international oppression. It has been overlooked that visions of a pan-African conference were transformed from dream to reality in 1919 partly and critically because of the resources, contacts and organization of a transracial and international socialist movement. Du Bois articulated, years before the Labour Party did, that domestic racism was an outcome of international capitalism. He and the early NAACP served as a model for the party's realization of the advantages of interracial collaboration. Today, we underestimate the importance of socialism in the first two decades of this century in bringing together dispersed radicals and the importance of the early pan-African meetings. These conferences, which took place at the high point of European colonialism and imperialism, were not easily organized.

Our point is evident when the pan-African meetings in 1900 and 1914 are compared to the 1919 conference. In 1900 Du Bois's statement in the *Report of the Pan-African Conference,* "To the Nations of the World," is really very mild. This document did not have the kind of systematic critique that was in the 1919 statement, nor did the 1900 conference have the attendance, support, follow-up, or impact of the 1919 conference. Nothing came of this first meeting. The 1914 meeting really did not occur. In 1914 just before World War I, Duse Mohammed Ali and Du Bois attempted to organize the conference but were told that Paris was under martial law and the conference could not be held at that time. So the conference had to wait until after the First World War. But by 1914 Du Bois would not have written the same kind of protest and appeal for decency that he did in 1900. In this fourteen-year period he had come to see much more clearly the relationships between capitalism, imperialism, and racism at home and abroad—they are all interconnected and cannot be separated from one another.

Virtually every issue of *Crisis,* edited by Du Bois, had comments on domestic and foreign affairs—and not just on Africa, but Europe, Asia, South America, and the Caribbean as well. When Du Bois organized the massive 1917 antilynching parade in New York, it was meant not only to be a protest against a domestic outrage but also to bring international pressure to bear on the United States. This is why Du Bois marched at the front of the parade down New York City's most famous avenue, Fifth Avenue. If this had been simply a racial protest with no interest in attracting international attention, the parade could have been held more easily in Harlem. In fact, because of Du Bois's fine knowledge of how capitalism, imperialism, and racism worked at home and abroad, he was able to anticipate both world wars as logical outcomes of these processes. Another way to appreciate Du Bois's growing world perspective and how domestic affairs related to it is to compare the content and approach of *The Souls of Black Folks* with the greatly ignored little book *The Negro* (1915). *Souls* has a domestic focus and is introspective, whereas *The Negro* is international, bridges geographic and historic divisions, and was and still is essential background work for a real postcolonial and postneocolonial pan-Africanism.

Unlike the earlier meetings, the 1919 pan-African conference attracted the active opposition and concern of the president of the United States, Woodrow Wilson. Wilson was concerned not simply because Du Bois wrote to him, informed him that the meeting was going to take place, and asked for his support. The 1919 meeting was a threat precisely because it raised the specter of a domestic front of blacks, whites, and socialists united in their criticism of capitalism and imperialism. But now this domestic threat was becoming international. Col. Edward House, a Wilson aide, and Maj. F. P. Schoonmaker of the U.S. Army closely monitored Du Bois's movements around Paris. Not surprisingly, Du Bois was having a great deal of trouble getting permission from the French to hold the conference. That the conference happened at all can be attributed to the support of Blaise Diagne, who, according to George Padmore, was the most influential colonial politician in France and a close friend of the French premier, Georges Clemenceau.[6] It probably also helped that Du Bois's plans were viewed by the French and other observers as utopian, without revolutionary intent, and with no chance of influencing the delegates at the postwar Paris Peace Conference. While the 1919 Paris Pan-African Conference did not dissuade the great powers from their practice of colonialism, it did achieve a less ambitious goal. Educated Africans came together to get to know each other and to lay down plans to address the eventual emancipation of Africans.

Du Bois represented a radical and interracial NAACP at the 1919 Pan-African Conference that supported his leadership role—imagine such a leader and organization today. Unlike the 1900 pan-African meeting, in 1919 Du Bois represented an organization that claimed 300 branches, and 88,448 members, half of which were in the South. By 1919 *Crisis* magazine had a circulation of more than 70,000.[7] An independent but important related development was the rise in socialist and union memberships during the decades leading up to 1919. Members of socialist and union organizations represented the core of domestic opposition to capitalism, were supportive of antiracism, and supported blacks as members in their organization. Given this fact, Woodrow Wilson had good reason to take notice and to be concerned.

Personal Relationships

There was no behind-the-scenes relationship between Booker T. Washington and W. E. B. Du Bois. For most of Booker T. Washington's career, those whom he could not control, he spied upon by bribing people close to them. Washington also attempted to destroy their reputations and livelihoods through well-placed lies and misinformation in the press. Booker T. Washington's behind-the-scenes attempts to oppose Jim Crow and the lynchings came relatively late in his career, after he had compromised opposition to Jim Crow in its earliest and most vulnerable days. Washington's opposition to Jim Crow was independent of and in opposition to all the groups that opposed the political and educational disenfranchisement of blacks in the South from the start of Jim Crow. For decades, he tried to destroy Du Bois, nearly succeeded in destroying the Niagara Movement, and fought the NAACP by publishing lies about black men and white women having sexually suggestive dances and dinners together.

Booker T. Washington recognized Du Bois's potential to oppose him before the publication of *The Souls of Black Folks.* Washington tried to control Du Bois by offering him a professorship at Tuskegee. Du Bois asked what he would teach but never got a clear response from Washington. Washington later regretted not responding and saw this as a lost opportunity to gain control of Du Bois. Booker T. Washington also tried but failed to get Du Bois the position as superintendent of colored education in the District of Columbia as a way to control him.

Then there was the 1903 meeting of black leaders sponsored by Andrew Carnegie in New York City. Carnegie paid for all the leaders' expenses, except Du Bois's. At this meeting, Carnegie appeared at the beginning, welcomed everyone, and then left. Another time after an attempted reconciliation meeting between Washington and Du Bois in New York City, Du Bois spoke of a conversation he had with Booker T. Washington while they rode a trolley together. Du Bois asked Booker T. about Andrew Carnegie. Booker T. responded that Mr. Carnegie talked very little but had a great deal of money. At this meeting, they made plans to develop some kind of partnership and organization. But Du Bois would not have anything to do with it because he knew that Booker T. Washington was corrupt and could not be trusted. They published a couple of pamphlets together and that was the extent of their collaboration. Du Bois believed that Washington was very much aware that Andrew Carnegie was interested in him only because of the coal and iron mining prospects in Alabama. Carnegie wanted free access to these resources and did not want black labor agitation. Carnegie's relationship with Booker T. Washington paid off—Birmingham, Alabama, became the center of Carnegie's U.S. Steel Corporation. Booker T. Washington was trying to discredit the NAACP and Du Bois right up to his death in 1915.

Very few people know that Du Bois, along with Alain Locke, was also a father of the mistitled Harlem Renaissance. It was mistakenly identified as only a Harlem event when in fact the arts and letters among blacks flourished in St. Louis, Chicago, and New Orleans as well. It was a national renaissance. In the 1920s there were very few great black artists, writers, poets, or singers whose careers were not supported by Du Bois. He wrote about them in *Crisis,* and the writers and poets were able to use *Crisis* as a forum for their work. They included Marian Anderson, Langston Hughes, Arna Wendell Bontemps, and especially Elizabeth Prophet. Du Bois first published Langston Hughes and Countee Cullen, and set up the *Crisis* group of writers and scholars, as well as the first serious live theater in Harlem, the Negro Theater. During the 1920s he was an organizer, agitator, and the father of the black intelligentsia.

By 1930 Du Bois had worked vigorously for three decades. He was nearly sixty years old and had lived apart from his first wife since 1906, when she moved to Baltimore. Du Bois never moved to Baltimore, nor did Nina Du Bois and their daughter, Yolanda, move to New York. He visited them occasionally and corresponded with them. The letters were practical and focused on what Nina needed and how Yolanda was doing. Clearly they had grown apart. Nina Gomer Du Bois died in her sixties in 1950. At eighteen years old, Yolanda married Countee Cullen and eventually became a high school French teacher. It turned out that Cullen was a homosexual. He had his male lover with him on his and Yolanda's honeymoon. Du Bois did not know about the homosexuality, but he did find out that Cullen was not making love to his daughter and wrote a letter to Cullen on how to be gentle with her, how to make love and to care for her. Countee Cullen eventually married several other women, one of whom was very wealthy and lived on Fifth Avenue.

Marcus Garvey came to the United States in 1916 originally at the invitation of Booker T. Washington. He was in charge of a school in Jamaica founded on the same philosophy as Tuskegee: preparing students for practical work. But Booker T. Washington died in 1915 before Garvey's arrival. When Garvey finally got to New York, one of the first people Garvey wanted to see was Du Bois. Garvey knew Du Bois from one of Du Bois's trips to Jamaica to lecture. Garvey, a newspaper reporter and columnist, had interviewed Du Bois and been part of the welcoming committee. In New York Garvey went to Du Bois's office but Du Bois was not there. Garvey left a note and they continued to correspond. For the first five years of Garvey's career in the United States, Du Bois was favorably impressed with Garvey, who was an outstanding and militant anti-imperialist, pan-Africanist, and inspired orator and leader. You will find nothing critical in *Crisis* about Garvey until 1923. Before that Du Bois only expressed concerns about Garvey's business associates. There were thousands of supporters who sent a dime a month to Garvey's United Negro Improvement Association. Du Bois wanted to know where that money was going. No one questioned Garvey's honesty, but his business associates left much to be desired.

In the early 1920s Marcus Garvey changed abruptly from a militant anti-imperialist to a pan-African black capitalist and leader of black emigrationism. At the same time, Garvey began to be very critical of Du Bois and of the NAACP. Like Booker T. Washington, he attacked the NAACP's interracial composition. Garvey was also very derogatory about Du Bois. He compared Du Bois's lighter skin color to his own darker color, suggesting that Du Bois could not be trusted as a black man and leader because of his mixed blood. Garvey never really understood how color was viewed differently in the United States than in his native Jamaica. Du Bois tried unsuccessfully to explain the difference to Garvey in the *Crisis*.

Garvey and several associates were framed and arrested by the U.S. government for mail fraud in 1924. Several of Garvey's crooked associates testified against him and were not prosecuted. Only Garvey was convicted and sent to prison. This was one of the first cases J. Edgar Hoover was involved in. Hoover considered Garvey's domestic and international activities to be a threat to the United States and wanted to get Garvey. Robert Hill, who is editing Garvey's works, is finding more and more about Garvey's abrupt change and is trying to understand how and why he became increasingly conservative—to the point of having secret meetings with the Ku Klux Klan who supported Garvey's plan to take American Negroes back to African. The white supremacist U.S. senator Theodore Bilbo was also very happy with Garvey's position and recommended that the U.S. Senate support it. Garvey and Bilbo formed a united front for which Du Bois blasted Garvey in the opinion section to *Crisis* by asking if Garvey was "a lunatic or a traitor."

Organizational Leadership

By 1934 the NAACP had lost its radical potential. It became increasingly distant from its international mission, and its identity became primarily that of a black middle-class organization. All during this time, Du Bois maintained the independence of *Crisis,* a journal he had founded that became the official organ of the NAACP. Du Bois was the organization's most visible and well-known figure. His prominence was based largely on the centrality that *Crisis* took in shaping progressive black opinion. Du Bois, through *Crisis,* was the most consistent and critical black voice in the nation for more than two decades. Du Bois's views in *Crisis* had survived Booker T. Washington, Marcus Garvey, and a host of others. Du Bois described *Crisis* as "a little monthly magazine that would discuss the Negro problem and would tell both blacks and whites what the NAACP was about and what it proposed to do." In doing so he made a lot of enemies, both inside and outside the NAACP. But the magazine was financially self-sufficient. It paid for itself and Du Bois's salary, and cost the NAACP nothing while it provided the NAACP with national and international exposure.

In addition to editing *Crisis,* Du Bois wrote weekly columns for the *New York Amsterdam News* and the *Chicago Defender.* He also traveled around the country in the 1930s, including the South, making militant speeches. Few people could have imagined that Dr. Du Bois spent years driving through the South, relieved himself in the woods, carried sandwiches to eat, traveled with a pistol and was prepared to use it, wore coveralls, and repaired his car himself. This is what you had to do as a black man traveling in the South—Du Bois was no exception. Besides being a genius, the man had seemingly endless energy. Du Bois was an extraordinarily talented and driven man—one in a million. He also had fantastic creativity.

Once when I went to interview Norman Thomas, who knew Du Bois, Thomas said to me that the main thing about Du Bois was that he was a prophet. Du Bois planned his work not just for months at a time but for a decade in advance. In his Atlanta University studies of the Negro family, health, crime, and so on, Du Bois laid out what he hoped would be a century of studies. He had hoped these studies would be redone periodically to see what had changed. Du Bois realized that Atlanta was a marvelous social laboratory of a suppressed people. He was not only a scholar but also an activist who passionately wanted to see his people free in the United States and Africa.

In addition to his work as an activist, Du Bois also produced pioneering scholarly works, including *John Brown* (1909), *The Negro* (1915), *Darkwater:*

Voices within the Veil (1920), *The Gift of Black Folk: The Negro in the Making of America* (1924), and *Black Reconstruction* (1935). Between February 1910 and May 1921 alone, Du Bois wrote 571 magazine editorials, articles, and commentaries. This is roughly about half his lifetime's work in this category. He also wrote two historical novels during this period—*The Quest of the Silver Fleece* (1911) and *Dark Princess: A Romance* (1928). This record of productivity does not include pamphlets, edited works, and chapters he wrote for others. Du Bois had no difficulty moving between activism and scholarship. His only complaint was over being barred from using certain libraries because of his race. Despite all that he did, Du Bois was not able to do the research he would have liked to do because of racial restrictions. Du Bois was pursuing what he felt his purpose in life to be, and there was no distinction in his mind between scholarship and activism.

Tension had grown between Du Bois and the NAACP leadership because he was much more radical than they. The NAACP had become mildly reformist and a gentlemanly organization, which only worked consistently to oppose the crudest forms of racism—lynchings. Du Bois wanted the organization to have a much larger mass following and to be more radical. During the New Deal socialists in the CIO and the National Negro Congress were pushing Roosevelt toward progressive reforms. Twenty years earlier the NAACP might have played this role. Du Bois felt that the New Deal had both positive and negative aspects for black people, but the NAACP leadership was unable to make such distinctions. Du Bois tried but failed to change the NAACP by getting his own people on the NAACP board of directors. By 1933 the socialist radicals were gone, and white liberals such as Joel Spingarn, whom Du Bois held in high regard, dominated the board. After failing to change the NAACP, Du Bois resigned; he did so without criticizing the leadership. The NAACP acknowledged his historic work with them.

What Du Bois did not know was that Joel Spingarn was an army intelligence officer in World War I, still maintained his government connections, and was directed to keep track of Du Bois. When Du Bois began to organize the 1919 Pan-African Conference, the Russian revolution had already begun, and intelligence officials in this country were concerned that there might have been some connection between the Soviets and the pan-African movement. No one knows to what extent Spingarn made reports to Washington, but he clearly watched Du Bois for years. Du Bois loved Spingarn and would have been very hurt to find this out.

In 1934 Du Bois was more than sixty years old and became an Atlanta University professor again. During the next decade he published *Black Folks*

Then and Now (1939), *Dusk of Dawn* (1940), and *Color and Democracy: Colonies and Peace* (1945). He wrote several hundred more magazine and newspaper articles, and he taught in and chaired the Atlanta University Department of Sociology. He continued to be radical, outspoken, critical, and was still regarded by many as a national leader. In 1944 the Atlanta University Board of Directors fired him. He was astonished.

Du Bois and the Cold War

One of the great ironies of Du Bois's long career is that he went back to the NAACP after being fired from Atlanta University. He was invited back to head their new research unit. He saw this as a renewed opportunity to turn the NAACP into a force against colonialism. World War II made this hope possible. It was a war against racism, against fascism, against Hitlerism, and for democracy. These were all things that Du Bois and the NAACP supported. But this period of elevated consciousness and unity ended when the war ended, and by 1947 big business and government were trying to reestablish the prewar status quo. Du Bois found himself at odds again with the NAACP leadership. He was not the only one who found the postwar years repressive. I was an officer assigned to a black artillery battalion during the Second World War. By 1947 President Truman took away my commission because of my views and friendships with Negroes—which just confirmed for them that I was a subversive.

The major difference Du Bois had with the NAACP leadership was over their support of President Truman's Cold War against the Soviet bloc nations. The head of the NAACP, Walter White, believed that by supporting Truman there would be domestic civil rights concessions from the federal government. Du Bois asked what could the NAACP possibly gain from supporting Truman's policies, which were only a continuation of Western imperialism and colonialism? The tension between Du Bois and White over the position of the NAACP on U.S. foreign policy became evident when they served together with Mary McCloud Bethune on an advisory committee for the founding of the United Nations. Their committee represented black people in the United States. What did they encounter at the founding meeting in San Francisco? The United States, France, and Great Britain dominated the meeting. Nehru of India and the Soviet Union's V. M. Molotov tried to have an anticolonial policy instituted from the beginning. They failed due to opposition from the big three. Du Bois noted the United States' support of continued colonialism, and the contradiction between the UN's charter and the admission of fascist Argentina to the

United Nations. Du Bois tried, unsuccessfully, to convince the United States delegation to support the fight against colonialism. He then came out publicly in opposition to U.S. procolonial Cold War foreign policies. But Walter White and the NAACP board supported Truman's foreign policy. So in September 1948 Du Bois was again dismissed from the NAACP.

Du Bois did not give up nor did he go into retirement as he approached his eightieth birthday. By 1948 Du Bois joined Paul Robinson as cochair of the Council on African Affairs. This was a small but important postwar public policy effort and the only voice of Africa in America at that time. Du Bois did a lot of public speaking for the council. They eventually published *Decision in Africa* (1957) written by Dr. W. Alphaeus Hunton. Hunton, who had been fired from Howard University for being too radical, was modest to a fault and highly regarded by Du Bois. The council kept alive the postwar protest on Africa, especially the case of South Africa as apartheid was being institutionalized. The council worked to educate the public and to influence U.S. foreign policy until McCarthyism closed the council and forced it into bankruptcy. Some of the council members went to jail. Alphaeus Hunton got six months for refusing to turn over the files and records of the council to J. Edgar Hoover's FBI.

In 1950 Du Bois was still an influential national voice that helped shape progressive public opinion in the United States. He was a candidate for the U.S. Senate and got 250,000 votes against a fairly progressive Herbert Lehman. I recommended to him that he run for governor of New York instead—that was a race he might have won. Du Bois was also a leader in the United States in the fight against the continued development and deployment of the atomic bomb. He was chairman of the Peace Information Center, which was the U.S. arm for the distribution of the Stockholm Appeal. This was a worldwide effort to stop the development of the atomic bomb. In three paragraphs, the petition pleaded with the United States not to develop the bomb, urged the U.S. to ban its deployment, and charged that the first nation to use an atomic weapon was a criminal against humanity. Two million people signed the appeal in the United States. Millions more signed it in the world community. The response of the U.S. government to the Stockholm Appeal came through President Truman's Secretary of State, Dean Acheson. He accused Du Bois at the age of eighty-one of being an unregistered foreign agent. Du Bois was indicted, arrested, and fingerprinted. This was in 1951. Du Bois got cables of support from all over the world. Ghana's Nkrumah asked Truman if the United States had gone insane in arresting Dr. Du Bois. India's Nehru asked the same question of the president.

Before the trial, the government offered Du Bois a deal. If he would plead guilty to being an unregistered foreign agent, they guaranteed they would drop the charges. The government had no idea whom they had arrested. Du Bois wrote back saying that he had been offered many deals in his life but before he would lie to his government, he would rot in jail. He went on to say that some jail time might do him good. Du Bois believed that this was a matter of freedom of speech. He was a fanatical believer in the Bill of Rights from his early Massachusetts rearing. Fortunately, he had good attorneys. The judge had a lot of integrity—like an old-fashioned Republican. Du Bois was indicted under the McCormick Act, not the McCarran Act. The McCormick Act requires substantial proof of the charge. The McCarran Act does not have such a requirement—it is a bill of attainder. The government presented its case, which was no case at all. After a short time, the judge asked the prosecution if they had proof that Du Bois was a foreign agent—was there something in writing, a group of witnesses, or any other substantial evidence? They had to answer that they had none. All they had was an informant named O. John Rogge. The judge denounced the prosecution in open court, told them that they had wasted the time of the court and the taxpayers' money, and acquitted Du Bois. The case never went to a jury. This was one of the first victories against McCarthyism.

All during the late 1940s and 1950s efforts were made to hang the "Communist" label on Du Bois. Secretary of State Acheson continued to accuse Du Bois of being a dupe of the Communists, asserting that the Stockholm Appeal was a Communist plot. The NAACP leadership refused to assist in his defense at the trial because they believed he was guilty and because it would have jeopardized their relations with Truman's administration. The government, the NAACP, and many others did not understand that Du Bois advocated his own brand of socialism, independent of any ideology or sponsorship. Fundamentally, he was anticapitalist, antiracist, anti-imperialist, and anticolonialist. He believed that production for individual profit was a failure as a just way to organize society, that it was immoral, selfish, and wrong. What he believed he said and said often—this is all in his writings. The overwhelming subject of his newspaper and magazine articles, public speeches, and scholarship after 1948 was the international context of race and class. He had a dual devotion to peace and to the struggle to end Western economic oppression. People who are comfortable with Du Bois as merely a domestic race scholar and activist either do not know about his anticapitalism and internationalism or cannot deal with that side of Du Bois—they believe what the government said about him. These readers focus on his work before 1934 and ignore his more mature work. The late career of Du Bois is evident in *The World and Africa: An Inquiry into the Part Which Africa Has Played in World History* (1947) and *In Battle for Peace: The Story of My Eighty-Third Birthday* (1952).

How much of a threat was Du Bois's work, and how convincing was the government's effort to discredit him? One measure of both was that from 1948 until his death in 1963 the *New York Times* did not mention Du Bois's name, and then the mention was brief. The leading association of American historians through their review journal, the *American Historical Review,* has not to this day reviewed his great history book *Black Reconstruction.* He became unmentionable. All during his time as a pariah in this country, Du Bois continued to write books and to send manuscripts to publishers who had accepted his work in the past—Viking, Harper, and Harcourt Brace. Now he either got no answer or got rejection post cards. I was on the editorial board of *Masses and Mainstream,* which published his final books, including *In Battle for Peace.* He also wrote another historical novel, *The Black Flame* (1957–61), which I edited. This three-volume set sold ten thousand copies.

For many Americans it may come as a shock to learn that the forty years of a massive Cold War defense buildup, the development and deployment of nuclear weapons, and the isolation and separation of domestic from international affairs were totally unnecessary. The Soviet Union did not initially pose a military threat to the United States or to western Europe. Du Bois traveled to the Soviet Union several times to see for himself and saw no evidence that the Soviet Union was doing anything other than rebuilding itself after the war and defending itself against threats from the West. He asked what country would want to be a military threat to anyone after suffering 27 million dead and the destruction of all the European USSR during World War II? What were they going to do to the United States, which escaped World War II with no damage and became the leading economic and military force in the world? In 1947 when Truman began the Cold War, the Soviets were absolutely no match for the United States.

The Cold War was manufactured by the very industrial and military elites that President Eisenhower warned of in the 1950s. The Soviet threat and the spread of world Communism were all exaggerated, and this fact is now slowly coming to light. This point has been admitted in the *New York Times*—the CIA exaggerated the Soviet threat for years. And now Robert McNamara tells us in his *In Retrospect: The Tragedy and Lessons of Vietnam* (1995) that the war in Vietnam could not be won and was unnecessary. President Harry Truman deliberately began this hysteria. Du Bois knew it, called it what it was, and opposed it.

The Cold War was necessary in order to preserve pre–World War II economic and political control over former colonies that aspired to be free and looked to the Soviet Union rather than the United States for anticolonial leadership. The purpose of the Cold War was to prevent the real stirring of liberation movements throughout the world, in particular in Africa and Asia. These movements would have prevented the massive expansion of capitalism overseas into the former colonies that has very effectively choked the development of Third World domestic economies. The outcome of this expansion of capital, which begun shortly after World War II, has been neocolonialism, where Third World nations were granted political independence but continued to be economically dependent upon European mother countries. In more recent years with the collapse of Soviet socialist opposition, neocolonialism has been intensified. Third World nations are now nothing more than labor and resource reservations for the modern global economy. The very world economic system we are looking at today would not have been possible without the Cold War isolation of the socialist potential and the perversion of countless national liberation movements into pro- or anti-Western Cold War factions.

We now know that the socialism of most national liberation movements was secondary to their nationalism. Vietnam is one of many examples. The French and then the United States conducted the war in Indochina on the premise that all socialists were alike, were united, and posed a threat wherever they were. So peasants in Vietnam who only wanted their national independence presumably posed such a threat to the United States and France that there were serious plans to use atomic weapons to suppress the Vietnamese struggle against France.[8] The only reason the atomic bomb was not used was because the English opposed it. All this is in McNamara's book. This is why I went to North Vietnam in 1965 and Du Bois traveled to the Soviet Union and China in the 1950s—to get the facts to oppose this insanity.

Du Bois anticipated neocolonialism. He, Alphaeus Hunton, and the Council on African Affairs saw the strategy of neocolonialism developing. The emergence of neocolonialism was evident in the United States' support of France's efforts to maintain colonies in Africa. The whole point of the council was to educate the public and, unlike the early pan-African conferences, to raise money to support the liberation struggle in South Africa. It turned out that during this time in the 1950s Max Yergan, a member of the council and president of the National Negro Congress, was a paid agent for the government and kept them informed of our plans.

Was there a connection between the Cold War and Jim Crow's ability to continue in the South after the Second World War? Absolutely. The Cold War gave the federal government an excuse to abandon the New Deal programs after World War II, to ignore poverty at home, and to put off the political enfranchisement of blacks to some unspecified future date. The exploitation of black people is fundamental to the history of the United States back through the colonial period of enslavement and up through the period of de facto enslavement (sharecropping and Jim Crow). Exploitation is not an aberration on the part of the nation. It is fundamental to the organization and conduct of this country. Du Bois not only understood this but also articulated it better and more often than anyone else in this century. The brilliance of Martin Luther King Jr. was that he turned the Cold War's Jim Crow on its head. By unmasking and making evident the South's fascist practices for the entire world to see on television, King turned Cold War politics against Jim Crow practices and interests. The South became an embarrassment to the United States in the ideological struggle against socialism—how could the United States stand for freedom, democracy, and liberty in the world community when black people in the South were denied these basic rights?

Du Bois saw the connection between the intensification of urban racial ghettos and the Cold War. As Jim Crow was to the southern poor, the Cold War was an excuse for abandoning the urban poor, who reflected capitalism's abuses more directly than anyone else. The high point of the New Deal was the possibility of eliminating the scandalous poverty of white and black people in this country—the richest in the world. This is what the early socialists, the CIO, the National Negro Congress, and the later civil rights movements were about. Du Bois was aware of this and was also aware of what could have been done instead of spending billions upon billions of dollars on preparation for war and the development and deployment of atomic bombs. This is what the Stockholm Appeal, the Council on African Affairs, and the U.S. Communist Party were about—pointing this out and opposing such madness. To "ban the bomb" meant opposition to Washington's foreign policy with its inevitable effects on neocolonialism, world poverty, and domestic ghettoization. If Du Bois were here today, he would not speak of one of these realities without showing the connections, influence, and importance of the others.

The drug trafficking and self-destruction that we are witnessing today in poor black communities is not a new development, nor is it unconnected to economic exploitation overseas. Those today who see black drug trafficking and abuse as simply a domestic race problem or as simply black people's moral or cultural problem would not be pleased to read Du Bois's comments on ghettoization in the 1930s and 1940s. As far back as 1924 Du Bois focused on the forces that created ghettos rather than the self-destructive behaviors that followed in the ghettos. Nothing like drug trafficking, that is both national and international in scope, simply happens independent of powerful self-interests—ruling-class actions. When I was in North Vietnam, I was told that one of the ways the French tried to prevent the Vietnamese liberation movement from developing was by pumping drugs into Vietnamese communities and encouraging gangersterism—just like what we have in the United States today. The French deliberately tried to corrupt the Vietnamese youth. Those in power in the United States today welcome the present chaos among blacks. The power interests and their families are not being impoverished, raped, drugged, and murdered on the streets. While this goes on, there are no significant challenges from blacks. Any sober people with unbought leaders and a history such as black Americans have would immediately challenge ruling-class control, which is necessary to prevent corrective actions from being taken.

Dr. Du Bois knew that the Cold War, ghettos, poverty, capitalism and profits, black disenfranchisement, racism, and the bomb were all unnecessary. These horrors are not in any of our interests to produce or defend, and if left to our own choices, we would not have created them. These monstrous developments all exist so that the few can control and benefit from the many. One does not have to be a Communist or even a socialist to know this and to oppose such interests. Du Bois more than anyone else in this century had the potential to get this across to black and white people alike. This is why he was hated, why those in power tried to send him to jail, and why he was ostracized in his own land. Martin Luther King was quickly moving to the same place that Du Bois had been for years, namely, that all the demons are interconnected—the real exercise of power in the United States, domestic and international racism, capitalism, the war in Vietnam, and neocolonialism. King was assassinated because of his potential, like Du Bois, to challenge powerful interests and the institutions that mask them.

The Final Years

While traveling in the People's Republic of China in the 1950s, Du Bois and his second wife, Shirley Graham Du Bois, were received by Chairman Mao. Dr. Du Bois was traveling as a leader of the international world peace movement. After this trip, the U.S. government forbade him to travel outside the United States. The rumors and campaign against him, the government effort to discredit him, and the growing belief among domestic civil rights leaders that there was no connection between domestic and foreign issues, isolated Du Bois from the influence he had exercised for decades. The U.S. government also took Paul Robeson's, Shirley Graham Du Bois's, and my passport as well. Not long after the travel restriction was imposed, Du Bois joined the Communist Party as a protest. He wrote a long letter explaining why he joined and what he expected—the letter is in the Du Bois correspondence. He knew that those who wanted to use the Cold War as a key to advancing domestic poverty and racism could not ignore his action. He wanted this gesture to be one of defiance.

In the fall of 1961 Du Bois and Shirley Graham left for Ghana. I drove them to the airport. In June of that year the Supreme Court upheld the McCarran Act, which permanently banned him from travel. Du Bois was already in the process of preparing to go to Ghana to edit *The Encyclopedia Africana* at Nkrumah's invitation. There was a ninety-day period between the time the Supreme Court upheld the McCarran Act and when the travel ban came into effect. Fay and I attended an emergency meeting at the Du Bois home to support whatever they decided to do. Shirley Graham and Dr. Du Bois decided to pack up and leave within ninety days. A note was sent to Ghana to see if they could come early. The response from Nkrumah was that Ghana and Africa would be honored whenever they came. Travel money was raised. The airline tickets were purchased. Several thousand of his books were bought by Fisk University. Dr. Du Bois asked me to take the files of his correspondence, since I had already agreed to edit his work. In the files were one hundred thousand documents, unsorted. Fay and I spent more than a decade just sorting and organizing these materials.

At the time of Du Bois's departure he was ninety-two years old. At the airport Du Bois told Jim McManus of the *Guardian,* who came to cover his departure, that *The Encyclopedia Africana* was to be ten volumes and that it would take him about a decade to do each volume. Of course, he said this in jest. Earlier that week, while Fay was delivering the airline tickets, she and Dr. Du Bois sat in the garden of his home in Brooklyn. Du Bois told Fay that he would be so happy if he could just stay in the United States. He knew then that his health would not permit his return.

It is false to assume that Dr. Du Bois went to Africa because he gave up the struggle to end racism, to end the insanity of capitalism and the Cold War. His plans to write *The Encyclopedia Africana* dated back to 1909, and finally he had an invitation from Ghana's president, Kwame Nkrumah, to come to Africa to begin this great work. Du Bois had to go to Africa to start *The Encyclopedia Africana* because he simply could not get the project funded in the United States. He had had stationery for the project for decades. Franz Boas was to be part of it. The closest he got to getting this project funded was in the 1930s when the Phelps-Stokes Fund provided money for an *Encyclopedia of the Negro* (1945), edited by W. E. B. Du Bois and Guy B. Johnson. This book was just an outline of what an encyclopedia devoted to blacks should have been. *The Encyclopedia Africana*, devoted to the whole of African peoples' past and present, was the project Du Bois was most eminently qualified to do, but it had eluded him for his entire career. An offer to finally begin this project simply could not be refused.

If Du Bois's health had not failed him, he would have come back to continue the struggle and fight the travel restriction. But he was not well when he left. After a long illness and period of hospitalization in England and Ghana, Dr. Du Bois wrote *An ABC of Color: Selections Chosen by the Author from over a Half Century of His Writings* (1963), twice. The first manuscript was lost in the mail between Ghana and the United States—we suspect the hand of the government in this. So he wrote the book again and lived to see it published. He also finished *The Autobiography of W. E. B. Du Bois* (1968). This manuscript was also lost for several years and surfaced after Dr. Du Bois had passed away.

Dr. Du Bois died in Ghana on August 27, 1963, on the eve of the March on Washington. He was ninety-five years old. His funeral was an enormous state event. All the major governments were represented, except the United States. Nkrumah and the world were in tears at the loss of the great doctor.

Postscript

There are some frequent questions about Dr. Du Bois's life and career that are not answered directly in this short review and reflection. Some of those questions are answered below.

- Does the loss of travel rights still stand? I sued the U.S. government for denying me a passport. This challenge went all the way to the U.S. Supreme Court in *Aptheker vs. Rusk*. I was to go to jail for ten years if I got a passport under the McCarran Act. But the Supreme Court ruled 6 to 4 in 1963 that Secretary of State Rusk was wrong in denying my right to travel and declared that part of the McCarran Act unconstitutional. Now anyone should be able to get a passport, even to Cuba.
- What did liberation mean to Dr. Du Bois? His concept of liberation changed as his life changed. There were three phases. During his early years, it was opposition to Jim Crow, to the lynchings, and to the compromises of Booker T. Washington. In the second phase, it became

more global as he become more socialist in his thinking, and he saw liberation as freedom from domestic and foreign political and economic colonialism. Then finally, after World War II, he was clearly a socialist and saw that liberation was dependent upon letting the world liberation movements run their course. To do so, he had to challenge the Cold War and educate as many people as possible about the Cold War's real underlying motives and goals. Within this sense of liberation came his desire to see African peoples united and able to determine their own destiny. It was very appropriate for the father of pan-Africanism to challenge capitalism, imperialism, and their modern sheep's clothing, the Cold War.

- What was Du Bois's socialism? Du Bois was much too independent, creative, and knowledgeable to be a follower of anyone else's socialism. He had his own. He was a member of the Socialist Party for only one year; he left because he could not change the party's racism. Du Bois's socialism was very conscious of the race issue. Many of the white socialists were racists. There were many in the dominant faction of the original Socialist Party who were notoriously racist. But their vision of some kind of civilization where you did not exist to exploit someone else or just to make money was correct. This is the only conclusion any clear-thinking and moral person can come to—how can one believe and then support a system of profit for the few at the expense of the many? It was this thinking that led Du Bois to socialism by 1910. This is why he did not stay with the NAACP in 1934 once it accommodated itself to the system and when there was a real opportunity to institutionalize socialist reforms in the United States. A person who might have influenced Du Bois's socialism and many others in this thinking was Mary White Ovington. She was significant in what we then called "the Negro question," as well as socialism. Ovington was from a very wealthy family that disowned her because of her views, work, and Negro friends. She lived alone for many years in the hotel St. George in Brooklyn. She was a remarkable woman for whom Du Bois had the highest regard.
- What is your response to Harold Cruse's portrayal of W. E. B. Du Bois in *The Crisis of the Negro Intellectual* (1967)? When it was fashionable for black intellectuals to be members of the Communist Party in the late 1930s, Du Bois was not. He had already arrived at his views on the Party. He wrote about this in *Dusk of Dawn* (1939). He states that the Scottsboro Boys could have been saved without the great international campaign the Party mounted. This was not an attack on the

Party. Du Bois in fact admired the Party's work, but he believed that much of what it did was not practical and would not be implemented. Fay Aptheker believes that Du Bois then still had some faith in the United States and the New Deal. He was also an official of the NAACP, while most other black intellectuals were not. Du Bois's position in the late 1930s was closer to the moderate socialism of Norman Thomas, whom Du Bois knew.

With regard to Harold Cruse, I have a great deal of difficulty with his work. It is very inaccurate. He has some other agenda than letting the facts speak for themselves. I was once the invited guest of the Association for the Study of Negro Life and History in Washington and spoke at their breakfast meeting. Charles Wesley, former president of Wilberforce College, was then president of the association. He presided over this meeting. When I began to speak, Harold Cruse stood up and began to berate me and to criticize the association for inviting "this Jew." The audience began to murmur against him; finally he was led out of the meeting still yelling and waving his arms. Whatever was bothering him then is certainly reflected in his work.

- How was Du Bois able to be such a prolific writer? There are several reasons. First, he believed intensely in seeing an antiracist civilization in the United States in his lifetime and the liberation of his people. He had strong hope for the society we could have become, not what we are today. His hope was for all people to have enough food, shelter, opportunity, and other basics to be decent and not be compelled to turn on one another as we are now witnessing. Once Arthur Spingarn asked Dr. Du Bois, "Why don't you go live in Paris?" Du Bois responded that "you don't understand me . . . you don't know why I work." Second, he was a disciplinarian. When it was time for class, the door was closed and locked. He also had tremendous self-control. I have seen Shirley Graham Du Bois lose her temper, but never Dr. Du Bois. Third, he had precise work habits and did his own research. Fourth, whenever he traveled, he would combine it with research, and whatever he was doing, he always set aside time to write. Finally, he always had an excellent secretary. His longtime secretary, Irene Diggs, eventually got her Ph.D. in Havana with Du Bois's help and became a university professor. It is ironic that the racists had his books in the library, but he along with all other blacks was banned from going into the same libraries. Later in his life he dictated his works to his next secretary, Elizabeth Lawson, who transcribed from his dictation.

- How did you come to edit the Du Bois papers? Dr. Du Bois asked me in 1946 to edit his papers and his work, and Shirley Graham Du Bois supported his request after he died. I was honored that he asked me. I have devoted most of my career to his contributions. There was a book published by the Howard University Press some years ago that claimed I was paid some enormous sum of money to edit the Du Bois papers. This is absolutely false. The fact of the matter is that the University of Massachusetts gave $100,000 to Shirley Graham Du Bois for the Du Bois papers at my urging. I was present when they signed the contract. Fay and I never owned the papers. For years we were trustees of the papers, which we kept in the basement of our Brooklyn home. I urged Shirley Graham to get the papers out of our house, especially after our basement flooded. The University of Massachusetts bought the papers from her, not from me. I never got a penny for them. Fay and I considered those papers to be sacred. We never got paid, never asked for nor expected money for our trusteeship.
- What were Dr. Du Bois's work habits and how did he deal with his emotions? Du Bois was a driven man all the time I knew him, and I got no sense that he had ever not been so. Though he was driven, he had a set routine. He went to bed at 10:00 P.M. sharp. If he was a speaker at an event and they did not call on him by 10:00, he would leave. He was a moderate eater. He smoked three cigarettes a day, one after each meal—no more and no less. He watched what he ate. He always had breakfast and had some fruit at most for lunch. Du Bois was also very much aware of what his purpose was in life, and it was important that he take good care of himself. He was afraid of what would happen if he were not here. He owned a pistol all his life, took good care of it, and had a permit for it. Fortunately, he never had to use it. Though he stayed calm, he was not a mild man; he was capable of anger but did not display it. He was able to write and speak to get out his frustrations. Also he was able to organize and see results.

Mrs. Aptheker pointed out that the only time she saw him excited and really enthusiastic was in Moscow after he had just returned from China in the late 1950s. Remember that Du Bois was a loner, a genius, and though he was a well-trained scholar and social scientist, he was at heart a poet. He was exacting in all he did. We found among his papers little scraps written by Du Bois on how one is to conduct oneself in life and in different situations. They were written as little poems and are now in a book published by the University of Massachusetts Press.

The poems were written for his students. Some are a line or two, and others are whole pages, dated around 1910. The book has been a best-seller and does well during Christmas.

- How did he live to be ninety-five years old? Like everything else in his life, this was calculated. He was very conscious of longevity, and in fact, was a lifelong member of a longevity institute. He went to their retreat every year, got advice from them, and he took vacations regularly. He began this routine in the 1920s after he had a kidney removed. Finally, he explained to us that the director of the institute told him that they had nothing else to teach him—by this time Du Bois was about ninety years old. He managed to live to ninety-five years of age and on one kidney for forty-six years.
- Did Du Bois see any errors in his views? He came to believe that the gradual use of the courts as a way to make social change—the NAACP's approach—could not address the broad structural abuses of capitalism, imperialism, and racism. Du Bois believed that he had overrated the moral character and integrity of those who rose up from the masses to lead and to serve. He felt that he underrated the power of bribery in its many forms, both direct and subtle, to buy off the "talented tenth." He realized that talent removed from the masses could be easily corrupted. This is why real social change over the long run must have mass involvement. A country as rich as ours can afford to buy off most potential troublemakers. He also gave up on trying to change the imperialist powers. Each successive pan-African congress was more radical and critical than the last. For most of his life, Du Bois had enormous faith in the power of reason. He believed that the truth was so manifest that it had to prevail and that the problems of this country could be overcome with reason. He came to see that this was not true. Those in control have tremendous holding power, no morals, would not hesitate to corrupt anyone if it serves their best interest, and are not moved by reason.

The point at which Du Bois realized the depth and depravity of those who rule was when the U.S. government put Ethel and Julius Rosenberg to death as spies for allegedly giving secrets of the atomic bomb to the Soviets. The government knew damned well that Ethel was innocent and that they had been framed. There was not one Jew on the jury of a trial held in New York City. Only the judge and prosecutors were Jews, and after the guilty verdict, the judge and prosecutors were all rewarded with promotions. This was a monstrous act, and it was at this point that Du Bois realized that those in control who benefited from the Cold War would do anything to get their way. Shortly afterward, Du Bois joined the Communist Party in protest. The Rosenbergs' execution had a devastating effect on many people. Many left the Party shortly afterward, not out of fear, but because they had lost hope. They became convinced that there was no use; the system and those in control could not be changed.

- What is the strategic value of the socialist extremes? It is necessary to take a radical and far-out stand in order to allow more moderate views to take a more progressive stance than they normally would. We on the Left did this consciously and as a service to social change. For example, social security would have never happened without our extreme view. When U.S. Representative Ernest Lundeen originally called for social security in 1935, his call was dismissed outright. Lundeen was on the far left. The Party knew that such a radical measure would not be accepted. We served as the front line in advocating social security and, in doing so, created the conditions for a more moderate bill to pass. But without our more extreme view, the moderate proposal would have been seen as too radical. This is how liberals can be a restraining and moderating influence. This was the game. We knew it. We knew that those in power were not going to give us everything. But we created the conditions where they had to give up something to benefit the masses. This is the same in labor strikes; you ask for the maximum in order to get some improvements.

What many Americans do not realize is that whatever benefits they enjoy, such as social security, health care, unemployment insurance, workplace health laws, minimum wage, and universal education, were gotten through struggle. And if they plan to keep them or improve on them, *they* will have to struggle. All the positive developments in this country were gained by mass radical struggle. Now that there is no Soviet threat and the Left is no longer effective, look at what is happening. Those in power no longer have a reason to maintain the social gains of the past. For these reasons, what we are facing today is without strong opposition with an alternative ideological base. The time is right for opposition to emerge. There is going to have to be a new national struggle, and black Americans will be in the forefront of it. It is a simple fact. Blacks have suffered more than any other group, except Native Americans, and are being put into a position where they have no choice. Blacks are also closer than any other

> group to knowing how the system works and what should be done about it. Part of having this advanced realization and knowledge lies in the life and writing of W. E. B. Du Bois.

I close by stressing W. E. B. Du Bois's courage, his absolute and unquestionable integrity, his profound honesty, and his personal devotion to justice. Du Bois personified virtue.

NOTES

1. Marable, 7.
2. Ibid., 11.
3. Ibid., 14.
4. Ibid., 46.
5. Ibid., 70.
6. Ibid., 100–101.
7. Ibid., 97.
8. McNamara.

REFERENCES

Marable, Manning. *W. E. B. Du Bois: Black Radical Democrat.* Boston: Twayne Publishers, 1986.

McNamara, Robert, with Brian VanDeMark. *In Retrospect: The Tragedy and Lessons of Vietnam.* New York: Times Books, 1995.

10

Vindication in Speaking Truth to Power

Herbert Aptheker

I was born in Brooklyn, New York, in 1915 and was the youngest of five children. At the time of my birth, my family was quite wealthy. I had health problems, so very early in my infancy my mother hired a woman to take care of me and to work in the house. She was a black woman from Trinidad named Angelina Corbin. She lived with us, and her bedroom was adjacent to mine. She took care of me—bathed me, dressed me, and fed me—until I started school. She was employed with us for many years. When my father lost most of his money and we could no longer afford to employ her, she remained a friend of the family. We all loved her. My mother, in particular, loved her as a friend. She was of great significance in my life. Where we lived, there were no black people, only some Italians who did truck farming.

My experience growing up with Angelina, with her permission we called her "Annie," made a lasting impression on me. I took a business trip with my father to Alexander City, Alabama, in about 1930 when I was around fourteen years old. We went by car, and in those days there were no thruways; so if you made two hundred miles a day, you did well. When we got to Washington, D.C., I saw Jim Crow racial segregation for the first time and was astonished. As we continued deeper into the South, the racism became more blatant. This was during the depression, which was terrible for white people but devastating to black people. There was one incident that has remained fastened in my mind. In Georgia, we stopped and I got out of the car. A short distance away, there was a doorless shack. Standing there was a big black woman, who reminded me of Annie. There was a boy in the field about my age. We saw one another. He was in tatters and very thin. I moved toward him. He stayed still and she watched. I had a bag in which there were cookies that mother had baked and given to us.

As I approached him, I took out a cookie and handed it to him, thinking that he would take it. But he did not. He came forward and took a bite from the cookie and left the rest of it in my hand. I was embarrassed and did not know what to do. We faced each other for a few seconds. I do not remember his saying anything. Then I returned to the car and papa. That encounter made an indelible impression on me.

After we drove home, I began to look into this question of black people like Annie, Jim Crow, and the terrible impoverishment and suffering. I had a column in the Erasmus High School newspaper and used my interest in journalism to investigate these issues. I discovered to my amazement that all this was known; it was in all the government documents and papers. So I devoted my column to what I called "the dark side of the South." Week after week, I wrote about it. I do not know if any one read it. But that was the beginning of my discovery of racism and the suffering of black people.

One day while coming home from high school, I saw a crowd. There was a wagon with a man on it, talking with a funnel speaker. Beside his wagon was a cage like in the zoo. In the cage was a man. A pamphlet next to him explained that there was a young man, named Angelo Herndon, in prison in Georgia. (See Charles Martin, *The Angelo Herndon Case and Southern Justice* [1976].) He was about to be executed because he helped organize black and white people, and had demanded either food or jobs. He was convicted in the 1930s under the slave insurrection rule of 1860. The man with the wagon and cage was part of a movement to defend Angelo. I wrote about this case in the school newspaper and later came to know Herndon. He was from the North and went down South to change things. They had knocked out his teeth when they arrested him.

Becoming an Activist Historian

I graduated from high school in three years and wanted to go to Columbia University. At that time, Columbia College, uptown, did not accept Jews. But Columbia University had a ghetto college in Brooklyn that was called Seth Low Junior College. Seth Low had been a president of Columbia College and a mayor of Brooklyn before it became a part of New York City. There, we were all Jews or Italians, and one Syrian, who was killed early in World War II. The instructors and books were the same as the ones from uptown. If you successfully completed two years, you were permitted to go uptown to be part of the university, but not Columbia College. I was very active with the school newspapers and covered the news when thousands demonstrated against the Italian invasion of Ethiopia and the Spanish Civil

War in the 1930s. Uptown at Columbia, I became interested in sciences such as chemistry and geology. My interest in geology was partly fostered by the geology professor's daughter; she attended all the classes, and I was attracted to her. I ended up getting a bachelor of science degree in three years, not the usual four. Though my father was no longer a millionaire, we were still quite well off. I stayed on at Columbia for an advance degree.

At Columbia, there was one black student, Lorenzo Greene, who was studying for his doctorate. He was much older than I and was my closest friend. He got his Ph.D. the year before I did. His book *The Negro in Colonial New England* was published in 1942, and my *American Negro Slave Revolts* was published in 1943. By this time I had decided that I wanted to study and write what we then called "Negro history." Therefore, I was attracted to Carter G. Woodson and his Association for the Study of Negro Life and History, which I joined as a graduate student. Once when I went down to Washington to use the Library of Congress, Dr. Woodson met me at the train. He was about fifty, very tall and distinguished. I remember on this first visit we had lunch at the counter in Union Station because we could not eat anywhere else. He asked what I was working on and ended up inviting me to visit with him again. The next time I met him, he took me to a restaurant in the ghetto. It was down some stairs and through a dark corridor; I felt some apprehension. He must have sensed that and said to me, "Herbert, you may eat with us; we are civilized." That was the beginning of a very close relationship and frequent correspondence I had with him.

Another decisive influence on me was my friendship with Louis Burnham who did not live far from us. He was very active in the Left. I was already moving toward the left in my thinking and began teaching at the workers' school in New York; this is probably where I met him. Around 1937 he asked if I would like to join him on an organizing trip through the South. This was right after my little booklet came out, "The Negro in the Civil War." We took hundreds of copies, put them in the rumble seat, and went off into the South. In Memphis I was invited to speak at the all-black LeMoyne Junior College. In the auditorium we put out copies of the booklet and the students swarmed onto them. Then I spoke. Louis arranged everything. I believe he was a genius for being able to organize such activities right there in Boss Crump's town. This booklet was very important because it challenged the idea that black people were dormant in the Civil War. It also challenged the dominant view in American history that blacks were passive. The fact is that black people immediately began to demand the right to fight against the Confederacy. At the same time, there was a massive flight of tens of thousands of slaves from the South. The pamphlet documents the active participation of black people in the effort to crush the Confederacy and to emancipate themselves. Lincoln stated in writing, twice, that the contributions of black people were decisive in the victory of the Union against the Confederacy. About 180,000 black men enlisted in all-black units. I also showed that the so-called all-white units had blacks in them. There were about 20,000 blacks who fought in the navy, and about 250,000 worked for the Union forces as nurses, carpenters, drivers, and so forth. This half million were decisive in the outcome. International Publishers published the booklet and distributed it for ten cents. Tens of thousands read it.

The next thing I finished was "Negro Slave Revolts in the United States, 1526 to 1860," based on my dissertation research. After I submitted it to *Science and Society,* a new quarterly journal, the editor said the board wanted to publish it but it was too long and should be cut. I wrote back that I would not. So they arranged a meeting with three or four of the editors. I told them that this work was breakthrough research and should not be abridged. They agreed and published it in two parts. The article showed that Nat Turner was not an exception. His was just one of a whole series of slave revolts. In fact, black people as slaves had not been quiescent, as the dominant historiography had insisted. They actively sought in every way to get their freedom, and this included sabotage, poisoning their masters, and killing black infant girls to keep them from being humiliated and from having slavery perpetuated. Though incomplete, it was a pioneering study that Du Bois called "a good beginning." Copies sold for fifteen cents.

In 1939 I completed "Maroons within the Present Limits of the United States" and got the nerve to submit it to Woodson's *Journal of Negro History.* Maroons were fugitive slaves who escaped from the plantations, formed communities in outlying areas, and attracted others to those communities. The dictionary defines "Maroons" as fugitive black slaves in Jamaica and the West Indies. They were not just in Jamaica and the West Indies; they were in Virginia and North Carolina and so on. This too was a breakthrough study. To my surprise, I got a fifty-dollar prize from Woodson's association. Woodson told me that I had to go and pick up the prize. The annual association meeting was somewhere in the Midwest at a black church and was attended by two hundred to three hundred people; I remember the travel costs were more than the prize money. The prize was very important to me. It affirmed the continued development of my theme that it was a vicious fallacy that black people in the United States embraced slavery and were docile as suggested in the work of U. B. Phillips, at the time the outstanding historian on this matter. The same year I also finished "The Negro in the American Revolution," in which I showed the active participation of blacks during the war. By the way, Du Bois's great-grandfather was a soldier in the Revolutionary War. Thousands of blacks fled to the British in Nova Scotia; still others fought for the Revolution.

My friendship and activism with Louis Burnham helped shape my early scholarly interests. By traveling with him in the South, I could see more deeply its reality and the need of accurate but liberating history. We worked to organize sharecroppers and tenant farmers, especially in Virginia. At the time, I did not know that he was in the Communist Party. He never mentioned it to me. He never tried to recruit me. He could have, if he had tried. I saw him at our home the day before he died. I have a vivid memory of him as he stood at the door and said, "I will see you soon."

Another early experience that shaped my career was my work against peonage. (For an overview, see Pete Daniel, *The Shadow of Slavery: Peonage in the South, 1901–1969* [1990].) At the same time that I was active with Louis Burnham, William Henry Huff, a black man from Chicago, visited me in 1938. He told me about peonage in Oglethorpe County, Georgia, where he had come from. There, people were held in slavery and something had to be done. Peonage is a form of debt slavery where the workers (sharecroppers or tenants) lived on what the landowner gave them. They were supposed to produce the crops he wanted, and of course, the landlord kept the books. The tenants were always in debt. This indebtedness bound them to the land, to the landlord, and to their condition. It was a form of slavery that was very common in the United States before World War II. There were close to 4 million peons, most of whom were black.

I knew William Patterson very well; he was called Mr. Civil Rights up in Harlem. I took Huff to see Patterson, and he did what I knew he would do. He said, "We need an organization. Let's call it the Abolish Peonage Committee. Herbert, you are the secretary, and Huff is the chairman." Then Patterson said, "I know Marcantonio in Congress. He will be the honorary president. We will start raising hell about this goddamn peonage." That was the beginning of the 1930s campaign against peonage. We began meeting in homes and demonstrated.

We got to a point that someone had to go down there to get some of those people out so they could speak about the conditions. I went back down South in 1937 as a traveling salesman. The people there had been informed that someone was coming who could be trusted. I stayed in a different house every night. I met people at night on the second floor of a whorehouse, above all sorts of drinking and carrying on. Black sharecroppers would meet with me by appointment. I would give them bus tickets to get out of town. We had white allies in New Orleans who ran a bookstore. Sharecroppers took the bus to New Orleans. They were to sit in the back, be quiet, and cause no trouble. I told them, "When you get to New Orleans, these people will meet you and you can trust them with your lives." They did, and then they got tickets to Nashville where there were other white allies, and from there, they went on to Chicago. I used the name Beale. We got close to twenty or thirty people out. Then one day on such a mission, I was shaving in a small washhouse. A black man working there said to me, "Go home." I said, "What did you say?" He looked up and said louder, "Go home now." I left immediately. That man saved my life. I hope to God he was not discovered. What ended peonage was the invention of the mechanical cotton picker by the Rust brothers and World War II, when they started drafting people. I am still proud that we had a part in that mass campaign.

Controversial Publications

After the peonage campaign and my work with Louis Burnham, I continued to be active with Angelo Herndon, whom I had first learned about in my youth, and Richard Moore, who owned a bookstore in Harlem. We formed what was called the Negro Publication Society of America. One of the first things we published was Frederick Douglass's *Autobiography* about 1940. Then we published Kate E. R. Pickett's novel *The Kidnapped and the Ransomed* [1941], an account of the enslavement and liberation of a black person from Alabama. Then we published Frederick Douglass's speech at the opening of the statue to Abraham Lincoln in Washington, D.C., not to be confused with the Lincoln Memorial. This statue was funded completely by black people. Our publication society published their pamphlet.

Around 1936 I did research at the Brooklyn branch of the New York Public Library. My older cousin Fay lived across the street. I was very attracted to her and visited occasionally, once with the excuse that I needed paper. That began the most important relationship in my life. We were very close, and for a long time our families did not know about our relation. We got married just after the war. Interestingly, Fay was a member of the Communist Party before I was. She was a labor organizer. But she was not instrumental in my joining the Party.

Grace Hutchins was an early organizer of the movement and an assistant in the Labor Research Association. I knew her when I was about twenty; she was very helpful to me in my research. Also Elizabeth Lawson, who wrote *Twenty Years on the Chain Gang? Angelo Herndon Must Go Free* (1935), was important to me and to the Left. She is neglected in the history of the Left. Elizabeth was a tall, white woman who had organized in the South. She had been imprisoned and put in solitary confinement for a long period with only the Bible to read. She was a pioneer in what was then called "Negro history." She produced a sort of mimeographed textbook used by the Left on black history. For some time, she was a secretary for Du Bois. The Party was her life; she never married and she had no children. She lived a spartan life in a cold-water flat in New York. When the abuses in Russia under Stalin became public, she killed herself. She was a model Communist and very effective.

I joined the Communist Party as an intellectual decision after the peonage struggle. After having lunch with V. J. Jerome, who was the editor of the Party organ, *Political Affairs,* which was then called the *Communist,* I walked with him to Party headquarters. I asked him how one joined the Party. He looked at me and said, "You are not in the Party?" I said no and asked again how one joined. He asked if I had fifty cents. I reached into my pocket and gave him fifty cents. He said, "Well, now you are in the Party." That is how I officially became a member in 1939.

Virtually all the writing I had done to date went against the grain of dominant historical writing at the time about blacks. At the center of that historiography was U. B. Phillips. What do you think the "U" stood for in Phillips's name? It was for Ulrich, but that was not his name given at birth. His real name was Ulysses. He was raised in Georgia. When he found out that the man who defeated Robert E. Lee was also named Ulysses, he insisted that his name be changed. This tells you something of the man's bias in his writing. His book *American Negro Slavery* (1918) was the standard text that we all used at the time. It is a chauvinistic work, filled with ideas of the docility and passivity of the Negro in the United States, unlike the Negro in Jamaica and Haiti. This was nonsense but was very influential and very important in the United States at the time. Correcting his errors would be something I would devote myself to. I began with the only slave rebellion that was known at the time in the United States, the Nat Turner rebellion.

The standard works dismissed Nat Turner as a crazy person. So I decided to study this Nat Turner and the insurrection of 1831. I went to Washington, to Virginia, to the archives, and to the old newspapers, and then I wrote my book-long master's thesis, "Nat Turner's Slave Rebellion." It was not published until the 1960s. One of my points was to show that Nat Turner's effort was simply the high point of the whole period of slave unrest beginning in the 1820s. Then it occurred to me that if this was true in the 1820 and 1830s, what about other periods? What about the entire history of slavery in the United States? U. B. Phillips falsified the whole subject. Nat Turner was not an exception; he was an example. I demonstrated that, and it became my Ph.D. dissertation—"American Negro Slave Revolts." My wife, Fay, typed it in five copies when we were in Louisiana; it was a very difficult job with footnotes. It was submitted in 1942, accepted, and published by Columbia University Press in 1943. I do not know if Columbia University Press knew what it had. I called it "American Negro Slave Revolts" because Phillips's classic work was called "American Negro Slavery." I do not think most people noticed, but my title was deliberate.

While I was in the army, a distinguished southern historian in North Carolina, Joulhec de (J. D.) Hamilton, reviewed my dissertation in the *American Historical Review*. In his review he said that this was a conscientious work that was thoroughly wrong. I got word of this review late, was incensed, and wrote to the editor in reply. The editor sent me a very nice letter informing me that he had received another communication similar to mine with details refuting Professor Hamilton. A young professor at Vassar named Kenneth W. Porter wrote the refutation. The editor suggested that it would be better if they published Porter's response. I agreed, and it was a good critique. Porter became a professor at Oregon where I lectured in the 1970s. Before his untimely death, he did very important work on Negro-Indian relations. Columbia University Press published a second edition of my dissertation in 1944 and a third edition in 1945. Then came the Cold War. Columbia University Press pulled the book, because by then I was notorious. So around 1950, I went to a Party publisher, International Publishers, and persuaded the editor to purchase the rights to my book. He did so, and the book has never been out of print. It is now in its fiftieth anniversary edition with corrections and additions. I think that I am correct in saying that it is now standard and that Phillips's work is in the trash can where it belongs.

World War II

I learned that the Japanese had bombed Pearl Harbor as I was going home after a lecture; there was great excitement at the train station. I was teaching then at the Jefferson School. I canceled my lecture engagements and told them at the school that I was going to enlist. There was a problem with my mother because I knew she would be opposed. I explained to her that this was what I had to do. It was a question of Hitler and what he was doing to our people. By that time I had my master's degree, was in the Woodson Association, had my experience against peonage, and was with Fay. I took a handbag to Whitehall Street, took the induction test, and did very well. The sergeant said to me that they needed people in field artillery. I told him that I did not know one gun from another. It did not matter. I was put in field artillery and went into basic training at Fort Dix, New Jersey. After basic training, they sent me to North Carolina to learn artillery. It was very difficult for me because I was overweight. All I had done for years was sit and write. For a while I thought I would not make it. But I did, and I am proud of that. I got down to 150 pounds. I finished artillery basic training and was promoted to corporal.

One day an officer came up to me and said, "Aptheker, you are going to Officers Candidate School (OCS)." Off I went. What was interesting about OCS then is that it was integrated. There were a few young black men who were also becoming officers. We were completely integrated. There were some whites from the South who could not take it; they were told to go home. There were five officer candidates to a tent. After I became an officer, they asked if I had a particular desire for placement. I told them that I wanted black troops. So they assigned me to black troops in Louisiana. I later learned that they were very happy to do this, because they knew who I was. The black troops in Louisiana had mutinied a few weeks earlier, had torn up the town of Alexandria, and had been suppressed with great brutality. Many were killed. I am sure that figured into why they were happy to send down the maniac Aptheker. So there I was. Now that I had a commission, Fay and I could be together as long as I was based in the United States. My black troops gradually discovered that I was a human being; I knew what was in their minds. So I did not rush it. Sergeant Stewart sensed this, and soon the men knew that they had this strange officer. I came to love them and would have gone into combat with them. Later, they did see action, but I was not with them.

We had a racist battalion commander named McEwen. Our breaking point came one day when two black officers were assigned to our outfit. Up to that time all the officers were white. They came to the dining room and waited to be seated. They knew there would be a problem. I was watching this. They were put in chairs as near the kitchen as possible. They got up and left. I said something about it to the commanding officer, who responded with something vile. So I got up and left as well. I refused to eat again with him. The next day, I went to one of the men at breakfast, Sergeant High. I asked High if he would mind if I ate with them. He said, "No sir. I would be honored." So the next day I came in and they had a separate table for me. Then I noticed that the tables in the mess hall were not arranged in the regulation way. They were arranged in two **V**s—**V** for victory at home and **V** for victory abroad. I said nothing. I sat at a separate table and finished breakfast. I called High and said two things: "First of all, I do not want to sit at an officer's table. If the men do not mind, I will eat with them." He said, "Yes, sir." Then I told him I was aware of how the tables were arranged. It was not regulation, and we did not have to look for trouble. So I asked him to fix the tables according to regulations. He said, "Yes, sir." I came in the next day and they were set up regulation style.

Before you go overseas, you have to pass the Army Ground Forces (AGF) test. Part of it is a twenty-five mile march with full pack to be completed as a unit in eight hours. Sergeant Stewart and I laid out the plan for the march. We would start out in the late afternoon after the hottest part of the day, and we would go through a town called Pollock, Louisiana. Pollock had a sign outside of it that said Nigger Stay Out. In most of these towns, a black person, especially a male, was required to leave town by dark. But this town would not allow blacks in at any time. Stewart and I decided we would march through that town fully armed, with a white officer at the head. The guys were in full combat gear. We had no ammunition, but no one in the town would know that. We started out and got to Pollock around eleven o'clock at night. The men knew what was going on. When we got there, we started singing *John Brown's Body.* "John Brown's body lies a-mold'ring in the grave. . . ." There were 150 of us singing at the top of our lungs and the lights came on. They must have thought the Civil War had started again. We completed the march as a unit. There was one little fellow, the cook, who could not make it. Two of our guys grabbed him by the elbows and kept his feet moving. So he made it. I do not know how many miles I marched going back and forth. When I returned home, Fay had prepared a lunch for me, but I fell asleep at the table.

In my next assignment I was assigned to a white artillery outfit. The commanding officer, Theodore Parker, named after a great abolitionist (he knew it), called me into the office and told me that I could not go overseas with the outfit because I had asthma. He made a deal with me. I would go with him on a march with a full pack. If I made it, he would change my record and I would go overseas. I did it. Then he wanted to send me back to school; that would have meant that I would be promoted to major. Fay and I were excited about that. But before I could go, the opportunity was killed by Parker's commanding officer, Buell Smith, who was a ferocious anti-Semite. He knew that I was Jewish and had an opportunity to be assigned to a general staff school for promotion. So he canceled the recommendation and had me transferred out to some outfit in Virginia. Embarrassingly, Parker explained to me what happened. From there I went to

Virginia and then on to Fort Bragg with the 940th Field Artillery Battalion getting ready to go overseas.

We finally left for overseas; we were part of a great convoy that took nine days to sail to France. It was a very difficult trip. Once we got there, we traveled inland in trucks. We were soon put into action in support of the First Airborne during the Battle of the Bulge that January. We were never directly in battle; but we were there in case they needed us. The Russians took Warsaw and the Germans were defeated. We continued on through France and Belgium as the First Airborne advanced. In Germany we got to the Rhine. Our guys took the third of Dusseldorf on the western side of the river. But across the Rhine two-thirds of the city was held by SS troops who never surrendered. We had to blow them out. This was in March. I remember that the Germans had a celebration when Roosevelt died. So we added to their celebration by having the corps artillery fire on them. They stopped.

I came back from the Second World War as an army captain and had command experiences that included running refugee camps for the slaves we had freed from the Nazis. There were many Polish women; there were tens of thousands of them. When I got back to the United States, there were attacks on me from racists in Congress from Mississippi, and the army came to my defense. Some major general gave a glowing account of my performance. Also after fighting against the greed and barbarism of the Nazis, I was greeted by a greedy landlord who wanted to immediately raise our rent; there were store owners who were shortchanging our purchases; and there were gas stations that hoarded gas. I had to remind myself what kind of society we lived in and that the war made no difference. In the midst of all this, I got a letter from Woodson. He wrote that he was happy that I was home and that I had survived; he also said the journal was open to me. That meant a lot to me. After a short assignment with the army at the Pentagon to write a history of the wartime Army Ground Forces in the United States, I was discharged in April 1946 with a promotion to the rank of major. I immediately got back to my research and writing and activism. The war had convinced me all the more that it was needed.

In 1945 my prewar historical articles were put together in a book, *Essays in the History of the American Negro,* published by International Press. When I returned, Gunnar Myrdal's *American Dilemma: The Negro Problem and Modern Democracy* (1944) was considered to be the definitive work that settled the Negro question. I found this book to be wanting. There were some historical inaccuracies, but the main problem was the analysis suggested in the title. The thesis was that the source of the oppression of black people was not attributable to any institutions or political practices. There was some mystical and unknown source. Furthermore, the condition of the Negro could not be changed other than by time; eventually whites would change. So I wrote a book-length critique of Myrdal in 1946, called *The Negro People in America: A Critique of Myrdal's "American Dilemma."* I said that the oppression of the Negro people was intentional, had political and economic motives, and could be changed. My critique had considerable influence. It was published and republished. I had the pleasure some twenty years later, when I was a delegate to an international conference, of meeting Myrdal, who told me that my critique was valid. In 1948 I published *To Be Free: Studies in American Negro History,* which was another set of prewar studies on black resistance to slavery. In the early 1950s I published another pamphlet, "America's Racist Wars." This was the first full treatment of the existence of racist wars not only in the South but in the North.

The Cold War

I had been associated early in my career with a famous publication entitled *New Masses* that was in financial trouble because of declining subscriptions. In 1946 an effort was made to continue its work in a quarterly, called *Mainstream.* It lasted about a year as mostly a literary magazine. A group of us decided that with sufficient effort we could produce a monthly magazine that could be sustained. In the beginning, there were four editors. Samuel Silleh, the chief editor, had been a professor of literature, before being fired because of his radicalism. Another editor was a young black fellow, Lloyd Brown, a labor organizer who had been imprisoned because of his radical activities. He had been a sergeant who suffered the indignities common to black soldiers in World War II. The other was Charles Humboldt who had originally published under his given name, Clarence Weinstock. He was a literary expert and had great sensitivity for poetry. However, he was difficult to get along with. The four of us put out this monthly magazine, *Masses and Mainstream.* We began with very limited funds. With fund-raising, we succeeded in publishing every month. Some of the great names in American art were attracted to our magazine, and we published their work. But when we came under attack during the McCarthy era, it became difficult to publish. It is interesting that some artists held firm with us, while others disassociated themselves from us. Some great artists like Joseph Solman, Helen West Heller, and Jacob Lawrence stayed with us, and we continued to publish their work.

I was the political and ideological affairs editor on the magazine and wrote a column entitled "Ideas in Our Times." In this column I came to grips with the leading ideas and people of the time, such as Walter Lippman and Arthur Schlesinger Jr. I had an impact. We had a circulation of fifteen to eighteen thousand every month. I was also out lecturing two to three times per month. I remember one particular lecture I did after I published a critique of Arthur Schlesinger. With great difficulty, students at Harvard arranged a debate between us. The audience was packed when I criticized his liberal reformist views as opportunistic and shallow. It was clear that I had the upper hand, and he was reduced to vicious jokes to entertain the young people and to cover his embarrassment. He turned to me and said privately that this was something he would not do again. I had a debate in Philadelphia with another Harvard professor, Nathan Glazer, in the 1970s. I got the best of him as well. I was effective because I offered a radical critique of the present social order in the United States and, in particular, racism. Gradually, McCarthyism killed the magazine. It was not so much because of lost subscriptions; we depended upon financial contributions from the Left in general. They subsided and we eventually had to close the magazine. I anticipated a period of repression and wrote about it in "Why Defend the Rights of Communists," published in 1949 and widely circulated. This was at the time of the Smith Act prosecution of Party leaders.

The McCarran Act passed in 1950, and the top leaders of the Communist Party U.S.A. were arrested. Their trials were held at Foley Square in New York City. I was the Party's chief witness; it was my job to explain what Marxism was and that the use of violence came from the ruling class. While Marxism was not pacifism, it did not advocate violence. But it did insist upon resistance to the violence of the ruling class. I was the expert witness and testified in many cases brought against comrades. It was my point to especially explain the capitalist basis of racism. One of the last cases was that of the singer Pete Seeger. Fortunately, the case against him was called off; he was not indicted. The prosecutions began to decline around 1955. Juries began to refuse to convict. This was when the most virulent aspects of McCarthyism began to wane. Finally, they stopped bringing people to trial altogether. But by 1960 there had been thirty to forty convictions. Many went to prison, like Elizabeth Gurley Flynn, a historic figure. The United States actually sent her to prison. Her fellow prisoners always addressed her as "Miss Flynn." They showed great respect for her.

Then there was the case of Gus Hall. He was convicted and fled to Mexico with the help of comrades. He was met by comrades in the Mexican army, one of whom was a U.S. agent. So the U.S. government knew exactly where he was hidden and sent agents across the border to arrest him, violating Mexican sovereignty. Four young comrades with an older leader were already in Mexico waiting for Gus. When he was captured, they were left in Mexico with little money and few provisions. I was asked to go to Mexico with money to get them out. I accepted, knowing that it was a very dangerous undertaking. In Mexico, I met a comrade named Magel, who was a correspondent for the Czechoslovakian press. He knew where the others were and took me to them. I got the money to them and helped them get back to the United States.

During this period I received a subpoena to testify before Senator McCarthy. The House Committee on Un-American Activities was part of his effort to repress writers, artists, and professors. He was out to silence whoever was associated with the Left. He would get them as witnesses to tell about the Party. His assistant, Roy Cohn, was his chief inquisitor. It was summertime and McCarthy was late for my testimony. Cohn asked me the initial questions; none of which were substantive. He had several of my history books that were supposed to be subversive. He picked up one or two of them and asked if I had written them. I answered, "Yes, I did. Did you read any?" Others on the committee included Senator Symington of Missouri, who was especially hostile to the Party and who had presidential ambitions. He was what we called a liberal Democrat. He took over the questioning and tried to make it substantive. I cooperated with him, and we actually had a conversation. Cohn and McCarthy were becoming frustrated with this. So they stopped Senator Symington and asked me if I still refused to answer their questions. I said, "Yes, of course, I refuse to answer." McCarthy responded that I would hear from them.

As I left the Senate building, a man up in the balcony called "Aptheker, Aptheker." I stopped and he came downstairs. He was a lawyer from Wisconsin in Washington on business and had read in the newspaper that McCarthy was having a hearing. He said that he admired McCarthy, thought that the hostility against him was from the eastern newspapers, and thought he was a fighter. But he was very disappointed; the way he questioned me was wrong. He told me that he admired my response and activities. The point that I want to make is that all during this period of persecution and having to be underground, there were many instances when people expressed sympathy privately. When I came home from the McCarthy hearing and was going up in the elevator, a woman who lived a floor below us turned to me and said to me that she admired me and so did her husband. These kinds of experiences recurred. At the end of my lectures to student and faculty organizations, people would come up and express support and encouragement. Quite often, department chairs initiated the faculty invitations. It is significant that I would be invited in the first place. It was an act of courage to associate with me in those days. People did this especially during the McCarthy period and the war in Vietnam. One time in the Midwest, the department chair invited me to dinner. Afterward, we went out to his car and all the tires were slashed. I apologized; he responded that it was all right. It was worth it. This kind of thing happened, and I do not think that enough has been written on this aspect of the period of the 1950s and early 1960s. I got hundreds of invitations to speak all over the country; people wanted to hear what I had to say.

In the late 1950s the editor of *Political Affairs* was V. J. Jerome. He was a Smith Act defendant and his time was taken up with his defense. He asked me to help put out *Political Affairs.* So for sometime I served as acting editor. He went to prison, and at some point I became the editor. *Political Affairs* was the organ of the U.S. Communist Party with a circulation of about twenty-five thousand. It was very difficult work during this period. Much of the Party leadership not in prison was in hiding. I frequently had to leave for secret meetings without telling Fay and without calling her once I had gone. I had an assistant, Nemmy Sparks. He was very instrumental in getting us continued support. From time to time, he and I would sit and edit text. *Political Affairs* came out every month and on time. I was very proud of that. It also held its circulation. It is an important source of the history of the Left during the McCarthy period. By the early 1960s much of the terror of the McCarthy period was over, and I asked to be relieved of this position.

I found in my travels around the country that there was intense interest in Marxism, especially among the young. I thought we should establish some sort of Marxist institute that would be a center for the study of Marxism and related subjects. I put this to the leadership of the Party and they agreed that it was a good idea. They said, "Do it, but we cannot financially support it." So I went all across the country explaining this idea of a leftist research institute and publishing forum. The organization I started was the American Institute for Marxist Studies (AIMS). I already had contact with professors and groups in the places I had lectured. There was a favorable response. I sought help and tried to think of someone who was well known and could bring attention to AIMS. The name William Appleman Williams came to mind. He greeted me and asked if I had a million dollars; I looked at him and realized he was serious. I told him no, that I had raised about $40,000. He laughed and said he did not want to be associated with the enterprise. I started AIMS anyway in rented loft space off Fifth Avenue in an old building. Friends and comrades came to set up the offices; they did carpentry work, put in carpets, found furniture, and so on. A very dear friend, who was important in my life, was Louise T. Patterson. She joined me in this effort. She was one of the officers and served as my executive secretary. When I was away, which was often, she was in complete charge. She was a leader of the Harlem Renaissance and was married to William L. Patterson, who headed the civil rights struggle for the Left at that time. She died in 1999.

Publications and Activism from 1950

A Documentary History of the Negro People in the United States was first published in 1951. I started work on it right after I came home from the war with the help of a Guggenheim Award for $2,500. Fay told me to go back to them because that was not enough money. I did and was pleased to get an additional $500 only to have Fay ask why I did not ask for even more. I did not know at the time that I was working on volume 1. It ends with 1910, which I saw as the beginning of the modern period. It was well received, so I began thinking of subsequent volumes. There are now seven volumes; the final one concludes with the murder of Martin Luther King Jr. If there are to be other volumes, others will have to do them. I think the only volume out of print is volume 1. In these volumes, I wanted black people to talk for themselves. I did not want others to talk about them or for them. They spoke for themselves. It makes for exciting reading. I spent years doing the research: there are leaders, many women, children, organizations, conservatives, liberals, and radicals. All views were represented. I knew my bias, so I was careful not just to select material for points of view that I agreed with. It would have been wrong to have only the radical point of view.

One advantage I had in doing *A Documentary History* was that I shared an office with Dr. Du Bois. He invited me to do so shortly after I returned from the war. His desk was no more than ten feet from mine, and he told me to ask him questions any time. He came in regularly at nine o'clock and brought a sandwich to avoid eating in the local restaurants. So I brought a sandwich as well and we would talk over lunch. He was a trained historian with a mind that was encyclopedic. Across the street from our office on Fortieth Street was the main branch of the New York Public Library with one of the largest collections in the world. This was a wonderful situation that lasted for a year and a half until the NAACP fired Du Bois. Du Bois was unwilling to support Walter White and the NAACP's deal with Truman: that the NAACP would withdraw from activism and commentary on international relations (i.e., support the U.S. Cold War) in exchange for the president's support on domestic matters.

In my activism, I traveled a great deal. So when I would go to, for example, Madison, Wisconsin, I would go to the historical library there, or when I was in Columbia, South Carolina, I would go to the state archives. There is a story here. When I began visiting Columbia, I had already published some things. Interestingly, whenever I asked the woman archivist there for material, she would tell me that either they did not have it or they could not find it. I soon realized that they were keeping me from materials; they knew who I was. I did not know what to do. While in Columbia, I stayed with the great Modjeska Simkins, a radical black woman leader, whose basement was a center of revolutionary activity. I told Modjeska my problem. She called up the archive janitor. Since he was black, he was called the janitor, but in fact, he was the archivist. She told him that he could trust me. I explained the problem to him. He told me to meet him in the front of the archives Sunday morning and he would give me whatever I wanted. That is how I got many documents in *A Documentary History,* especially those related to the Vesey insurrection. Everything was there in the archives, including the original Vesey trial court records. Of course, when I finished the books, I could not acknowledge their help. I imagine those whites are still wondering how I got that material.

Modjeska knew everyone. I was not quite thirty, and Modjeska asked me if I would speak at some of the Negro colleges. I said certainly. So she called up the president of Benedict College and told him that a very distinguished person was visiting and was willing to speak at his college. After I spoke at Benedict, she did the same thing at Allen University. But there, she told the president that this distinguished person spoke at Benedict, certainly he would want me to speak at Allen as well. That is the way she would arrange things. Some years ago, I realized that I had not spoken with Modjeska in a long time. So I called and asked to speak with her. The woman on the other end said in a sad voice that Modjeska had just passed away. She was a civil rights leader in the 1940s and 1950s, long before the 1960s movement. Ironically, she was treasurer of the Republican Party in South Carolina and used that position to cover her activities. She was a Republican like I am a Republican.

In 1954 I wrote *The Labor Movement in the South during Slavery.* It also opened new ground because it pointed out that there was a labor movement in the South during slave times, primarily in cities like Charleston, Baltimore, and New Orleans. It was quite radical and distressing to employers. Until then the major writing on labor in the United States, even in the work of John R. Commons, ignores this pre–Civil War, southern, free, white labor movement in the cities. Also in 1954 I published a critique of dominant American historiography called *Laureates of Imperialism: American Big Business Rewrites American History.* That work was aimed at Allan Nevins who was one of my teachers. Then I did a large book in 1955, *History and Reality.* It was reprinted in 1962 under a new title *The Era of McCarthyism.* It is a defense of historical materialism as a valid approach to a study of the past. It also contains chapters on growing lower-class repression in the United States in the postwar period. The book is noteworthy I think because in the late 1950s Dr. Du Bois read it. He wrote me a very long letter about the introductory essay, which was on the defense of historical materialism. He wrote that he read the essay twice and it had convinced him that view was valid and had enlightened him. It was quite a letter.

Another book of some consequence was *The World of C. Wright Mills* (1960). Mills did one of the most influential critiques of American society in the postwar period, *The Power Elite* (1956). He was a professor at Columbia who was considered an outlaw. He told me that he was very badly treated by other faculty members. He wrote well and passionately and his books were widely circulated, especially *Listen, Yankee: The Revolution in Cuba* (1960). I got to know Mills well and from time to time we had lunch together. He did have one blind spot, and that was the African American. He came out of Texas, and when he wrote critically of the United States, he ignored its worst single crime, which was the treatment of the African Americans. I told him that, and I will never forget his reply. He said, "You know, Aptheker, you are a terrible sentimentalist." This comment showed how profound was his lack of comprehension. But compared to others who were subservient to reaction, Mills was a shining light. He was also very charming. I sent a copy of my manuscript to him for his criticisms. He responded with a long letter of appreciation and suggested a chapter reorganization. He went with his wife to the Soviet Union and told me that he was impressed. There were problems, but he thought it was a genuinely advanced society. He died at a young age. In 1962 I published another long book called *American Foreign Policy and the Cold War.* It is a critique of imperialist and racist U.S. policies on the foreign front in the postwar period.

The central literature on the 1960s civil rights movement gives the impression that the movement began in the 1950s. That is wrong. Its roots go back to the abolitionist movement. There were three provisions of the constitution of the American antislavery society. The first was the abolition of slavery. The second was the promotion of the condition of the free black population. The third was the rejection of racism. This is in the original constitution. The civil rights movement was more than one hundred years old in the 1930s. The National Negro Congress, begun around 1936, became an important and very militant organization by the 1940s; it was the first organization to propose a march on Washington. Its membership was primarily black, but there were white members as well. I was one. The Southern Negro Youth Congress was started in the 1930s; whites including me were members of this organization as well. We held integrated meetings with thousands throughout the South in defiance of Jim Crow laws. In Columbia, South Carolina, I was present when the sheriff told us that our meeting was illegal. About a quarter of those in attendance were white. Jim Jackson, Louis Burnham, and I showed him the audience. He gave up, because the audience could not be separated. One of the purposes of the meeting was to honor Du Bois who was there and was given an award. I had the task of speaking after Paul Robeson; I should have stayed home! My point is that we had such organizations in the 1930s and 1940s; they were militant, large, integrated, and antiracist.

In Brooklyn in the 1950s our daughter, Bettina, and Angela Davis, Margaret Burnham, and a young man named Charles picketed Woolworth's because they would not hire black people, even in stores where the majority of the customers were black. The youngsters would not let me picket with them because I was an adult. This sort of thing had been going on unrecorded for decades. There were thousands of black soldiers who had profoundly liberating experiences fighting in Europe and Asia. They also impacted thousands of whites who fought with them and who realized that blacks were not inferior as they had been told. When the war ended and these white and black men came home, the reimposition of segregation and racism was resisted. Black veterans were lynched and maimed, as blacks had been in the 1920s. But this time the racist could not always get away with it because resistance among blacks and whites was much stronger. The outrage and organized resistance against Jim Crow increased after the war. My *Documentary History of the Negro People in the United States* was welcomed in this context. Du Bois wrote the introduction. There was a meeting that hailed the book; a small play was put on based on the material in volume 1. These activities were not unique; they were part of the "soil" from which resistance in the 1960s grew. The 1960s movement did not drop from heaven, and it has two related threads. There was the student movement. Colleges and universities were still run like they were reformatories where the trustees had absolute power. The unrest on campuses was because of this, and I have to remind people that the student unrest was not just among whites. It was black and white and very militant. The Berkeley uprising was just an example. It was very effective and produced change. Then there was the antiwar movement, which was also closely related to the student movement. These, along with the black movement, characterize the uniqueness of the 1960s. There were demands for change on multiple fronts.

During the 1960s I was invited to campuses all over the United States. Special care was taken when I went to black campuses in the South, especially in Mississippi. I would not fly into the nearest airport. I would come in elsewhere and be met by three or four black students; they would drive me to their campus on back roads. I would be the only white and, often, the students were my guards. I would speak and then return to the airport the same way. They saw that I stayed alive and was not endangered. In one case, there was an enormous black audience with one white newspaper reporter who was drunk and scared out of his wits. I teased him during questions and answers. The black students took care of me. I always came back safely. The only time I was attacked and injured was in 1946 after speaking at the University of North Carolina.

I wrote a study pamphlet, "Dr. Martin Luther King, Vietnam, and Civil Rights," in 1967, not long before King was murdered. It was a critique of his analysis of the source of black people's oppression. King avoided the socioeconomic and historic roots of that oppression and focused more on the morality and psychology of oppression. In my critique, I was fully respectful of the historic contribution he was making. About two months before he was murdered, *Freedomways* magazine organized a celebration of the life of Dr. Du Bois, at the centennial of his birth. It was held in New York City's Carnegie Hall. Dr. King, who was the main speaker, knew that *Freedomways* was a leftist publication. In that speech Dr. King not only hailed Dr. Du Bois as a pioneer in the struggle for freedom, he indicated an affinity with (not an acceptance of) Marxism. In the speech he called attention to the fact that Dr. Du Bois was a Communist; that O'Casey, the great Irish writer, was a Communist, and that Pablo Neruda, the poet of Latin America, was a Communist, as was Pablo Picasso.

King did not profess an affinity with the Communist Party. What he affirmed was the relevance of the Marxist view in contemporary society as indicated by Marxism's influence on great writers and artists. King emphasized his plans for the mass demonstration in Washington a few months later, in which Negro people on relief and all those who were suffering would come from all over the country. His plan was to have them go into a park and stay there until Congress passed legislation relevant to solving their problems. This was the most radical speech Martin Luther King ever made.

Two months later he was assassinated. I am convinced it was a political murder because King was moving to the left and was going to use mass mobilization not only for civil rights but also for social and economic rights.

Then there was the war in Vietnam. I was one of the leaders in the antiwar movement and also a member of the World Peace Council. At the council meeting in Helsinki, some Vietnamese friends came up to me and extended an invitation to visit Vietnam. They asked if I could bring two non-Party members and, if possible, could one be a Negro. I accepted their invitation and told them I would do my best. Once home I called and invited Staughton Lynd, a well-known historian and man of great principle. He accepted and suggested that I get in touch with Bob Moses, the leader of the antiracist struggle. Bob came to my office. We could not speak there, so we went outside. I told him what I had in mind. I never heard from him again. It got close to December, so I told Lynd about Moses' nonresponse. He got Tom Hayden, a leader of the antiwar youth movement. We went to Paris and were met there by friends from Vietnam. They arranged for us to go from Paris to Prague. It was Christmas. In Prague, Tom asked me if they celebrated Christmas and if it was all right to go out for a walk. I said, "Why of course, it is." This is when I realized how ill informed Tom was about the "Communist" world. From Prague we went to Peking and then on to Hanoi. A delegation met us at the airport. As we walked, one of the Vietnamese asked me where was the Negro. I told the delegation that he did not come; they were very disappointed. We were the guests of the republic and met all the leaders, except Ho Chi Minh. He was visiting his "family." Since he did not have any blood relatives, he went from area to area and stayed at people's homes. We never saw him.

Party leaders invited me to their meetings where serious matters were discussed for fifty minutes. Then they would rest and have tea. I commented that this was very unusual. When we have meetings, we go on and on. Here they were in the middle of a war and they took a ten-minute break every hour. They said their work was more productive with such breaks. They arranged trips for us, but we had to move at night. We went south into the bombed area and saw the devastation. They asked me if I had any requests. I asked to see the oldest priest in the area. After formalities, he asked, "Why is your country bombing my country?" I did not know what to say to him. His question was right to the point, and I had no answer for him. I asked him how it was living under the Communists. He said that under the French, there was one mass for the French and a separate mass for the Vietnamese. To him this was not Christian, but now things were better. I asked him what he meant. He said, "Now with the Communists, we have one mass. People of all races may worship together; this is more like Christianity." As we toured the countryside, we could see how well prepared they were. There were bomb shelters everywhere; all the women were armed; and their morale was very high. I also learned in Vietnam how the French tried to continue their domination in French Indochina. They intentionally corrupted the youth through drug use. Then they would jail as many of these young people as possible under the pretext that they were criminals. This is exactly what is going on here. Black youth cannot get decent jobs and make a legitimate living. No one will look at them or educate them; everyone is afraid of them. What are they to do? The fact is that those who run the system do not want to employ black youth or allow them to take advantage of job opportunities. They would prefer to make criminals out of them and put them away. They are pleased when they engage in criminal activities.

While in Hanoi, I got a call from the *Herald Tribune.* The reporter asked, "You are in Hanoi?" I said, "Yes, that is where you are calling me." He asked, "Are you all right?" They asked about my physical condition. I told them about the bombing and that we were fine. I do not know what he imagined. We were there ten days. When we got back home, a large crowd met us. There was a lot of excitement in the newspapers and on television. One time when we spoke, they turned the cameras off when it was my turn to speak. At another mass meeting, they turned off the heat on a cold January day. There were thousands of people, all of whom had to keep their coats on. I spoke to thousands of people, but Tom and Lynd probably reached millions. Lynd tried unsuccessfully to talk with Senator Fulbright. Lynd had letters from American POWs for their families. We interviewed one of the prisoners and asked how he was being treated. He did not know what the war was about, all he knew was that he had been shot down and was being held prisoner. Our visit helped advance the antiwar movement. I was one of the people behind the demonstration that shut down New York City for a day. Fay and I were present on the sidelines during the march. One of the demonstrators stopped when he saw us and said, "You did all this." (See Herbert Aptheker, *Mission to Hanoi* [1966].)

The black community has been the basis of my support since the 1930s. At the height of the persecution of the Party in the 1950s, it made no difference to them. People would say, "Aptheker knows our history and he talks straight. We want to hear him." I was invited to black churches and organizations. I was honored many times, even by the NAACP. I received an award from them along with Shirley Chisholm, whom I knew quite well.

We both lived in Brooklyn. I ran for Congress the first time in 1966 in the Twelfth District of Brooklyn. I spoke widely against racism and the war and was invited on several occasions to speak at the Bronx Community Center. There were two attempts on my life there. In one, a fire was set above where I was speaking. Later the Bronx district attorney called me at home and told me they had arrested three people who were responsible for an effort to kill me. They were all convicted and given light sentences. In time, the Twelfth Congressional District was gerrymandered. It was the largest district in the United States and included Bedford-Stuyvesant and Staten Island, which was absurd geographically. It was to prevent Negroes from getting into Congress. Shirley and I participated in a movement to challenge the district reorganization and demanded that the boundaries be corrected. My campaign organization joined the legal challenge, and we won. That is how Shirley got into Congress. We conducted a successful campaign against gerrymandering. She was elected to Congress from the Negro community. She was the first black woman elected to Congress. I believe that she is not there now because she was dangerous to the powers that rule this country.

Early in 1966 I was finally able to publish *Nat Turner's Slave Rebellion* along with the so-called confessions of 1831. That book was a reprint of my master's thesis accepted by Columbia University in 1939. There is story here. In the foreword I said that William Styron was writing a historical novel about the revolt. I mentioned it because Mr. Styron had gotten in touch with me before the publication of my book. He said he was working on the Turner rebellion and had read my thesis in the Columbia University library. It would to helpful to him if he could have a copy of the thesis so he could study it. I sent it to him. He kept it about two weeks and returned it with a letter of praise, saying it was exactly what he needed.

When his book came out, *The Confessions of Nat Turner* (1967), the *Nation* magazine asked me to review it. To my astonishment it was a travesty and a complete falsification. I said so. This produced a long series of exchanges between Styron and me. He had the advantage; everything he said criticizing me was published in the *New York Times*. But the *New York Times* refused to publish my replies. The only places I got published were in *Political Affairs* and some student papers—nothing approaching the readership of the *New York Times*. Afro-American scholars became very interested in this quarrel and began to comment. My friend John Henrik Clarke, then associate editor of *Freedomways*, edited a book on the matter called *William Styron's Nat Turner: Ten Black Writers Respond* (1968). The book was a devastating critique of Styron, chapter after chapter, by a group of distinguished black scholars. Styron raised this issue again in an issue of *Harper's* magazine (August 2000) after John Henrik Clarke passed away. Of course, by not mentioning me and that I started the critique of his shameful work, he is attempting to vindicate himself by racializing the matter.

A Hollywood film company had given Styron a $400,000 advance for the rights to do a movie based on his book. John told me that he and other black scholars wrote a letter to the producer advising him not to film the Styron travesty. After the Clarke book, the film producer decided to change the title to simply Nat Turner, dropping the idea of a confession. However, other black people got involved. The only black cameraman in Hollywood led a group of distinguished people who also made known their displeasure. They demanded that such a film not be produced. The film was never made. Styron never forgave me. It would have been another *Gone with the Wind,* seen by millions.

I completed a book in 1970 entitled *The Urgency of Marxist Christian Dialogue.* It was widely commented on. It was reflective of a significant worldwide dialogue between the Left and the religious communities. There was also *Abolitionism: A Revolutionary Movement* (1989). The abolitionist movement has been treated in one of two ways: as an abomination by the racist historians or as a liberal reform effort. The latter did not have a real understanding of the revolutionary quality of the movement. It was revolutionary because it challenged the basic structure of the social order. To challenge slavery was a fundamental challenge to the very structure that this nation was built upon. Abolitionism, therefore, called forth severe repression and attacks against it. My other theme is that the abolitionist movement was a genuine black-white movement. The first abolitionists were, as one would suspect, black people. Their agitation educated white liberals, including William Lloyd Garrison, who at first took a position favoring colonization, which was a racist solution to the race problem. But Garrison attended a black antislavery convention in Philadelphia where he was educated. He left the convention a true abolitionist. This fact is reflective of the reality of the whole abolitionist movement and is the way many other whites became involved in the movement. I have noticed in the literature reference to it from time to time. I believe that in time this view will dominate the studies of the period.

Du Bois's Publications

My relationship with Du Bois dates to before the Second World War. While I was an editor of *New Masses,* I did a review of his *Dusk of Dawn* (1940). I was critical but respectful. Du Bois wrote to me. He thought the review was one of the best. From then on, we communicated. After the war, while we worked in the same office, our relationship grew, and he got to know my work and me. He lived near Fay and me in Brooklyn, and we visit him and Shirley on Sundays. Bettina, our daughter, loved to visit him. He was very fond of her and they loved to play baseball together even though he was well into his eighties.

Around 1946 Du Bois asked me to edit his published works and correspondence. Fay and I considered this charge to be sacred and a great honor. Shirley Graham, Du Bois's wife, had a letter written by Du Bois indicating that I was to be his editor. I sent out letters and published one in the *Nation* asking for correspondence from Du Bois. While he was living, I tried to get support to publish his works. I got some positive responses, but they seemed to fade away. Arno Press, owned by the *New York Times,* was interested. The editor came to our home and looked at the files in our basement. They seemed ready to do it, but soon afterward backed out. Lippincott Press accepted the manuscript of what was to be volume 1 of Du Bois's correspondence. I had a contract in hand and was waiting for galleys but did not get them. They may have even paid Shirley Graham Du Bois an advance. I got in touch with the editor; he said to me that it was called off. I do not think it was a coincidence that Lippincott went public on Wall Street just before the Du Bois project was called off.

I was having great trouble getting his work published. I told him so and suggested that perhaps he should seek another editor. I was simply too notorious. Since he was also notorious, it would be better to get some well-established faculty member to edit his work. He said to me, "Herbert, I want you to be my editor. The time will come when it will be possible to publish my work." That settled that; I continued to make all sorts of attempts. Fay and I worked on his papers in our basement for years. There were tens of thousands of letters. They were in our basement because Du Bois had gone to Ghana. While we were helping him make travel arrangements, he said to me that since I was going to edit his papers, could he send them to my home. Fay and I agreed since we had a finished basement. Characteristic of Du Bois, he had saved copies of every letter he sent as well as the replies and his responses. There were more than one hundred thousand letters to and from Du Bois. But they were haphazardly organized in rough chronological order in boxes. Fay and I spent thousands of hours rearranging and cataloging them. It was a tremendous task, but we did it.

This is the way Du Bois would have wanted it. After he left the country, we remained in contact. Alphaeus Hunton, Du Bois's assistant, wrote me a letter after Du Bois died and asked if I would come to Africa and continue the Du Bois project. I was deeply honored but declined. I knew my place was right here in the United States. Right after that came the coup in Ghana; then Hunton became ill and soon died. He was one of the most perfect people I have known. We believe that his wife is still living on Staten Island. Du Bois did not "give up the struggle and go to Africa disillusioned." No, he went to work on a long-overdue project. After Du Bois's death, we grew concerned with having all his papers in our basement. I discussed relocating the papers with Shirley Graham. She had conversations with people at Fisk University, but nothing came of it. One day we had a flood in the basement. With visiting friends, we saved the papers after shoveling water all night. That danger persuaded me to get in touch with Shirley Graham again and convince her that we had had the papers long enough. They must be properly stored. She got to work, and the University of Massachusetts agreed to take them and to give her $100,000 for them. I was part of the group that signed for the university to take them. Following that there were all sorts of hostile rumors that the Jew Aptheker got a fortune for the papers. This was even published in a book. Fay and I did not get a penny; we did not want any money and did not ask for any. Shirley sold the papers to the University of Massachusetts. Now their library is named after Du Bois.

The real breakthrough came in the person of Leone Stein, then the director of the University of Massachusetts Press. I agreed to publish a two-volume series of Du Bois's selected letters. With her help we got some very distinguished names to support the project. One was C. Vann Woodward. Elliot Rudwick and August Meier were two others who were also to be advisers. But one by one, they withdrew. I believe they did so because of my notoriety. Mrs. Stein even went to the National Endowment for the Arts for funds. At a meeting with the director over lunch, he replied in a loud voice in the restaurant that she was ridiculous for asking. The National Endowment would not help a notorious Communist. After that, I would not have been surprised if she had dropped the project, as did the others. But she stuck with it. *The Correspondence of W. E. B. Du Bois: Selections, 1877–1934* was published in 1973. The book was well received. Mrs. Stein was eager to get the *New York Times* to review it. They refused. The book sold so well that I was asked to do volume 2, *Selections, 1934–1944,* which was also well received. The final volume, *Selections, 1944–1963,* was published in 1978. All this was made possible under the directorship of Leone Stein. I later found out that someone on the *New York Times* editorial board asked why the Du Bois works had not been reviewed. This had become something of a scandal, so they reviewed volume 3. We had the good fortune of having a distinguished historian, Eric Foner, do the review. It was excellent and led to the book's being selected as one of the ten best books of 1978. Foner mentioned in the draft of his review that the *New York Times* had not reviewed volumes 1 and 2. They cut that sentence out of the published version. Leone Stein was vindicated; the Press did not lose any money on Du Bois. In fact, they did quite well. All three volumes are still available and are also in paperback.

My work was not over. Kraus-Thomson took an interest in the published writings of Du Bois. At long last, in 1973 I annotated the first volume of all Du Bois's published writing. It cites everything Du Bois published, all his magazines, journal articles, newspaper articles, and books. Then I edited thirty-nine volumes of Du Bois's publications. This was a massive undertaking that consumed the first half of the 1980s. The last volume came out in 1986; it was a collection of Du Bois's pamphlets. Simultaneously, I saw that Du Bois's unpublished books were made available. In 1975 Monthly Review Press published *The Education of Black People: Ten Critiques, 1906–1960* by Du Bois. I was the editor. Another unpublished book by Du Bois was called *Prayers for Dark People,* which was published in 1980. These were prayers he had delivered to his students in Atlanta as sermons on different occasions. We found them on slips of paper in a manila envelope; most were hand-written. I put them together and dated them. This little book is still in print and sells well around Christmastime. Black people often buy the book as a gift for their children. Another unpublished Du Bois work that I titled *Against Racism: Unpublished Essays, Papers, Addresses, 1887–1961* came out in 1985. The University of Massachusetts Press published all these books.

Activism and an Academic Career

I had been such a nuisance to the U.S. government for so long, I believe that J. Edgar Hoover and company bought some prostitute historian to write a critical review of me. The FBI published this work in a pamphlet called "Herbert Eugene Aptheker, Historian." Whenever Fay or I would get a letter or telephone call addressed to Herbert Eugene Aptheker, we knew the mailing list could be traced back to the FBI. I never use that middle name. They knew that while I was editing the Du Bois works, I was traveling all over the country trying to start a revolution and running the American Institute of Marxist Studies (AIMS).

AIMS published several books that I edited. One is entitled *Marxism and Democracy*; another is called *Marxism and Christianity.* Then there is *Marx-*

ism and Alienation. They were all published in the 1960s. They contain essays by scholars and public figures of various persuasions. For example, *Marxism and Democracy* has an essay by Eslanda Robeson, Paul Robeson's wife. Another very important book I did, edited by Lee Baxendall, is called *Marxism and Aesthetics* and is on Marxist writings in literature, art, and culture. For a time Fay served as the librarian of AIMS. There were several thousand volumes. When we gave up the institute, it was sold for ten thousand dollars to the Communist Party of Japan. This helped us settle our debts.

In 1976 I ran for the Senate against Daniel Patrick Moynihan. My campaign had very limited money. There was only enough for one comrade to serve as a bodyguard. He went with me on an upstate tour to Syracuse and Rochester. Surprisingly, I got 25,360 votes; that was the most of any minority candidate, despite the fact that you could hardly find me on the ballot. I talked my heart out against racism and reaction. During the campaign, a man attacked me with a knife. A neighbor walking her dog saw the struggle and yelled for him to "leave the doctor alone." She probably saved my life. I managed to fight him off, but I was seriously injured. He was a professional, was very calm and deliberate, and just walked away. The attack happened across the street from our home. I could not hide it from Fay. Because I was campaigning, I did not go to the hospital. Fay took care of me and was very shaken by the attack. That is when we decided to leave New York City. It had become more and more difficult to live there. We found the snow especially difficult. Fay was insistent that we move. Our daughter, Bettina, was already in California and asked us to come out to San Jose. She selected the house; we put a deposit on it without ever seeing it. We have been very happy here since 1977. The neighbors have been wonderful and very supportive.

Huey Newton and Bob Seale invited me to lecture while they were still in high school, before they formed the Black Panther Party. Then I spoke at a mass meeting supported by the Black Panthers in Oakland with thousands in attendance. It occurred while Huey Newton was in prison. I was the only speaker. I asked Bob Seale how long should I speak. He told me as long as I liked. He also asked that I explain why there was the race problem in the first place. I spoke with Panther guards all around me and explained the oppression of black people: why it existed, how it came about, and what had to be done to end it. There is no way to end oppression except through political struggle with blacks and whites together. This is very difficult for many to accept, but there is no other way. True liberation cannot come about by burning down cities; if you burn a few cities down, what have you got? Nor will liberation happen after returning to Africa. If you go back, what would that do to change the domestic source of oppression there and here? Nothing. There is no way out except through the unity of black and white people to fight against this monstrous condition of enslavement and the maintenance of upper-class privilege though racism. That was the essence of what I said. I spoke of the unity that came at different periods in the 1890s and 1930s. This is evidence that black and white unity against oppression was, can, and must be done. There is no other way. Fanaticism and assassinations cannot bring down a system of oppression. New cities can be built, and assassinated leaders can be replaced. There are no substitutes for social and political struggle. Bob Seale wanted this. Bobby has given up; and the others were killed. Now youth like Bobby and Huey go to jail. This is the ruling-class solution.

I had three college appointments; they were all temporary. One was at Bryn Mawr College. I am sure I got that position because of Mindy Thompson Fullilove. Her father, Ernie Thompson, was quite an organizer. In the late 1940s when Mindy was only an infant, I taught black history to groups in New Jersey at their home. Now Mindy was a college student at Bryn Mawr and one of maybe thirty black students. I remember the president spoke with me and was serious about the appointment. She asked me what day I would like to teach. I said whatever day would be best for the college. She was shocked at my response; she was not used to hearing that. She suggested Tuesday afternoon. So I began teaching Negro history at Bryn Mawr. Mindy used to meet me at the train station. The first day of class the room was packed with visitors, students, and television crews. The head of the department, Arthur Dudden, did not know what to do. I asked everyone who was not a student to please leave and I would meet them in the history department office. Dudden whispered to me that they did not have an office. I insisted that this was not a circus; it was a history class. I started teaching the class with mostly black students and only a few whites. When it was over, one reporter had stayed. He was black and from a local newspaper. He asked me some questions. The *Philadelphia Inquirer* wanted an interview with me. I told them, if they wanted me to speak on Negro history, I would. But that was not what they wanted. They wanted to know why a Communist was teaching.

One day before class started, an elderly gray-haired woman was waiting outside the classroom. She asked if she could sit in on my class. I told her that I had no objection. The subject of that day's class was slave rebellions. That is a stirring lecture. The next week, I met the department chair in the hall and he said, "Herbert, Herbert, you are in." I answered, "What do you mean?" "Do you know who was sitting in on your class last week? That was Mrs. Cadbury." It turned out that she was a member of the family that owns Cadbury chocolates; they were major donors and trustees of the college. "She was enthusiastic about your class. So you are in. Do not worry about it." Then there was a dinner of about twenty faculty members to welcome me—I am certain that Dudden had something to do with it. Sitting to my left was a Prof. Helen Manning, the daughter of President William Taft. Professor Manning asked me what I thought of Theodore Roosevelt, Woodrow Wilson, and William Taft. I knew she was his daughter. Fay will tell you that I am slightly crazy. So I answered, "I would have had Roosevelt shot; Woodrow Wilson, I would have hung; and Taft, I am not sure what I would have done with him." Everyone stopped talking. I figured I said what they expected me to say. That was quite a dinner. I continued teaching and they asked me to take another class. After three years, I told Mindy that we had to get a black person to teach the class. So that was arranged and I left after four years.

About the same time, a very dear friend, Eugene Meyer, came to me. He was a professor at Hostos Community College, part of the City University of New York in the Bronx. He arranged for me to get a part-time job there teaching history. The student population was 99 percent black. They were college students, but I discovered to my horror that most were functionally illiterate. They knew very little and could barely read. I put names on the board of famous people and presidents of the United States; they did not know who they were. This was scandalous. They were serious students and wanted to learn. I changed my course and made it an elementary introductory history course. I ended up teaching history, economics, and sociology—three classes. In each one, I found the same thing in terms of poor academic backgrounds. There were usually one or two students in the class who had skills and who had read. Most had finished high school only because of "social promotions"; they knew nothing. By the way, I participated in a struggle by the faculty against Albert Shanker, the trade unionist who headed the teachers union and who was praised by the *New York Times*. We had a chapter at the college opposed to him.

From time to time, I lectured in the community. One time I was lecturing at a leftist bookstore in New Haven. At the end of the lecture, a black woman came up to me and asked if I wanted to teach at Yale. I forgot about it. About two weeks later, I got a telephone call from a professor at Yale, who also asked if I was willing to teach at Yale. I said yes. It was all arranged and I was prepared. Then about a week before the class, I got a call from the same professor. He told me that my class was canceled because there had been objections raised to my appointment. I told him that he had not heard the end of it. I made the cancellation public, and the Yale students were aroused. Every week after teaching at Hostos, I would go up to Yale. I would make speeches; there was a mass movement; and a button was even produced in support of me. It turns out C. Vann Woodward opposed my appointment in the history department. The political science department was so outraged by this move, they appointed me instead. I went up to New Haven once a week, taught the class, and stayed overnight. The pay was very low. It covered the travel, overnight costs, and not much more. I took such a low-paying appointment as a matter of principle. My class met on the third floor of an old wooden building. The room was jammed. When I learned that the administration had limited the enrollment to fifteen students, I announced that all the others were welcome to sit in and participate. Every week there were fifty to sixty students there. The course was on W. E. B. Du Bois. Vann Woodward never forgave me. He released a statement that Aptheker was completely competent to teach at a community college but not at Yale. Staughton Lynd was a history teacher at Yale, and he was in favor of my appointment, as were many of the younger faculty. The students issued a letter published in the Yale paper that they all signed stating that my class was the best they had ever taken at Yale.

After we moved to San Jose, California, in 1977, one of our dinner guests was Angela Davis's sister, Fanya. She was a student at the University of California Berkeley Law School. She asked me if I would like to teach at Berkeley and, if so, what course. I suggested to her racism and the law, but reminded her that I was not a lawyer. Soon afterward I got an official request to be interviewed at the Law School. The committee consisted of about fifteen faculty and students. I am very proud that I first proposed to teach racism and the law, and now that course is taught in many law schools in the United States. Laws that upheld racism fill American history. I started teaching the course in 1978, and it focused on the relationship between the law, slavery, Jim Crow segregation, and so forth. I taught that course for ten years. They gave me a certificate of appreciation. I think they did so because they paid me so little. Fay and I would drive up to Berkeley; many times we had dinner together with the students. In time, the students at Hastings Law School in San Francisco heard about my class and would come to it. Soon I got a request from Hastings. I could not resist lecturing and teaching. It is my life; so I said yes. Fay warned me that it would be too much. We would leave home in the morning and have lunch in San Francisco. I would teach the class at Hastings. Then we would go over to Berkeley, have dinner, teach, and make the long drive home. In time, we realized that I could not teach at two different locations. So I dropped Hastings.

About the same time, another Berkeley professor approached me and asked if I would be willing to teach undergraduates. I said yes again. So I began teaching Afro-American history in the history department.

In the meantime, I had been invited to speak at Santa Clara University. Prof. Gary Okihiro asked me if I would teach a course there. Again, I said yes. I taught a very crowded course there for a term and loved it. But then I got a call from the dean who told me that they would not renew my contract. Gary told me that someone who gave forty thousand dollars a year to the Law School would stop donating money if I continued. So I was fired from there. Note that African American students at Bryn Mawr, Yale, Berkeley, and Hastings initiated all but two of the appointments I received. Black people have always encouraged my work and me.

I had a stroke on April 1, 1992, and was in the hospital for a month. Fay's quick response is what saved me. The stroke affected my short-term memory. In 1992 I completed *Anti-Racism in U.S. History: The First Two Hundred Years*. I had conceived of it as a longer book before my stroke that spring. The book outlines and discusses the extent of antiracism among white people from the colonial period through the Civil War. Some years ago, John Hope Franklin was a visiting professor at Stanford. He called me and we had lunch together. He asked me what I was up to. I told him that I was writing about antiracism. He immediately realized the importance of this work and told me, "Very good. You should focus on white people. Do not bother about us. We [black people] are, of course, antiracist." He confirmed for me that this was an important new book, which has opened a new field. It shows that the questioning of racism and outright opposition to it existed among many whites, especially women. I show that in this book. Antiracism existed even among some prominent whites such as Alexander Hamilton. Common men also opposed racism. A number of the white abolitionists rejected the idea of the inferiority of black people. They included Wendell Phillips and William Lloyd Garrison.

I believe in time *Anti-Racism* will have almost the same impact as my *American Negro Slave Revolts.* When I wrote *Slave Revolts,* the historical literature accepted the alleged racial unity among white people. This is false. In this new book, I document that there were significant antiracist feelings, agitation, and organization among white people. White women, in particular, were important in expressing antiracist sentiment. It would seem natural given the persecution of women based upon the idea of their inferiority. It is not surprising that they would become leaders in a movement against racism—the assertion of inferiority of another group. The whole antiracist movement is exciting and challenges the historical view of the unity of whites in accepting racism. In which case, someone like John Brown was not a maniac, any more than Nat Turner. John Brown's armed rebellion was a black-white effort; there were black people with John Brown, and they were hung with him. They spoke of him as a brother, a leader, and as a father. This speaks well of him and his wife, Mary, who was as fiercely abolitionist as he was. They had lost two sons in the Harper's Ferry raid. She took his body back to upstate New York and was harassed afterward. She left New York and came out to northern California to Saratoga, not far from San Jose, to live with her daughter. It is important to know that this movement was supported by blacks and whites. People need to know that the struggle against slavery was a militant black struggle as well as a black-white struggle. It is important to know that many whites, especially women, saw the horror of slavery and spoke out against it.

I have been collecting evidence of post–Civil War antiracism. My study is filled with thousands of pages of notes. I am not at the stage of writing yet; I am still collecting materials. I plan to end volume 2 at 1920, after World War I. One of the things about the early NAACP was its explicit commitment against the idea of racism and the concept of racial inferiority of black people. I do not think this is in the literature enough. But it is in the constitution of the NAACP that started out as a militant black-white organization. A white woman leader like Mary White Overton centered her work on demonstrating that Negroes had the same capacities of any other people. In fact, many of the early pioneers of the NAACP were white people. My next book will end with a focus on the NAACP. What is left for me to do is go through the *Crisis,* started in 1910, and pay very close attention to the appearance of antiracism among whites. By the way, the relationship between the abolitionists and the early women's movement deserves a book; there was a natural alliance then and still is.

In more than sixty-five years of activism and scholarship, I never had a full-time academic appointment. The lectureships paid very little. Despite all that I wrote, the royalties were not enough to live off. As editor of *Political Affairs,* I was paid seventy-five dollars per week, but they did not pay all the time. When we founded the American Institute for Marxist Studies, my salary again was seventy five dollars per week, and again, it was not always paid. My secretary earned the same amount. The only source of real money I gained was from lectures years ago. At the height of McCarthyism, black churches and clubs would give me twenty-five dollars for speaking. I never asked for it, but we needed it. I was able to do what I did over the long term because Fay always had a job, except right after the war when we had an infant. When I was in the army, Fay saved all the money I earned as an officer. Her love and commitment to the struggle, and Du Bois's confidence in me, made it all possible. Fay and I have had an extraordinary career, a real impact on history and the struggle, and would not do anything any different. In time Du Bois's work will be the basis of a new society. I am proud to be a part of this legacy.

Fay Aptheker passed away on June 15, 1999.

NOTES

This chapter is based on transcripts from videotaping done by Leslie James and Peter Shiver in San Jose, Calif.

A book in honor of Herbert Aptheker includes a number of important analyses of his work and contributions. See Herbert Shapiro, ed., *African American History and Radical Historiography: Essays in Honor of Herbert Aptheker* (Minneapolis: MEP Publications, 1998).

11

Catching History on the Wing

A. Sivanandan as Activist, Teacher, and Rebel

LOUIS KUSHNICK and PAUL GRANT

My grandfather was one of the smallest of smallholders in the arid north of Ceylon, where nothing grew except children. His chief ambition was to send his sons to an "English school" so they could learn English and thereby find proper jobs and some sort of economic and social mobility. That was the ambition of most people in the north and in all Tamil areas. My father finally made it from the Tamil-medium school to an English-medium school and at sixteen entered the postal service as a clerk. His ambition, in turn, was to send his children to the foremost English schools and give them a better chance of entering the professions. Because my father disrupted my education by being transferred from place to place (the British raj didn't like dissidents and transferred him from one malarial station to another), I was sent to school in the capital, Colombo.

I was aware that my first duty, as the eldest son of a fairly poor family, was to go through school and college, hopefully to university, and then get a good job and so be able to help my parents to look after the family. That sense of responsibility—that sense of what Nyerere meant when he said, "we must return our education to the people who gave it to us"—underscored most of my conflicts. For my life was full of contradictions. I came from a poor peasant background; I attended a Catholic "public school" and lived with an impoverished uncle in a Singhalese slum. I was a Tamil and a Hindu having to attend Catholic religion classes, sometimes attending mass and benediction, and at the same time going to temple on a Friday with my uncles, aunts, and cousins. Inside me, then, Western culture and religion were mixed up with Hinduism, the urban with the rural; the aspiring boy who wanted to become middle class was learning the culture of the slum. And I was also desperate to belong to my village in the north, which we went back to every year for holidays. Because I went to the Colombo school, I had a prowess beyond the boys in the village. And a searing gap developed between my contemporaries and me as we grew up; this gap was very painful. And then there was the other side of me—the one that wanted to belong to Colombo and my English school and pukka friends. I remember most acutely my sense of betrayal when I disowned my favorite aunt when she came to visit me in school. She looked shabby, was without shoes and a proper blouse under her sari, and I made out that she was some sort of family servant.

My politics and commitments probably sprang out of all these forces and conflicts. I think it's a mistake to think of colonialism as a one-way street, as something that is done to you, something so powerful you can't resist it. There is always a resistance somewhere that comes out of your own culture, your language, and your religion. And that resistance first takes the form of existential rebellion—rebellion against everything that goes against your grain. I remember how much I jibbed when some of the Fathers forced me to attend catechism classes and go to church.

I suppose I could have gone one of two ways—become totally Tamil, totally Hindu, totally Ceylonese. I could have gone into the kind of reactionary nationalism that tries to put the clock back and pretend that the British, Dutch, and Portuguese have not influenced every aspect of our culture. (And there was a feeling in me that if I went back to the temple and my culture I would find refuge from Catholicism, from colonialism, from the British raj.) On the other hand I knew that if I wanted to get places, to look after the poorer members of the family, to become a barrister (as I once wanted), to go to England some day to the Inner Temple, then I had to go along with the system. By the time I entered university in Ceylon I was veering between being a nationalist and being a cosmopolitan.

I was not really political then in a conscious way. But all colonized peoples have, all the time, a subliminal sense of politics, a sense of powerlessness. University formulated that politics—especially because I studied political science and economics. What opened me up was looking at various political theories and the writings of people such as Hobbes and Locke, Rousseau, Owen and Proudhon and Fourier, and finally finding Marx. Or rather finding dialectical materialism and, in it, finding a way to analyze my own society, a way to resolve my own social contradictions, a way to understand how conflict itself was the motor of one's personal life as well as the combusting force of the society one lived in.

This was after World War II, when our countries were becoming independent, and nationalism in both India and Ceylon was anti-imperialist and pro–working class. Many of our lecturers had been educated at the London School of Economics, and they came back with very radical ideas. They had absorbed some of the British Left traditions and became the conduits through which those traditions passed on to us. We imbibed Harold Laski's *Grammar of Politics* (1938), the thinking of Maurice Dobb, Joan Robinson, the Webbs, and the Fabians through these teachers—many of whom were also members of leftist parties in Ceylon. They opened us up to a leftist British culture that was antisubjugation and spoke to the British working-class struggles for liberty and equality.

I left university with a degree, but not a very good one. The sports I loved—football, tennis, badminton, table tennis—the debating society and Trotskyite Left party that everyone belonged to, all these seemed more exciting than my studies. And because I did not come from a rich family and have the necessary connections (nepotism was the way into the sought-after professions), I went into teaching. I was so poorly paid I could not meet my family obligations, so I finally got into a bank as a staff officer and soon deputy manager. Those of us who had degrees were few and far between then, and as the banks were being nationalized they were looking for Ceylonese nationals who could be put straight into management.

In 1958 the riots broke out between the Singhalese and the Tamils (my wife was a Singhalese). My father's house was attacked. I saw people killed, burnt alive. Our Sinhala Buddhist government did nothing to end the violence; educated people in high places did nothing; the press and radio did nothing. Singhalese-Tamil friendship ceased at the midnight hour. I couldn't take it any more. So I chucked my job and pushed off to England.

I came to Britain in 1958 in the wake of those riots in Ceylon and walked straight into the race riots in Notting Hill, where I had gone to live. It was a double baptism by fire, which, I believe, set the course of my career and my commitment. I was in my thirties by then, married with three children, and I found it very difficult to get either accommodations or a job. I had been a bank manager in Ceylon, but they did not want "coloreds" in banks here. Besides, if I wanted to challenge racism I needed another career—as a teacher, perhaps, or writer. I ended up, instead, as a tea boy in a library in Middlesex. But I qualified as a chartered librarian a few years later and, in 1964, found myself at the Institute of Race Relations (IRR).

The "Old" Institute of Race Relations

In the early days the Institute of Race Relations was more concerned with looking at race relations abroad—at the question of race relations in Third World countries, in the colonies and former colonies—than race relations at home. It had been set up in 1956 as a department of the Royal Institute of International Affairs, and many of those involved understood race relations as an aspect of international affairs. A few years later, the Race Relations Department moved out of Chatham House to become an independent institute, but it still continued to look at race relations as a factor in persuading Third World countries after independence to allow new investors to come in and proceed with recolonizing them. Hence the Tropical Africa Project was financed by Shell, for instance. The institute also received money from the Nuffield Foundation and later the Ford Foundation.

In the colonial period the whole question of race and race relations was one of superiority and inferiority. White racism was expressed through the beliefs that white people had a superior culture, a superior language, a superior religion, and so on: the natives had to be rescued from themselves and taught to govern themselves. With independence, however, and the natives' coming of age, the colonial view of race relations, where natives were subordinated to the ruling power, ceded to the neocolonial view of race relations, where we were all equal but some were more equal than others. And an organization such as the Institute of Race Relations was necessary to prepare the way for such an understanding. A number of books published by the old IRR speak to that exercise.

The race riots of 1958, however, brought race relations back home—and the institute began to concentrate on domestic issues. So it wasn't an accident that the first IRR publication on Britain was on the 1958 Notting Hill riots. The institute now began to look at the question of how the study of race relations in Britain should be funded in its own right. It was, at the time, the only such research organization in Europe, and it started off with a fairly liberal outlook. But the contours of that outlook were defined quite quickly when the passing of the Immigration Act of 1962 restricting immigration from the new (i.e., nonwhite) Commonwealth required the institute to have a point of view. At first, it said nothing, but when the act was endorsed by the Labour government in the white paper of 1965, the institute's director declared that there had to be immigration controls because the newcomers couldn't be easily assimilated. "We have to take them a mouthful at a time" was essentially how he put it in a *Guardian* article.

I entered the institute in 1964 and soon became conscious of the contradiction in the organization between intent and action, between the declared objectivity that the institute pursued in the matter of race relations research and its action in siding with government policy to one degree or another. This didn't look like independent research to me, especially given the fact that it was siding with immigration acts that were clearly racist.

Thereafter, I began to look more closely and critically at the research the institute was doing and the books it was publishing—on Africa, South Asia, the Caribbean, and on other Third World societies with "race relations" problems. But by then, the institute's reputation as the foremost think tank on race relations in the Western world was growing—and the institute was expanding. A lot of new people were coming in. An International Research Unit (IRU) was set up as a companion to the Survey of Race Relations in Britain. The latter did a great deal of research on race relations in London: transport, employment, education, social services, and so on. Its findings were published in 1969 in the book *Colour and Citizenship* by E. J. B. Rose and others, which in its comprehensiveness claimed to be Britain's Gunnar Myrdal. The survey, and later the IRU, brought a few radicals into the institute—this was the 1960s, mind—and some of them began to question the nature of the research being carried out by the institute—and the premise of *Colour and Citizenship* itself, predicated as it was on empirical research based on preordained notions.

When I joined the institute, as its librarian, the library was only open to members of the IRR and its council. But this was a period of political activity in the streets, with grassroots groups such as the Universal Coloured People's Association, Black People's Alliance, and various other self-help organizations emerging. And they were asking all sorts of questions but had nowhere to go for the answers. So I opened the library to all these kids from off the streets and people from these groups. They wanted to understand what the hell was going on around them. They wanted to know about the impact of the immigration acts. Why were they being discriminated against in schools and jobs? Why were black children disproportionately being placed in schools for the educationally subnormal? Who is this man Elijah Muhammed and is black separatism a good thing? What about the Black Panthers? Where can we read Malcolm X, since his writings aren't in public libraries? They had all these questions, so I began to get the journals and newspapers that would answer them, such as the *Black Panther Party Newspaper, Muhammad Speaks,* and *Black Scholar.* I would get journals from Third World countries, about the war in Vietnam, about Indochina, about the movements in Indonesia, and so on. As the revolutions in so-called Portuguese Africa developed, I would get material about those struggles and about Amilcar Cabral and Mondlane, and later about Walter Rodney and the Rastafari movement. And, of course, there was always, always Frantz Fanon, probably the greatest influence on my life at that time. (In fact the then-director of the institute called me Fanonandan!)

That was the literature that I began to provide in the IRR for people from these various black groups who would come to use the library after the institute was closed. I, the librarian, provided the material they wanted, and they, the kids from the streets, gave me a feeling for their lives and a new consciousness. It was a two-way process: I was exposing them to literature, and they were exposing me to their experience.

I already had a politics, the politics of anticolonialism: the politics of left-wing groups in Ceylon (as it then was), an understanding of the Indian national movement and how that affected Ceylon, and of other Third World struggles for independence. My experiences had been, up to then, more or less, the experience of the movement for colonial freedom. Now I was getting an experience, even if at one remove, of the fight against racism in the inner cities and the ghettos, in the *favelas* of this country. These kids were giving me an understanding of what was going on, and I began to get involved with the Black Unity and Freedom Party (BUFP). The institute was getting press cuttings about racial incidents all over the country, and those too were part of the politicizing process.

It was just a coincidence, I suppose, a historical accident, that the librarian of the IRR was, at a time of growing racism, institutional racism, state racism, being brought into increasing contact with the denizens of the inner city. The first gave me an understanding of how the power system worked and why racist policies were being formulated; the second made me feel the impact of those policies on ordinary people. I was seeing both ends of the spectrum, as it were, at the same time, and that blinded me. Or rather, the opposite: it opened my eyes. I was in the system, but not of the system, and that position allowed me, I think, to see the symbiosis, not only between theory and practice but also between race and class.

I was beginning to locate the whole question of "race relations," as it was then defined, as a relation of power and to see that relation of power as tied up with the question of wealth and poverty. And I had to wrestle with the implications of this within myself. I had been born poor, but had, through education, gone to university, become a teacher and then a bank manager—and become "bourgeoisified": in Ceylon I had had a car, house, and servants. So there was another symbiosis there, between the political and the personal. And what that told me was that I was a jumped-up middle-class shit who had come from a poor family and had forgotten where he came from. I had in Eliot's grand phrase, had the experience but missed the meaning. (Although he's a conservative poet, there are things about his work that have resonated in my own life.)

What I'm trying to say here is that my own colonial education, like reading T. S. Eliot at university, hadn't become practical, material until I met with the extraordinary racism in his country, and then Eliot was cast in a different light—although he would have been horrified to know that I was quoting him in favor of liberation. In a sense, it pleased me, because I was driving the white man not only out of his own language but also out of his own literature; I was purloining the white man's language and the white man's literature. And it was in becoming conscious of all those forces that I came to write what for me was a vitally important essay, "Alien Gods." This was important because it was an exercise in decolonizing myself, a purging of my colonial soul. Vital, because it was a crucial taking-stock exercise: to view, from my own experience, the place of the black intellectual in the fight against racism, hence its subsequent publication as "The Liberation of the Black Intellectual."

Looking back, in writing that piece I also became aware of my role, my immediate role, in the struggle. It was a sort of prelude to struggle. There was my role on the streets with the BUFP, but there was also my role in my job at the IRR. I had found that, as librarian, I could provide the material that ordinary black people needed to understand their own lives and to help them connect with the experiences of other like-minded people all over the world. Now, because that experience cast light on my own self and who I was, I asked myself, what's my role in this place and what's happening here?

The Struggle for an Independent Institute

Here was a so-called independent institute justifying the ways of the state to man, as it were, and I began to ask how we could change it. In a philosophical way I began to realize that the goal might be a nonracist society, the goal might be a socialist Valhalla, an egalitarian society without oppression or exploitation, but if I were simply goal-oriented, I would end up in hopelessness. I shouldn't lose sight of the goal, but I should begin from where I was. I didn't have to be a great revolutionary, but I could move pebbles and hope they would start an avalanche. I felt I should try to bring about changes in the institute to the best of my ability.

It began, strangely enough, with a fight over luncheon vouchers. The institute gave us luncheon vouchers, which were supposed to be in addition to our pay, but were really in lieu of it. But we could only use them in the restaurant at Chatham House, at the Royal Institute of International Affairs, of which we were once a branch. Now the Royal Institute was posh, and the people who came to eat lunch there were posh people, in suits and ties and with posh accents. I felt completely out of place, and I wasn't going to eat there. I found that others on the staff, a Chinese woman and the black receptionist, also felt uncomfortable there. We couldn't go and eat anywhere else with those vouchers, so we demanded money in lieu, and that was our first battle. It taught me something about an issue that would unite people; it had brought all the employees together across race and color and provided a foundation for our next struggle.

When the IRU was set up, other employees of the institute began questioning the type of research the institute was doing. For example, Robin Jenkins, one of the researchers in the unit, read a paper at the British Sociological Association, "On the Production of Knowledge at the Institute of Race Relations." In this paper he told black people that when researchers came from IRR with their questionnaires, they were really spying on the black community and should be told "to fuck off."

The council of the institute argued that Jenkins, in attacking the work of the institute outside the institute, was guilty of gross disloyalty and should be sacked. At the same time, *Race Today,* under Sandy Kirby, a former priest, was opening up its pages to black voices and criticisms of dominant race relations organizations and views. It published critiques of the government's Community Relations Commission and Race Relations Board, despite the presence on the IRR's council of its former chairman. It also gave a free advertisement to the antiapartheid movement on the back cover, and put on the front cover a photograph of Lord Goodman, the government's negotiator in Rhodesia, with the headline, "Five million Africans say 'No.'" The council was furious about this, because, don't forget, at that time it was run by the lords and ladies of humankind, and they were in cahoots with the government.

So, although we started small, with the luncheon voucher revolt, we quickly learned that we could have a broad agreement on issues that were common to us and that a common cause could be the basis of action. And there were two issues on which all the staff agreed. One was academic freedom: should Robin Jenkins be allowed to express his opinions as an academic or should he be censored? The second was journalistic freedom: should Sandy Kirby be censored or had he the freedom to write what he wanted in the journal he edited? On the basis of those two liberal concepts, we got nearly all the members of the institute on our side, and an ongoing battle around those principles took place first within the institute's membership and then in the pages of the national press.

The council tried to divide us, offering a carrot here and wielding a stick there—but it failed. And although it had powerful press connections, we had widespread support throughout the black community and among a wide range of whites. There was a general commitment to an independent institute, which finally, in April 1972, forced the council to put the issue of management versus staff to an extraordinary general meeting of the members. And in the hall, academics, journalists, and community and social workers spoke up for our cause—and we won the day. In one sense, it was a Pyrrhic victory, because the council took the money and left us with the library. But in another, it established that in future, the staff, the workers of the institute would run the organization and not the management council. And that tradition has lasted to this day.

The second stage of the palace revolution began when we were forced to move out of our posh premises in the Fortnum and Mason belt into an old warehouse in the precincts of Pentonville Prison—and people who were not really committed to the cause of fighting racism were leaving the institute. So we did not have a purge, the institute purged itself, because the money went and people who didn't want to work for the cause went with it. We were finally left with a bare shell of an institute, with a marvelous library, three staff members, a small management council (headed by its first black chairman, the Reverend Wilfred Wood) that worked alongside the staff, a host of volunteers, and a black community group keeping the library open for black kids in the evenings.

We had taken over the institute and, as the slogan at the time put it, we had become "a sparer, leaner, more relevant institute." We had realigned the institute, with *Race Today* doing grassroots work and the library catering to black and Third World kids. But the most difficult fight was to wrench the institute's quarterly journal, *Race,* from the clutches of the academics and make it relevant to the struggles of ordinary black and Third World peoples—predicating, in the process, a symbiosis between race and class. From this arose the precepts "the function of knowledge is to liberate" and we must "think in order to do and not think in order to think." A series of articles and pamphlets looking at racism (and not at the *study* of racism) from the subaltern's point of view came out of that understanding—most important Jenny Bourne's "Cheerleaders and Ombudsmen: The Sociology of Race Relations" and my "Race, Class, and the State: The Black Experience in Britain."

"Race, Class, and the State" and the Problem of Race Relations

Until the publication of "Race, Class, and the State" in 1976, race relations had been popularly viewed as relations between people of different hues and habits, with the British people as a largely tolerant, reasonable lot, who were prepared to put up with the darkies so long as they knew their place and did not overcrowd this little island. The academic sociological view was not much different except that it attributed "colored immigration" to Britain to the push-factors of poverty in the Caribbean and Indian subcontinent and the pull-factors of prosperity in Britain and Europe.

What "Race, Class, and the State" did was, first, define the problem not as one of race relations but of racism—and state racism in particular. And, second, challenge the academics' push-and-pull theory of immigration and point out that "colored immigration" to Britain should be seen in its historical context as a continuum of colonialism: we are here because you were there. This allowed us to analyze what colonialism had done to our countries, how much it had cost us to "produce" our workers back home (and deliver them ready-made to Britain), and how it was that the removal of our capital to the "mother country" had brought us here—textile workers from India to Bradford, for instance. Labor follows capital.

The pamphlet also looked at how postwar immigration began and how the Nationality Act of 1948 had lifted all citizenship restrictions for Commonwealth immigrants because a war-ravaged Britain needed all the labor it could lay its hands on. Whereas the rest of Europe had to resort to Gastarbeiter labor, Britain had its colonies to dip into, and that is why the act established that every citizen of the Commonwealth was a citizen of Britain. But at the point of entry we automatically became second- and third-class citizens. We were not people, but units of labor, to be fed into the maws of the factories and the service industries: Asian and Afro-Caribbean workers were needed for the postwar reconstruction of Britain. But by the same token, when that period was over, Britain began to shut off further immigration with a series of immigration acts that excluded all but the skilled workers that Britain still needed.

"Race, Class, and the State" also pointed out that setting up the Race Relations Board and Community Relations Council ostensibly to smooth out race relations, would only serve to induct Afro-Caribbean and Asian people into ways of controlling their own, of buffering protest, of absorbing struggle and negating it—creating, in the process, a managerial class of black people who would manage racial discrimination within the purview of law. In the matter of language or terminology, too, "Race, Class, and the State" established an important point: that we were no longer "colored immigrants" but black settlers. And that, in turn, established our right to fight for our rights as equal citizens: we were here to stay, here to fight.

That fight was already in progress—and the common experiences of independence struggles back home and against an undifferentiating racism here were bringing Afro-Caribbean and Asian people together to forge a black identity. That identity as a people was then reinforced by the working-class jobs we did. Even if we were educated, when we came here we got working-class jobs. I became a tea boy in a library, as I couldn't get a job in a bank though I was a qualified banker. Asians and Afro-Caribbeans were forced to live in the most dilapidated areas of the inner cities—so that gave us a class orientation. All this and the struggles we entered into—on the factory floor for trade union rights and in our communities for decent housing, schooling, and so on—made us a people and a class and a people for a class. And black was the color of our fight, our politics, not the color of our skins. We might have, in our lifestyles and our beliefs, defined ourselves culturally, but in our fight against racism we defined ourselves politically. What separated us was not as important as what joined us.

The very success of those struggles—coupled with the state's anxiety that a British-born second generation was not going to put up with the discrimination their immigrant parents had put up with—frightened the government into action. It put money into the inner cities by way of Urban Aid and, in the process, bought off a whole lot of self-help groups—which now began to be responsive to the fund-givers and not to their communities. And backed by the findings of the ethnic sociologists and the new breed of "cultural Marxists," the government proceeded to set out its multicultural stall—of the saris, samosas, and steel bands variety—in the course of which, the fight against racism became a fight for culture.

That, however, did not still the discontent of the never-employed youth of the inner cities who rose up in riot against Thatcher's police state in 1981. But most of the reports and analyses and commentaries that came out at the time saw it as being instigated by a handful of troublemakers or, at best, a result of unemployment, and not as a culmination of years of resistance to the double bind of poverty and racism that black youth had been cast into. And it was as a riposte to that sort of "victim historiography" that I wrote "From Resistance to Rebellion: Asian and Afro-Caribbean Struggles in Britain." Its importance, I suppose, was in the fact that it was the first history of blacks in Britain written from the subaltern point of view.

Racism Awareness Training

There was a chance in 1981 that the Scarman inquiry into the Brixton anti-police riots would identify racism, and institutional racism in particular, as the cause of the uprisings. But Scarman insisted instead that there was no such thing as institutional racism—and, as for racism, there was of course the occasional prejudiced police officer . . . and so on. The problem, he maintained, was one of cultural or ethnic disadvantage. It was to take another eighteen years before the Stephen Lawrence campaign and the Macpherson report would finally put institutional racism on the nation's agenda.

In the meantime, culturalism and ethnicism, revitalized by Scarman, descended into skin politics and identity politics, and black struggle descended into racism awareness training (RAT) exercises for white people in positions of power—on the grounds that racism was really prejudice plus power. And since power was defined as personal power, the exercise would involve training white officials out of their inherent racism. For all whites were, by virtue of being white, ipso facto, racists. It was ingrained in them, part of their collective unconscious, original sin. But racism awareness training could at least render them "antiracist racists." That was what was claimed.

And so a whole multitude of RAT consultancies and groups, deriving from their American prototype and headed by Afro-Caribbean and Asian "trainers," began to put forth—creating, in the process, a whole profitable industry based on white guilt and supported by local authorities and NGOs who knew no better. All of which helped middle-class blacks to get places but had nothing to say to poor black people whose lives were being blighted by systemic, institutionalized racism.

That, perhaps, was what triggered my anger and caused me to write "RAT and the Degradation of Black Struggle." The Uncle Toms were living it up again. These were the people who had had the experience of being black, of being oppressed, exploited, and poor—and then forgot it when they made it or, even worse, made money out of it, as in the case of many of those involved in RAT. Besides, the whole RAT thesis was based on the same type of biological/genetic argument that white (scientific) racists had used against blacks. And here were these people using the same tools of oppression ostensibly to overcome theirs. They were not only betraying the black condition but also the human condition. The fight against racism is the fight against privilege and class, but it is also the fight for what Fanon calls " the universality inherent in the human condition." And that is what these people turned away from. They should have been fighting for a greater justice for everyone, not just for themselves. If we are at the bottom of the barrel, as black people, for example, then by lifting ourselves we must be able to lift others.

Racism particularizes us; class and gender exploitation particularize us—but in fighting them we should not ourselves become particularist and self-seeking. Through our fight against particularity, we should be able to envisage the universality that Fanon speaks of. To fight racism is not to become racist ourselves; to fight privilege is not to become privileged ourselves. And what is worse is to use our race or "underprivilege" to pull rank over others in a hierarchy of oppression. As I argued in my piece on RAT, there developed a whole politics based on "I'm more oppressed than thou" and "I'm blacker than thou" type positions linked to the whole RAT thing. RAT allowed black people to pull rank on white people. The cause of black people has its own intrinsic merits; it does not need to pull rank on anybody else. It might have been white people who invented RAT, but black people became collaborators in it.

The essay on RAT was a polemical piece, an interventionist piece. I am essentially a pamphleteer, who writes for the time, writes to change the times—not a theoretician writing for all time. And I think the pamphlet did succeed in alerting the public to the dangers of psychologizing racism and instigating a campaign against racism awareness training, which led to its official demise. Unfortunately, its psychologism sprouted elsewhere in mutant forms—among postmodern academics, in particular, which interpreted the racism of white youth in the inner cities as a crisis in white identity engendered in them by antiracists and antiracism. Hence my attack on postmodernism as an intellectual cop-out on engagement in "La trahison des clercs" followed by my polemic in "All That Melts into Air Solid: The Hokum of 'New Times.'" I consider the post-Marxists to be postmodernism's midwives.

The Shape of Things to Come

In the meantime, the global economic changes that were taking place as a consequence of the technological revolution were beginning to change the contours of racism and, at the risk of being called a functionalist, the function of racism. In the interests of a common market, the European Union was forging common racist policies to shut out "foreign" labor altogether and to repatriate, decitizenize, or both those who were already within its borders. For capital no longer needed labor in the same quantity or in the same place as before. New technologies allowed it to take up its plant and set it down in any part of the Third World where labor was cheap and captive and plentiful. And it could move from one labor pool to another, extracting maximum profit. And to guarantee such peaceful exploitation, Western powers, while preaching democracy, were in fact setting up or consorting with authoritarian Third World regimes—forcing dissidents to flee their countries and find refuge in Europe. But here they are being turned away as illegals or economic immigrants. My answer to that is that there is no such thing as illegal immigrants, only illegal governments.

Global capitalism ties up racism more directly with imperialism. Of course there was always a connection between the two. That is why the institute's journal *Race and Class,* which I edit, has, for the last twenty-five years, been emphasizing the relationship between black and Third World struggles (as the journal's subtitle, *A Journal for Black and Third World Liberation,* indicates). The "color line," which Du Bois identified as the problem of the twentieth century, is today the power line and the poverty line. Global capitalism, or imperialism under another name, has affected a symbiosis between race and class and power as never before.

It is these connections between global exploitation and racism and their implications for struggle that I began to examine in 1979 in "Imperialism and Disorganic Development in the Silicon Age" and continued in "New Circuits of Imperialism" (1989) and in "Heresies and Prophecies: The Social and Political Fall-Out of the Technological Revolution" (1996). "Globalism and the Left" (1999) is an examination of the implicit "West-centrism," if not racism, of the orthodox Marxists who continue to ignore the fact that qualitative changes in the productive forces, which the technological revolution has brought about, have also shifted the focus of exploitation, and, therefore, the focus of rebellion, from the First World to the Third.

Marxism for me is neither holy text nor dogma but a way of understanding, interpreting, the world in order to change it. It is the only mode of social investigation in which the solution is immanent in the analysis. No other mode holds out that possibility. That is what is unique about Marxism. But for such analysis to be current and up-to-date and yield solutions to contemporary problems, it must be prepared to abandon comforting orthodoxies and time-bound dogma. It must dare to catch history on the wing.

I grant that the working class in the Third World is not a fully developed capitalist working class and therefore not a revolutionary working class in the orthodox sense. It is partly feudal, partly capitalist, partly peasant, partly urban—involved in small-scale industries, service industries, or it may be doing menial work. These people are the superexploited, and they move from place to place, from village to free-trade zone, and so on. In all sorts of ways this is a fragmented, disorganic working class.

But global capitalism—through the structural adjustment programs and other conditionalities imposed by the IMF and the World Bank and through the adverse trade agreements imposed by GATT, NAFTA, WTO, and so on—has impoverished not merely the workers of Latin America, Asia, and Africa, but whole populations and blighted their future. The farmers have no land; the workers have no work; the young have no future; and the people have no food. The state belongs to the rich; the rich belong to international capital; and the intelligentsia aspire to both. Only religion offers hope; only rebellion, release. Hence the insurrections when they come are not class, but mass, sometimes religious, sometimes secular, often both, but always against the state and its imperial masters: hence the mass revolts in Indonesia, Zaire, and Nigeria; hence the continuation of such struggles by the Karnataka farmers of India, the Ogoni people of Nigeria, the Peasant Movement of the Philippines, and so on, against the WTO, G7, and other avatars of global capitalism in the United States and the capitals of Europe.

But the Marxist Left in the West is still wedded to the theory of proletarian revolution and is reluctant to accept that working-class resistance, whether in the Third World or the First, is but one component in an aggregate of rebellions that are slowly and surely being mounted against multinational corporations and global capitalism. But creating a conscious socialist movement out of them is going to take a long time. We are almost in a new society; we are at the gates of another history. There is an epochal shift in capitalism, and we have to understand that there's a qualitative change in the way that it operates. We can define capitalism in the orthodox way for the next five hundred years; I'm not interested in taxonomy. The way that capitalism impacts me and the way it operates in ordinary people's lives are what interests me.

What the Western Marxists are interested in is the identity politics of capitalism: what is capitalism; what are its problems; what are its internal contradictions; how is it going to fall on its face; what is its latest "crisis"? I'm not interested in these things. For me capitalism is what capitalism does. In everything I've touched on, that has been my constant theme: racism is what racism does. Fight racism; don't define it, because no definition is good for all time. Racism changes its contours, its inscape, its shape, its velocity, the way it impacts on people's lives and institutions. We must have a thousand different ways of fighting racism in a thousand places. There are a thousand ways to skin the cat; don't commit yourself to one. If one approach doesn't work. try another; otherwise you lose. Be firm in principle but flexible in tactic.

REFERENCES

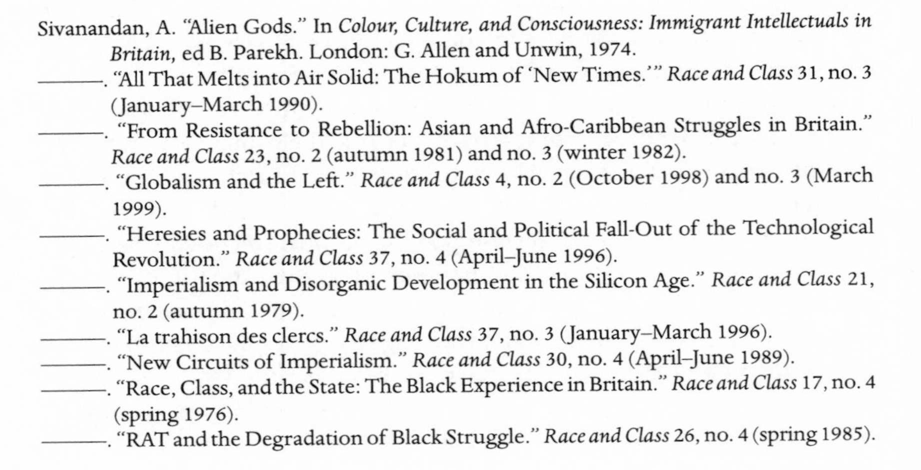

Sivanandan, A. "Alien Gods." In *Colour, Culture, and Consciousness: Immigrant Intellectuals in Britain,* ed B. Parekh. London: G. Allen and Unwin, 1974.

———. "All That Melts into Air Solid: The Hokum of 'New Times.'" *Race and Class* 31, no. 3 (January–March 1990).

———. "From Resistance to Rebellion: Asian and Afro-Caribbean Struggles in Britain." *Race and Class* 23, no. 2 (autumn 1981) and no. 3 (winter 1982).

———. "Globalism and the Left." *Race and Class* 4, no. 2 (October 1998) and no. 3 (March 1999).

———. "Heresies and Prophecies: The Social and Political Fall-Out of the Technological Revolution." *Race and Class* 37, no. 4 (April–June 1996).

———. "Imperialism and Disorganic Development in the Silicon Age." *Race and Class* 21, no. 2 (autumn 1979).

———. "La trahison des clercs." *Race and Class* 37, no. 3 (January–March 1996).

———. "New Circuits of Imperialism." *Race and Class* 30, no. 4 (April–June 1989).

———. "Race, Class, and the State: The Black Experience in Britain." *Race and Class* 17, no. 4 (spring 1976).

———. "RAT and the Degradation of Black Struggle." *Race and Class* 26, no. 4 (spring 1985).

Two collections of political essays, including some of the above, were published as A. Sivanandan, *A Different Hunger: Writings on Black Resistance* (London: Pluto Press, 1982) and *Communities of Resistance: Writings on Black Struggles for Socialism* (London: Verso, 1990). Sivanandan has also written an award-winning novel on Sri Lanka, *When Memory Dies* (Arcadia: London, 1997). *A World to Win: Essays in Honour of A. Sivanandan,* ed. Colin Prescod and Hazel Waters, was published by IRR as *Race and Class* 41, no. 1 (July 1999) and no. 2 (December 1999).

Conclusion

Of Jim Crow Old and New

This book tells the stories of eleven scholars and the times that produced them. The introduction and interview-essays highlight the interrelationship between individual biographies, the racist structure of early twentieth-century societies, and the historical circumstances of their development. Unsurprisingly, their biographies reveal broad similarities and striking differences in lives lived in the shadow of the race mountain.[1] The narratives also illustrate four types of critical intellectual engagement forged during the first half of the twentieth century to confront racism and racist policies. John G. Jackson and John Henrik Clarke represent the community scholars, whose primary interest was grassroots education in the communities in which they lived and worked. Frank Snowden Jr., John Hope Franklin, and St. Clair Drake are the university scholars, whose work focused on challenging the racism of their disciplines and the academy. The activities of Robert C. Weaver, Hylan Lewis, and Kenneth B. Clark aimed to redirect the activities of states and structures of power toward mediating racial and social inequalities. W. E. B. Du Bois, Herbert Aptheker, and A. Sivanandan reworked Marxist tools of analysis and political practice for black and Third World people. In this chapter, we revisit the stories to attempt three tasks: to compare and contrast the scholars on the basis of our framework of questions; to tease out the key themes from that evaluation of challenges to the old Jim Crow; and finally, to consider the challenges of the postindustrial Jim Crow.

Early Lives

The interviews were structured around five main areas. In terms of the scholars' biographies, we were primarily interested in the influence of their families and communities, and the events and experiences that led them to careers in scholarship and activism.[2] We also wanted to examine their struggles for higher education and the factors that distinguished them from their academic peers. There was also a concern to identify the conditions that brought their work to public and scholarly attention.

There is much in the interviews that supports the popular explanation for distinction in later life in terms of family background. However, each scholar's recollections reveal the structural conditions that shaped the lives of black families and constrained both the aspirations and achievements of whole communities. John Henrik Clarke and John Glover Jackson's families were among the least affluent and least educated of the group, and it is no surprise that neither of them went to college (not even to a black college in the South). It is no coincidence that their thirst for knowledge and justice was directed into community scholarship in the absence of opportunities or material resources to do otherwise.

Ironically, the only other scholar who came close in family poverty to Clarke and Jackson was the African American academic par excellence W. E. B. Du Bois. Jackson's and Du Bois's families were distinguished in and supported by their local communities, whereas Kenneth Clark's mother moved from Panama to New York City for a better life and greater opportunities for young Clark. Given current attitudes about the black family, it is important to note that both Du Bois and Clark grew up in single female-headed households. Rather than retarding their development, this experience was a resource for later intellectual sensitivity and singularity of purpose. In Drake's case, these qualities were derived from parental origins in the Third World. His father was a Garveyite preacher from the Caribbean who often hosted African and Caribbean visitors. Consequently, Drake grew up in a family that nurtured a consciousness of black cultures and ideologies. Sivanandan's was a peasant family in a poverty-stricken region of Ceylon. They became socially and economically mobile through education but maintained connections with their poorer relations. Like many of the other scholars, Sivanandan makes it clear that experiencing the contradictions of parental values and choices and family poverty in a racialized hierarchy was central to his political and personal development.

Some of these contradictions are to be found in the relationship between racial violence and social and geographical mobility. Although both John Hope Franklin's parents were college graduates, the family was financially poor. His father moved to Tulsa from rural Oklahoma to set up a new home just before the race riot that killed scores of blacks and leveled a prosperous community. Racial violence affected black families in different ways, and the means of avoiding it differed according to class and geography. Snowden, whose father was an army officer, came from a middle-class family. They moved out of the Jim Crow South to Boston to escape racial segregation and to embrace the educational opportunities in Boston.

Whereas Snowden, Weaver, Lewis, and Aptheker all came from solid middle-class backgrounds, all but Clarke's, Jackson's, and Du Bois's families had attained middle-class status before the great post–World War II expansion of the middle classes in the United States and the British colonies. The families of the interviewees sought to seize opportunities for social and educational advancement amid the chaos and violence of the depression and the war years. Their access to increased wealth and social standing, however, compounded the contradictions that shaped the scholars' political, intellectual, and moral development.

Education and Liberation

Although their family backgrounds were connected by experiences of racial exclusion and limited social mobility, in themselves these do not explain the development of activism or scholarship. The scholars also highlight the role of committed and extraordinary teachers in challenging a Jim Crow education system designed to reproduce existing inequalities, while creaming off the elite to manage it. John Hope Franklin was an English major at Fisk University but was so fascinated by Theodore Currier's history lectures that he changed his major to history. Furthermore, Currier sponsored Franklin's admission to Harvard and loaned him the first year's tuition fees. Although this combination of material, academic, and personal support goes far beyond what is currently understood by mentoring, it underlines the importance of personal relationships in professional achievement and development.

Weaver attributed his cum laude graduation from Harvard in 1929 and his subsequent doctorate to his time at Dunbar High School in Washington, D.C. However, it would be wrong to understand this as a matter of sentiment and altruism. The brutal facts of racial segregation meant that black graduates from the best colleges in New England, many with doctorates, ended up teaching at Dunbar during the 1920s and 1930s. As Hylan Lewis pointed out, Dunbar was a high school with a university faculty and the crown jewel of the Washington black community. The system that excluded black teachers from personal achievement ensured that future generations received an unparalleled high school education and the inspiration to question the system that made it possible.

For each scholar the exposure to education and knowledge seemed to compel some sort of active engagement in challenging the academic or social status quo, as did the very times in which they lived. The 1920s and 1930s were a period of tremendous social agitation, filled with the promise of change. For educated young adults of this period, activism was the norm rather than the exception. As denizens of turbulent times, our scholars attempted to resolve the contradictions of the times in their own lives.

Frank Snowden, who would not be regarded as a political activist, never hesitated to protest racial discrimination and segregation in debate and correspondence. Clarke and Drake were activist organizers early on in their careers. Henrik Clarke was a street speaker and fund-raiser for the Scottsboro Boys and later for the Angelo Herndon campaign. He was a non-Communist who worked in the Young Communist League because he believed these were the only people challenging such injustices. Drake did his organizing with Quakers and toured the South as part of a peace caravan, collecting signatures for the First World Disarmament Conference in Geneva in 1932. In the 1950s Drake was also deeply involved in community efforts to keep the University of Chicago from expanding into the Hyde Park area of Chicago.

Sivanandan was involved in the anticolonial struggle in Ceylon and became active in grassroots politics in the UK later in life. Although the race riots in Ceylon and England in the late 1950s formed the background to his activism, it was contact with ghetto youths in London that forced him to confront the racism that "kills bodies, hearts, and imaginations." Since that time, he has played a major role in the development and sustenance of grassroots campaigns in Britain, Europe, and elsewhere. John Hope Franklin, who contributed to the 1954 Supreme Court case ending legal segregation in public schools, said he became more of an activist in his later years, including marching with civil rights advocates in Selma and speaking out against Vietnam and the Gulf War.

Throughout their careers Weaver, Lewis, and Clark were heavily involved in promoting social change at the federal and local levels, as were Herbert Aptheker and W. E. B. Du Bois. Du Bois was one of the founders of the National Association for the Advancement of Colored People (NAACP) and the longtime editor of *Crisis* magazine. He also organized the initial pan-African conferences and later became a member of the Council on African Affairs with Paul Robeson. Whereas Du Bois joined the Communist Party out of protest toward the end of his life, Herbert Aptheker joined early on in his activist career. Aptheker did very dangerous antipeonage fieldwork and organizing in the South during the 1930s, led black troops during the Second World War, and ran for president twice as a Communist. Like the others, his passion for justice and penchant for activism have continued into old age: at well over eighty years old, he organized against the antiaffirmative action efforts in California.

For John Glover Jackson, activism geared toward influencing or changing government does not effectively counter the exploitation of blacks or working-class people. Government, regardless of whether it is Communist or capitalist, marginalizes and exploits the majority. Although these anarchist beliefs set him apart from the other scholars, there are deeper connections. Jackson agrees that people are their own best liberators, with meaningful change emerging from their efforts to transform the conditions of their own lives and environments.

Racism in the Academy

Under the old system of Jim Crow, regardless of merit or money, black students could not simply apply for admission to any college or university in the United States: race mattered. African American students with the means to afford further education went to black colleges and universities in the South. They could not go to a white college in the South and violate Jim Crow laws; nor could they go to most white colleges in the North and violate Jim Crow customs.

However, there were exceptions to the orthodoxies of segregation. Two such anomalies were Oberlin and Berea Colleges, started by abolitionists to show that racially integrated education was possible and desirable. While Cornell University's College of Arts and Sciences was closed to blacks, an occasional black student got an advanced degree from the School of Agriculture. Kenneth Clark was the first African American to complete a Ph.D. in psychology at Columbia University. The two major institutional exceptions were the University of Chicago and Harvard. The University of Chicago had a series of black social science graduate students in the 1930s, including St. Clair Drake and Hylan Lewis, and Harvard College trained a series of black students throughout the first half of the twentieth century, including Frank Snowden, John Hope Franklin, Robert C. Weaver, and W. E. B. Du Bois.

St. Clair Drake explained the University of Chicago's willingness to train blacks in sociology and anthropology in terms of the politics of the period. During the 1930s both business and government were concerned about the growth of large urban black communities, where enlarged worldviews and personal freedoms quickly translated into political activism and the embrace of radical causes. This was accompanied by a growth of political radicalism among black and white labor. The resultant wave of agitation and potential for rebellion threatened the stability of American capitalism and was best illustrated by the Scottsboro case, where blacks and Communists acted together.[3]

In March 1931 nine black men were tried and condemned to death for raping two white women. The men's trial itself took place in a mob atmosphere, where some ten thousand white men converged on the town to see the defendants lynched. The Communist Party, which came to the Scottsboro Boys' legal defense before the NAACP, organized protests all over the United States and Europe. This brought the case and its Jim Crow backdrop to world attention and put the United States government and white America on the defensive for the first time. Even so, black academics found it difficult to publicly support Marxist theory and politics, as nearly all were employed at conservative southern colleges unsympathetic toward radical ideologies.[4] However, the case of the Scottsboro Boys encouraged large numbers of young blacks to join the Party and black urban intellectuals to study Marxism and Communism during the depth of the depression and the heyday of the Popular Front.

In this context, private foundations, in particular the Rosenwald and Carnegie Foundations, wanted to use the social sciences to divert black militancy away from socialism and radicalism via a "race relations" industry. The Rosenwald Foundation sponsored the Race Relations Institute at Fisk University under Charles Johnson, making Johnson a new academic power broker. He was the gatekeeper to the Rosenwald scholarships for black and white students to attend the University of Chicago and be trained in the social sciences with a specific focus on race relations in the United States.[5] This was the institutional motivation and source of funding for Charles Johnson, E. Franklin Frazier, Horace Cayton, St. Clair Drake, and Hylan Lewis during the late 1920s and 1930s.

Harvard admitted blacks long before the radical threats of the late 1920s, due to a combination of history, tradition, and patrician arrogance. Although New England was no stranger to slavery, abolitionist sentiment was stronger in Boston and New England than anywhere else in the United States.[6] The very small black population was not seen as a threat to white labor, culture, or anything else, and was generally perceived as improvable through education and capable of living moral lives.[7] These historic and regional sentiments contributed to Harvard's early willingness to admit blacks, as did the fact that it was wealthy and independent enough to do what it liked as an educational institution. Nevertheless, not everyone overlooked race. Some white students and faculty opposed an integrated Harvard.

The barriers to higher education and training experienced by John

Glover Jackson and John Henrik Clarke, the community scholars, were the norm for most blacks interested in scholarly work. The few at the University of Chicago were there because white scholars could directly access neither the new black communities nor black opinion. Those who attended Harvard did so because it lacked a tradition of rigidly segregated scholarship. Thus even as the merits of the blacks who attended these universities were vitally important in their progress, they were also there because of interests and events that were larger than they were. For the many, though, there were very few institutional opportunities to develop themselves as scholars or to contribute to the well-being of their communities. The next section examines their capacity to produce so much critically important work and their struggles to achieve professional recognition against such formidable odds.

Of Work and Sacrifice

Each scholar was questioned concerning his work habits, the sources of his ideas, his projects, and the organizations he worked through. All were driven by a deep sense of personal commitment to their work, and there is a striking pattern of commitment to library work amid adverse circumstances. Aptheker reported that Du Bois's work habits were formed at Fisk University, where he would rise early every day to write according to a well-organized routine. By the time Drake was interviewed for this project he was a senior research professor and simply lived his work. This was to the extent that he could read and hold conversations at the same time, where what he read became intertwined in his conversation.

The scholars also developed institutional structures to express their commitment to research and social action. Kenneth Clark founded HARYOU in Harlem in the 1960s, the Metropolitan Applied Research Center in the 1970s, and worked closely with his wife, Mamie, in running the Northside Center for Child Development, all in New York City. In addition, Clark was professor of psychology at City University of New York. Hylan Lewis worked closely with Kenneth Clark in all three organizations, besides being a professor of sociology at the City University of New York. In contrast, John Henrik Clark and John Glover Jackson spent more of their lives as laborers and worked on their scholarly projects on occasional days, evenings, and weekends. John Glover Jackson said he would write every book and make every sacrifice all over again, even if no one read his work. What he did was for deep personal satisfaction and a sense of achievement. Sivanandan's experience of the contradictions of anticolonial struggles in Ceylon and the birth pangs of militant black politics in the UK shaped the Institute of Race Relations' emergence as a collective based on the staff's shared political commitment and practice.

Whether their work sprang from academic and professional values or took its meaning from its power to intervene and shape debates and policy, the scholars show a common dedication to something beyond themselves. No one said he would have done anything differently; no one regretted the path he had chosen or the opportunities he might have missed. However, each scholar was deeply aware of the impact of racism on his personal and professional life. Snowden had gasoline poured on his car and his life threatened for daring to ask why he was charged more than the pump price for gas. Franklin was called a "Harvard nigger" but was allowed to use a library special collection because of his good "southern" manners. As students at Fisk, Du Bois and Franklin were so traumatized by the racism in downtown Nashville, Tennessee, that neither went there again alone during their college careers and avoided the city for years after leaving the university. Aptheker was working against peonage in the South when a black man (who took a great risk in doing so) told him to leave town because other whites, angry about his activism, were planning to kill him. Sivanandan fled the 1958 anti-Tamil pogroms in Ceylon and walked into the race riots in London, where white mobs rampaged in search of blacks to attack. Class background and educational achievements were no protection against the violence endemic in societies based on racial hierarchy. And direct experience of racial violence and its ever-present possibility allowed these scholars to identify with the ordinary people who were "catching hell" and permanently shaped their theoretical and practical practices.

The community scholars were working people, without degrees or formal training, who did scholarly work on the side. There was little recognition for their efforts beyond the people in Harlem who supported and respected them. They were not even able to teach formally until very late in their lives. Jackson told of Willis Huggins's financial debt and eventual suicide because of the pressure and social alienation of the work. In contrast, all the university scholars and activists received degrees from renowned universities and worked with distinguished faculties, but they were not much better off than the community scholars in terms of the pressures they faced.

Snowden knew of blacks who committed suicide rather than go South to teach or embrace a career other than teaching. Many black scholars had to teach at poor, obscure teaching schools with ridiculously high teaching loads. The lucky ones that built reputations as exceptional teachers might be recruited to the primary black universities, Atlanta and Howard, but received no advantages because of where or with whom they had studied. They started out like all other black faculty, regardless of degrees and training; their promise as scholars was secondary. St. Clair Drake, Kenneth Clark, and Hylan Lewis, as younger members of this generation, were the exceptions. They received teaching appointments in Chicago and New York City after the Second World War. Aptheker never had a full-time teaching appointment and could only lecture now and then, despite his publications and position in his field.

Academic success requires sacrifices by scholars and their families, and in the context of the racially stratified societies of the first half of this century, those burdens were often nearly intolerable. To be married to politically committed scholars required a de facto vow of poverty and a willingness to be secondary to their husbands' attempts to change a world that did not even recognize them. It is no coincidence that Clark and Jackson in particular had difficulty in forming and maintaining marriages. Du Bois's research and organizing away from home and the physical threat of living in the Deep South took its toll on his first marriage. After the 1909 Atlanta race riot, Du Bois's home was invaded by white rioters and his wife and daughter threatened while he was away. Subsequently, he moved his family to Baltimore, but he lived and worked in Atlanta and then New York City.

Snowden, Franklin, Drake, and Aptheker had wives who understood their work, supported them throughout their careers, and were willing to make the necessary sacrifices to help them. Franklin said that many scholars in the South never realized their potential to make major contributions because their marriages could not bear the emotional and financial costs. Relationships were also strained by the black college professor's position as "black bourgeoisie" and its requirement that he live well, even if he did not have the means to do so. In most instances this led to a restriction on family size. The lack of children also meant the scholars could devote more of themselves to their professional work and the development of the institutions with which they were associated. Paradoxically, the renunciation of a "normal" family life allowed them to talk of the lives of ordinary black people and contributed to the breadth of their appeal.

Styles of Distinction

Although a focus on the little people was characteristic of many of these scholars, the connection between this sensitivity and the distinctiveness of their work raises some interesting questions regarding the relationship between the production of theory and larger social movements. For this generation of critical intellectuals, the key moments seem to be the radical politics of the interwar years and the civil rights movement of the 1960s.

For the community scholars, the black studies movement in the late 1960s brought new visibility to their work. This had a ripple effect: John Glover Jackson was not recognized until John Henrik Clarke became prominent enough to get a publisher to reprint Jackson's work. The movement also produced a sudden need for faculty who could address the critical questions regarding race, history, and culture raised by the new generation of black students and the prodemocracy movement that inspired them. Although Clarke became a senior contributor to programs at the New School University (for social research), Hunter College, and later Cornell University, the most important development was the publication of his writings. St. Clair Drake, who had retired from teaching at Chicago's Roosevelt University, was recruited to head the new black studies program at Stanford University, part of its response to student demands. His classic *Black Metropolis* (1945) was reprinted and the stage was set for *Black Folk Here and There: An Essay in History and Anthropology (1987–90)*. As communities came to a greater consciousness of themselves and organized to confront racism wherever it impinged upon their lives, there were sustained efforts to reclaim past scholarship and press it into serving contemporary needs.

For the activist-reformers, their reception has been mixed. Robert Weaver is still best known as secretary of Housing and Urban Development during Lyndon Johnson's administration. His scholarly work around and experiences of housing have yet to be either fully collected or appreciated, whereas Kenneth Clark achieved public recognition through the 1954 Supreme Court decision outlawing racial segregation in public schools. Clark also formed the first antipoverty program in the United States. Although Clark's model was successful, it was later compromised by local politicians and perverted by the rapid expansion of ineffective antipoverty programs by the federal government. Despite the fact that Hylan Lewis provided the theoretical support for Clark's antipoverty work of this period, he has not received the acclaim he deserves for his behind-the-scenes work. Even so, among those in the know, Lewis's expertise on issues of poverty and urban life among African Americans was highly sought after. Daniel Patrick Moynihan and Nathan Glazer attempted to recruit him to support their work on the plight of black families. He refused and continued to work on the margins, but with his integrity intact.

Two of the three university scholars, Frank Snowden and John Hope Franklin, were recognized in their fields before the black studies movement, partly as a result of their efforts at self-promotion. Since the early 1940s Snowden circulated copies of his papers to prominent scholars of the ancient world, seeking their comments, advice, and suggestions and establishing himself through a community of correspondence. Franklin did a similar thing. He wrote a monograph critiquing E. Merton Coulter's *The South during Reconstruction, 1865–1877* (1948) for the *Journal of Negro Education*, ran off 250 copies, and sent a copy to every prominent historian he knew of. Franklin attributes his initial professional recognition to that review, even though two years earlier the first edition of his *From Slavery to Freedom: A History of American Negroes* (1947) had been published. The former study, however, led to Franklin's invitation to address the then-segregated Southern Historical Association in 1949, the first black scholar to do so. Neither Snowden nor Franklin came to prominence due to the black studies movement; they were already established in their central disciplines because of unorthodox methods of self-publicity and their ability to exploit gaps in the armor of Jim Crow.

Sivanandan's work was greatly influenced by both the black power movement of the 1960s and the waves of anticolonial struggles that bracketed it. Drawing on the values and perspectives of that period, his writings have shaped the ways in which communities and political movements have understood and responded to major issues around racism and imperialism for more than thirty years. He is well known in Europe for the clarity of his analysis and the passion of his polemic and is becoming better known in the United States. Sivanandan has "caught history on the wing" throughout his career, ranging from the seminal essay "Race, Class, and the State: The Black Experience in Britain," which became the basis for understanding postwar racism, to more recent work on information capitalism and globalism.

Whereas Sivanandan did not begin his political writing until the 1960s, Du Bois was an important figure in black intellectual and political life before World War II. This was largely due to his long-term editorship of *Crisis* magazine: all the American interviewees read Du Bois in their youth. However, the postwar period saw his name disappear from prominence. From the McCarthy era in the early 1950s on, anyone who criticized the necessity for the Cold War or was associated with Communists became persona non grata. Du Bois did both. His stance in favor of national independence in the Third World and his refusal to bow to government-inspired anti-Communism sharpened the need to silence him.

Du Bois was not a Communist after the Second World War, but he refused to renounce his friends and associates who were and was arrested and tried as a Communist agent for it. Although he was acquitted in 1952, public opinion (and the organization he founded, the NAACP) had been turned against him, and his name disappeared from public view. However, as with the community scholars, the movement of the 1960s helped revive Du Bois's name and distinction. This revival received a further fillip with Herbert Aptheker's publication of his collected works running to more than forty volumes.

Although Du Bois mentored Herbert Aptheker and selected him to maintain and edit his papers, Aptheker is a prominent historian and engaged intellectual in his own right. A prominent member of the Communist Party U.S.A., Aptheker went to Vietnam to speak out against the war in 1966. Because of his association with Du Bois, his membership in the Communist Party, and his opposition to the Cold War, Aptheker was also ostracized. Regardless of his role as a major contributor to American history, Aptheker was excluded from university appointments, and only because of student demands did he get occasional lectureships. Aptheker attributes his extraordinary productivity to a combination of his wife's support and his isolation from the academy. He had no classes to teach, dissertations to direct, or department committees or appointments to distract him from his work. His prominence in the Party and on the Left was also a source of support over his many years on the margins of mainstream history and the academy. Aptheker is fond of saying that he and Du Bois dealt with their critics by simply outliving them.

Lessons and Research Suggestions

As a final question, the scholars were asked to give suggestions for future research. Generally this sparked a lot more than research ideas, and they shared lessons learned from a lifetime of scholarship and activism. The exception was John Glover Jackson, who simply said, "Read my books. All that I wanted and needed to say and offer is there." For him governments of any sort are, if not directly oppressive, easily compromised and incapable of tapping the virtues and intelligence of the common people. Jackson believes that government sponsorship of nuclear weapons threatens the possibility of any future in which we could discover and develop human potential and virtue. He feels that his writings contribute to the extension of that human future and world peace. In this sense, Jackson is much more than a scholar of the community; he is an uncompromising voice for global justice and peace.

John Henrik Clarke's vision is also expansive, inclusive, and very clear, and is accompanied by the most comprehensive and ambitious of plans. In his view, Eurocentric scholarship warps our knowledge of peoples and worlds, past and present. The task is to review our historical and cultural knowledge in order to identify and correct those distortions. This is a process that requires the inclusion of non-European peoples and points of view previously omitted or underplayed. It also requires the rewriting of European history from a standpoint where Europe is not at the center of the world. This would allow the world to be reflected in the history of Europe and allow European peoples to see themselves through the eyes of the world. The starting point for this grand scheme is the simple acknowledgment that Europe is not physically separate from the Asian continent and that its cultural, economic, and social roots are in Africa and Asia. For Clarke, this geographic reality in itself significantly undermines the popular European conceit that they are a separate, special, and historically superior people.

According to Clarke those ordinary people disregarded by white society and struggling to survive need this knowledge to help them work out where they came from and who they are. The acquisition of such insight is part of the process of mental and cultural liberation that precedes material liberation. Ironically, it is the community scholars who were the strongest advocates that a liberal arts type education (without Eurocentrism) be made available to all who will listen and participate. This process of communal self-education would free people of color from any sense of inferiority and allow whites to be liberated from their racism.

St. Clair Drake bridged the gap between the community scholars and the university-based intellectuals and offered a "new direction" in research that echoes Clarke's themes and suggestions. He calls for study of the points made by Cheikh Anta Diop in *The African Origin of Civilization: Myth or Reality* (1974) concerning the African genesis of human society and the origins of racism and color prejudice. Drake's view is that the dynamics underlying the present subordination of African peoples and cultures are best understood in terms of the distinctions between color prejudice, racism, and slavery. While each is distinct, with its own history and trajectory, in recent historical times all three merged in European colonialism. This is his central point in *Black Folk Here and There* (1987–90).

Frank Snowden Jr. has objected to many of the community scholars' assertions and perceptions regarding the ancient world throughout his career. Snowden is critical of their inappropriate use of the modern concepts of race and racism with reference to the classical period. He argues that the ancients did not understand race or express racism as we define it today; to write as if they did is to impose our reality and concepts on them and not to see the world as they saw it. Even so, like Clarke and Drake, Snowden worked to understand history without racist distortion and to communicate that knowledge as diligently as possible. He and John Henrik Clarke also agree that the lack of race prejudice among the ancient Greeks and Romans questions the presumption of innate race prejudice. Snowden also shares the community scholars' commitment to the continued critical review of scholarship that expresses and sustains European intellectual, moral, and material arrogance. However, the community scholars' "historical recklessness" raises serious difficulties for Snowden, whose research focuses on more detailed knowledge of the ancient Mediterranean and European worlds.

While John Hope Franklin is as much a specialist as Snowden in his field of the history the American South, his suggested areas of research were, by contrast, both extensive and detailed. One particular area that Franklin highlights is the paucity of historical research on the national black church organizations and prominent local congregations. For him, the black church is central to African American community life, as illustrated by the fact that leadership within the black community is consistently and disproportionately drawn from the church. Given this, the lack of historical analysis of black churches and faith-based organizations is a shocking omission and a strategic error.

Robert Weaver believes that government is the best institution to make fundamental changes in support of the constitutional right to "life, liberty, and the pursuit of happiness." He is a witness to what government can do to reduce racial inequity when it has the political will and imagination, as well as to what happens to antipoverty and public housing programs when the will is absent. These efforts "failed" because of government's lack of interest rather than any lack of capacity. Weaver argues that the claims made by contemporary conservative political leadership concerning the "limits of government" are fundamentally wrong and at core motivated and driven by racism. Economic inequalities in the United States cannot be addressed independently of racial inequalities; without racism, economic inequalities would be much more limited, and there would be a greater commitment to eradicating them.

Kenneth Clark agrees with Weaver's conclusion that the American state has the capacity to reduce racial and economic inequality and links the issue of political will among white leadership to one of Hylan Lewis's central concerns, the nature and effectiveness of black leadership. Clark notes that for every European ethnic group, more leaders and better political representation resulted in better-developed communities. However, although there are far more black political leaders than ever before, many black communities and regions are worse off now than they were before desegregation. Encouraging more effective leadership and more efficient use of the political process are key to advancing racial and social justice in this new century.

However, for Clark, there is a more fundamental difficulty to achieving these goals, a difficulty that echoes John Henrik Clarke's interest in understanding European culture and history. Clark believes that intra-European hatred and conflict underpin and mold their hostility toward blacks: Europeans would be at each other's throats without their hatred of blacks and other nonwhite groups to unite them. Without dealing with their ethnic animosities toward each other, addressing antiblack prejudice among white people will still leave them open to racism.

Hylan Lewis's suggestions are in line with those of Franklin, Weaver, and Clark, but with a stronger focus on black communities. Lewis believes that since the end of participant observation studies of the 1940s and his *Blackways of Kent* in the 1950s, there has been a loss of the sense of what is going on in black communities. His concern is to investigate the processes by which black "marginality" are constructed and maintained, that is, how black communities are denied participation in the economy and excluded from the larger society. Lewis also wants to understand how marginalization impacts individuals and their communities. Individuals and families cannot simply flee to a "promised land"; nor can they disappear, as income for housing, food, and clothes is a constant necessity, regardless of such circumstances as low pay, underemployment, or unemployment. Lewis believes that as their members lose the struggle to survive, communities undergo fragmentation; and if fragmentation goes on long enough, the very social structure of the community collapses outright. These are the outcomes of racially motivated economic policies, where structural racism and racial discrimination create ghettos of black communities and the attendant "pathologies" that Kenneth Clark so eloquently described in *Dark Ghetto: Dilemmas of Social Power* (1965). Lewis concludes that the scope and implications of this task are more comprehensive, complex, and critical than when he, Charles Johnson, E. Franklin Frazier, and St. Clair Drake were trained to do community studies in the 1930s and 1940s.

The works of W. E. B. Du Bois, Herbert Aptheker, and A. Sivanandan offer tools and vision for such a task of research, reclamation, and regeneration. Like Lewis, their basic assumption is that racial, class, and gender inequalities are not simply outcomes of prejudiced individuals, distorted cultures, and minor flaws in the structure and running of government. The inequalities that ravage the lives of black and Third World people developed from the very economies that they must rely on for survival. Other scholars in the collection make it clear that capitalism is no friend of equality and social justice in the United States; these writers point to the role of capitalism and imperialism in the impoverishment and exploitation of the majority of the world's people.

This type of analysis powerfully contradicts the usual explanations of racial inequality: the innate hatred of dark-skinned people; black psychology, low morals, and physiological flaws; and inept administrations and overgenerous welfare. Whereas the "blame the victim" explanations justified European racial supremacy and the rise and expansion of Western capitalism, analyses in terms of the new "globalism" suggest that the struggle to end exploitation and oppression requires an understanding of the global dominance of a new form of capitalism. If the conclusions of Du Bois, Aptheker, and Sivanandan are valid, then more basic work to eliminate racism is needed than any of the other scholars in this collection realize.

The Apthekers said that very late in his life, Du Bois confessed to having made major errors. The first was that he had overrated the moral character and integrity of those who rose from the masses, while underrating the power of direct and indirect bribery upon them. In these terms, Booker T. Washington was more the rule than the exception: an example of what happens when talent is separated from the masses in a country as wealthy as the United States. Furthermore, Du Bois felt it was a mistake to think that the gradualism of the courts could effectively address the broad structural injustices of capitalism, imperialism, and racism. He believed, according to Aptheker, that he had simply placed too much faith in the power of rationality, in the idea "that the truth was so manifest that it had to prevail and that the problems of this country could be overcome with reason."

After almost a century of scholarship and activism that spanned the interests of all our interviewees (the role and place of Africa and Africans in world history and cultures; the condition and status of black communities; the quality of black leadership; and the role of government in social change), Du Bois concluded that logic and evidence were insufficient to challenge structural injustices. Those who influence and benefit from these injustices have tremendous power, no morals, and little hesitation in crushing those who, like Du Bois in his later years, threaten their interests. The 1960s saw an increase in the power structure's capacity to act decisively against individuals and organizations that broaden the nature and direction of black struggle. Du Bois's life and those of Malcolm X, Martin Luther King, the

Black Panthers, and countless others who were harassed, silenced, or murdered by the system pose questions about recapturing anticapitalist and anti-imperialist impulses in the twenty-first century.[8]

Whereas Du Bois characterized the postwar period in terms of imperialism, Sivanandan writes of globalism, but whatever the term, the outcome is not the result of vast impersonal forces but of calculated human efforts. The political and economic systems that people look to to address their grievances and assist them in their everyday lives actually foster their exploitation and oppression. The activities of the U.S. government and international agencies such as the International Monetary Fund, the World Bank, and the World Trade Organization increasingly dominate world economic and political systems and reinforce what Du Bois called the "color line" on a global scale.

For Sivanandan, capitalism will have to be changed to root out the need for racism; the changing forms of capitalism and racism need to be understood to be opposed effectively. Capitalism is what capitalists do, and as Sivanandan says, "Racism changes its contours, its inscape, its shape, its velocity, the way it impacts on people's lives and institutions." Given that, there need to be myriad ways for fighting racism in a thousand different places, with the emphasis on firmness of principle and flexibility of tactic. This approach reframes some of the community concerns for detailed information on the lives and struggles of ordinary working people living under ever more oppressive conditions and offers a broader context for the debates around the capacity of local, national, and supranational states to improve their material and social conditions.

All four groups of intellectuals spoke against the knowledge that supports social injustice and racial inequality. Although from very different perspectives, the scholars were concerned to free minds imprisoned by ideologies that operated against their own best interests. For some, such as Drake and Clarke, this meant offering academic correctives to Eurocentric and class-biased historiography; for others, including Aptheker and Sivanandan, the task was to replace the Third World in analyses of racial exploitation; while others, such as Snowden, exposed the dangers of prejudiced scholarship of any hue. These scholars worked for reform, social justice, and liberation through committed research and reason and action based on the results. The race barrier was irrational and movable through education and social action. All believed that through hard-nosed intellectual work and grass-roots education, people can gain authority over, and assert the authority of, their experiences.

Clearly, the efforts of those who resisted the ideology and terrorism of

Jim Crow with organization, ideas, and their lives have made a difference. Many of the grosser aspects of racial injustice have gone. Formal Jim Crow racial segregation is largely outlawed; the number of lynchings has decreased dramatically; the precise etiquette of racial subordination in every aspect of life has been muted; and the formal racial barriers to college and university admissions and to public service are gone. In some areas, the beginning of the twenty-first century showed clear progress in America's movement toward racial equality, certainly in comparison to the start of the twentieth century. In these terms, scholars and activists of the 1930s generation have been vindicated in their belief that the race mountain could be moved.

The New Jim Crow and the Academy

But there are trends and changes since the 1960s apogee of social change that suggest the circumstances that made the triumphs of their generation possible no longer exist. Hylan Lewis was most thoughtful on this point. For him, education and research have become big businesses, and knowledge about race and racial inequalities is no longer a progressive endeavor, with a clear sense of direction and purpose. Now, it is only a small part of the information industry that produces ideas as commodities, like clothes, soap, or home appliances. Like so much fast food, ideas in the public domain are tasted and then quickly forgotten in the face of the next marketing campaign: what gets attention is that which is massively promoted and marketed by publishers. Consequently, what the academy produces has to compete with everything else, but without the authority it had between the 1930s and the 1960s. The role of the university as the site of research and teaching is shrinking, as career colleges and schools take over its teaching role, and research institutes with political agendas and soft-money ethics produce market-led public policy research.

The advent of the information revolution and the privatization of knowledge have accelerated the commodification of knowledge and its degradation into sound bites and infotainment. Lewis argues that there is no sense that ideas require engagement and work or that research reflects some underlying reality and truth, to be improved upon by subsequent study and action. In this new world, academic presses and scholarly work are creatures of tastes and fashions. In this context, what scholars consider knowledge concerning race and what is "real" in the streets are not the same, nor are they meaningfully connected. When major advances in race thinking do occur, there are no public outlets for them, and they remain in the academy or the research institution. Kenneth Clark's point about black politicians, that the many have little effect, now also applies to scholars and researchers. The more we have, the less knowledgeable are our communities and the less difference the new explosion of knowledge seems to make for our everyday lives.

For our four groups of critical scholars, the Jim Crow of blanket de jure and de facto racial segregation largely defined the black experience. This system of formal and legal control and exploitation was sustained by an ideology of scientifically and theologically ordained racial hierarchy and racial terrorism. However, black communities in the twenty-first century endure very different forms of social control and economic exploitation. This is a postindustrial Jim Crow, premised upon the so-called war on drugs waged by the state and the imperatives of advancing globalism.

A defining moment of the new Jim Crow was the sudden marketing and centralizing of drug dealing and drug use in urban black communities at the time of the 1960s urban riots. The government's strategy of massive police repression (to deal with both rising militancy and drug supply) proved as destructive as the drugs themselves to urban communities and the wider movement for social justice. Since then, drugs, police, and jails are the mechanisms that keep blacks and Latinos from fully participating in the economy and from confronting the racial discrimination endemic in American life. This is precisely what Jim Crow achieved in the South from 1890 to 1965, but the new Jim Crow is based on the narcotics industry, low-intensity warfare, and a prison-industrial complex. The prevalence of disinformation and the virtual privatization of knowledge sustain this structure of control and coercion. As more and more blacks and Latinos are locked up and their families divided, their communities are locked down; neighborhoods are ever more fragmented; and there is no consensus or common cause among scholars and researchers.

That the work of contemporary race scholars does not easily translate into background material for a general social movement to address the abuses of the new system is a contributory factor to the impasse in action. Their focus mirrors that of John Hope Franklin and Frank Snowden, with its emphasis on microanalysis: variations and varieties of historic experiences and the complexities and contradictions of specific events. However, without the macro or big-picture assessments to provide an overarching structure, microfocused work loses its value and usefulness. Paradoxically, narrow studies of ethnic relations and identities have replaced the primacy of "big ideas" and "grand narratives" about race and racism in the academic community, even as the global economy transforms the basis of domestic racism.

The distinctions between the national and international are blurred, as the marketplace for labor, goods, services, and subsidies is globalized. American businesses are partly owned by multinational corporations, and those corporations do business in the United States. Those global businesses tend to have their major manufacturing plants and the bulk of their employment in the Third World, where labor is cheaper. However, they also import skilled and unskilled labor into the United States and Europe to save labor costs whenever necessary. Consequently, whereas in the old Jim Crow at least the bottom of the economy was reserved for blacks, in its postindustrial form, there is no place for blacks and other locked-down communities at all.

As the underpinnings of racism are now globalized and vastly more complex, the responses have to be very different in comparison to measures taken from the 1930s to the 1970s.[9] If domestic racism has become international racism and neocolonialism in the Third World reimported into the First, then effective responses have to be both local and global in scope. Such analyses raise practical and theoretical questions about the responsibility for domestic economic inequality and racism, and the extent to which the federal government can act, even if there is the political will to do so. Although the answers to these questions will be born of practical political struggle in particular communities and movements, and are beyond a lone generation of black or domestically focused scholars, there is still much that can and is being done here and now.

Part of that task is to reclaim the past in order to build the future. The second volume of this series will examine the development of communities of resistance and the scholar-activists, women and men, who "grounded" themselves, as Walter Rodney did with the Rastafari and revolutionary nationalist groups in the Caribbean and as Fannie Lou Hamer did during the civil rights movement. Their vision was international and macroscopic, focusing on the big picture while intimately connecting it to the changing experiences of social injustice and structured exploitation in local communities.

The postwar years presented an opportunity for the first generation of scholars. The changed rhythm of national campaigns for civil rights and the internationalization of prodemocracy movements introduced surprising struggles that would have been inconceivable in the prewar years. No one could have predicted that there would be an effective nonviolent movement in the heartland of Jim Crow. Although led by a young black Baptist minister, this movement connected philosophy and tactics forged in South Africa and India against the British with the culture and aspirations of black women and men in the southern United States. Despite the largely male leadership, black women played a dominant role in community development and mobilization campaigns. In the same way, globalization represents a challenge to contemporary scholars. The key to an effective response to global inequality and racism may be in the very communications technology that is driving globalism. With distance reduced to seconds by the Internet, antiracist scholars and activists all over the world can more easily collaborate to understand racism and plan action against it. That is the challenge, and what is exciting is that there will be yet more surprises.

NOTES

1. Gaynor; Clausen.
2. Rossi; Elder; White.
3. Carter.
4. Meier and Ruddick, 102.
5. Robbins.
6. Melish; McPherson.
7. Cromwell.
8. Fairclough; Carew.
9. Bowser, ed., *Racism and Anti-Racism in World Perspective.*

REFERENCES

Bowser, Benjamin. "Generational Effects: The Impact of Culture, Economy and Community across the Generations." In *Black Adult Development and Aging,* ed. Reginald Jones, 3–30. Berkeley: Cobb and Henry, 1989.

———, ed. *Racism and Anti-Racism in World Perspective.* Thousand Oaks: Sage Publications, 1995.

Carew, Jan. *Ghosts in Our Blood: With Malcolm X in Africa, England, and in the Caribbean.* New York: Lawrence Hill, 1994.

Carter, Dan. *Scottsboro: A Tragedy of the American South.* London: Oxford University Press, 1973.

Clausen, John. *The Life Course: A Sociological Perspective.* Englewood Cliffs: Prentice-Hall, 1986.

Cromwell, Adelaide. *The Other Brahmins: Boston's Black Upper Class, 1750–1950.* Fayetteville: University of Arkansas Press, 1994.

Cruse, Harold. *The Crisis of the Negro Intellectual.* New York: William Morrow, 1967.

Elder, Glen H., Jr., ed. *Life Course Dynamics: Trajectories and Transitions, 1968–1980.* Ithaca: Cornell University Press, 1985.

Fairclough, Adam. *Martin Luther King Jr.* Athens: University of Georgia Press, 1995.

Gaynor, Cohen, ed. *Social Change and the Life Course.* New York: Tavistock, 1987.

Gergen, Kenneth. "The Significance of Skin Color in Human Relations." *Daedalus,* 96, no. 2 (1967): 390–406.

Meier, August, and Elliott Ruddick. *Black History and the Historical Profession, 1915–1980.* Urbana: University of Illinois Press, 1986.

Melish, Joanne. *Disowning Slavery: Gradual Emancipation and "Race" in New England, 1780–1860.* Ithaca: Cornell University Press, 1998.

McPherson, James. *The Abolitionist Legacy: From Reconstruction to the NAACP.* 2d ed. Princeton: Princeton University Press, 1995.

Robbins, Richard. *Sidelines Activist: Charles S. Johnson and the Struggle for Civil Rights.* Jackson: University Press of Mississippi, 1996.

Rossi, Alice. *Of Human Bonding: Parent-Child Relations across the Life Course.* New York: A. de Gruyter, 1990.

White, Robert. *Lives in Progress: A Study of the Natural Growth of Personality.* New York: Holt, Rinehart and Winston, 1975.